TEN COMMANDO

TEN COMMANDO
1942–1945

Ian Dear

Pen & Sword
MILITARY

Published in the United States of America in 1989
First published in Great Britain in 1987
by Leo Cooper
Reprinted in this format in 2010 by
Pen & Sword Military
an imprint of
Pen & Sword Books Ltd
47 Church Street
Barnsley
South Yorkshire S70 2AS

Copyright © Ian Dear 1987, 1989, 2010

ISBN 978 1 84884 400 1

A CIP catalogue record for this book is
available from the British Library

Typeset in Sabon 10.5/12pt by
Concept, Huddersfield

Printed and bound in England
by CPI

Northamptonshire Libraries & Information Service	
TOW	
Askews	

Pen & S ... *of*
Pen & Sword Av ... d Military,
Wha ...
Pen 8 ...

For a co ... *ct*

47 Church S ... ngland
F ...

Contents

Acknowledgments

The co-operation and hard work of many people made this book possible. Firstly, I would like to thank Henry Brown, Secretary of the Commando Association, who over a number of years has never failed to help and give wise counsel.

Next, I would like to thank the team of translators who struggled with unfamiliar military terms and phrases with unfailing good humour: Eve-Marie Wagner, Anne Griffiths, Marie-Madeleine Avit – and Caroline (French); Hedwig Woerdman, Daemian J. Van Doorninck (Dutch); Ellen Stevens (Norwegian); Mary Stephens, Ted Monsior, Jerzy Lisowski (Polish).

Then there are the many individuals who helped me in one way or another to gather the material for this book. George Lane and Dr John Coates both offered me encouragement in its early stages and gave me valuable leads. To supplement reports in the Public Record Office, or the books and articles that have been written about the different Troops that made up the Inter-Allied Commando, I have either interviewed, or corresponded with (directly or indirectly), the following, and I am extremely grateful for their co-operation:

French: Félix Grispin, Lt-Colonel Robert Dawson, Jean Zivohlava, Maurice Chauvet, Dr Guy Vourc'h, Alex Lofi, Mme Kieffer, Jean Pinelli, Laurent Casalonga, Rupert Curtis.

Dutch: Brigadier-General Jan Linzel, Rudy Blatt, Peter Tazelaar, Willem van der Veer, Nick de Koning, Martin Knottenbelt, Bob Michels, W. de Waard, W. Boersma, Bill de Liefde, G.P. Ubels, C. G. Offerman, C. de Ruiter, W. G. van Gelderen, J. G. van den Bergh, E. C. D. J. de Roever; the Secretary of the Dutch Commando Association; Dr P. H. Kamphuis, Lt-Colonel Leunissen, Guido Zembsch-Schreve.

X-Troop: Colin Anson, R. G. Barnes, K. W. Bartlett, G. Broadman, Keith Douglas, Vernon I. Dwelly, John Envers, Anthony Firth, E. H. Fraser, Manfred Gans, H. Geiser, R. Gilbert, Judge H. B. Grant, Ian Harris, George Kendal, George Lane, K. E. Levy, Peter Masters, Michael Merton, J. F. McGregor, G. P. Nell-Nichols, Harry Nomburg, Stephan Ross, Professor Paul Streeten, Peter Terry, R. W. Tennant, A. C. Turner, W. J. Watson, Roger Kingsley, George Saunders, James Leasor, Keith Thompson, Sir Maxwell Harper Gow, Michael Arton, Ken Wright; SOE Archivist; Brigadier Peter Young, Miss Pat Cleland, J. E. Day.

Belgians: Maj-General Baron Danloy, Carlo G. Segers, Paul Dufrane, Fred Laurent, George van den Bossche.

Norwegians: Arne Sørbye, Colonel Daniel Rommetvedt, Kaspar Gudmundseth, Arnfinn Haga, Alf Pettersen, Lt-Col Olav Gausland, Mrs Aslaug Risnes, R. W. Nilsen.

Poles: Ted Monsior, Maciej Zajaczkowski, A. J. Jedwab, Leo Licht, Zbigniew Gasiewicz; Archivist of Sikorski Museum.

Yugoslavs: Mario Mikolic, Press Attaché, Yugoslavian Embassy; Director of the Muzej Revolucije Naroda, Beograd; Librarian of the Canadian War Museum; Ronald Mitchell.

The following also gave me general information on the Inter-Allied Commando: Dr John Coates, Lt-Col. Godfrey Franks, Maj-General Tom Churchill, Lord Lovat, Thomas Connolly, Group-Captain K. S. Batchelor, William Beynon, John Miller-Stirling, Donald Bradford; Archivist of Broadlands Museum; Secretary of the Special Forces Club; Philip Ziegler, Lady Laycock, Dr Tony Hodges, the Hon Mrs Miriam Lane; and Paul Powell, who took enormous trouble in tracking down the citations for British decorations awarded to members of the Commando.

Finally, there are those who very kindly vetted the manuscript or parts of it: Brigadier-General Jan Linzel, Maj-General Baron Danloy, Colonel Daniel Rommetvedt, Lt-Colonel Robert Dawson, Félix Grispin, Dr Guy Vourc'h Arne Sørbye, George Lane, Carlo G. Segers, Peter Masters, Peter Terry.

Foreword

It hardly seems possible that there is a non-fiction subject connected with the military aspect of the Second World War that has not been covered by historians, biographers, autobiographers, hagiographers – or novelists.

Yet while I was researching a book on the Royal Marines I came across a brief reference to a unit called 10 (Inter-Allied) Commando. Intrigued, I turned to that excellent reference book on the Commandos, *The Green Beret*, by Hilary St George Saunders. It is 362 pages long, but not more than twelve are devoted to the Inter-Allied Commando. Yet he said enough to tell me that it must have been one of the most unusual units to have operated from Britain during the war, for it was made up of men whose own countries had been occupied by the Nazis. Even odder, to my mind, was the fact that the unit also contained a Troop of Germans!

I wanted to know more, but no detailed history of the unit had been published. So I checked every Commando history and then every published memoir, and from a page here and a page there the vaguest of outlines emerged. While I was doing this James Leasor published his book, *The Unknown Warrior*, which was based on information given to him by Lord Mountbatten and by Maj-General Sir Leslie Hollis, Senior Military Assistant Secretary to the War Cabinet and Chief of Staff Committee during the Second World War. This told the story of Stephen Rigby, who, according to Mountbatten and Hollis, had been a German member of the Inter-Allied Commando. It showed me that many members of the Commando were still alive, sane and, apparently, approachable.

But what really clinched it for me was the day I met George Lane. We had been introduced about an entirely different matter. Because I mentioned I had just finished my book about the Royal Marines George told me that he had been not only a member of 10 (IA) Commando but of the mysterious X-Troop which contained enemy aliens who spoke perfect German; that he was in fact a Hungarian by birth who had changed his name from Lanyi to Lane. I discovered later that he had been captured during a pre-D-Day reconnaissance raid, had been taken before Rommel for interrogation without betraying his real identity and had subsequently been awarded the Military Cross. I knew then that if the Inter-Allied Commando had been made up of men like this I had a book to write.

It has not proved an easy task, for practically all the published literature on the Commando is in Norwegian, Polish, Dutch and French, and it all had to be translated to extract the necessary information. Published details of X-Troop were sparse, so surviving members had to be interviewed and I also talked to many members of the other Troops, several of whom married British wives and settled in Britain; while others, of course, returned to their own countries and I had to track them down there. A third and vital source was the Public Record Office at Kew whose files yielded a treasure trove of information on the unit's activities, much of which has never previously been published.

From these three sources I have managed to piece together the story of what must surely have been one of the most extraordinary units to have been formed during the Second World War. But I hasten to add that it is not the complete story, not the definitive history I set out to write. Too much time has passed, memories have grown hazy or unreliable, too many of its members are dead or have simply vanished, and, inevitably, the official files now in existence were culled before being placed in the Public Record Office.

I believe, though – late in the day as it is and incomplete as it may be – that this book could not have been written before now. If I, or someone else, had started to research it twenty or thirty years ago – and certainly if it had been mooted directly after the war – many members of X-Troop for a start would not have been willing to talk as freely as they have done now. (As it was some were reluctant to co-operate: one, quite understandably, refused to talk to me as he is currently the Chairman of a German shipping company based in this country; another, recently retired after working for almost 40 years in military intelligence in Germany, has not, equally understandably, allowed his name to be used, though his story is in this book.) The habit of secrecy ingrained in them would almost certainly have prevented even the partial picture I have presented here.

Secrecy was not the only reason I found some members of the Inter-Allied Commando reluctant to talk. None wanted to be cast as a hero, and even those who had – fortuitously for me – written accounts of their wartime experiences, thought that what happened over 40 years ago was no longer relevant. I, of course, don't agree with them and by the very nature of the unit I am writing about I have had to emphasize the role of its members in any particular action, however small their numbers were numerically. This may sometimes make it seem as if it was those from the Inter-Allied Commando who won a particular battle, played the crucial part in a certain patrol or operation. This, of course, is nonsense, and unintentional. If my narrative does occasionally err in that direction it is entirely my fault, not that of those from whom I have had to extract their stories – or whose stories I have been forced, through the reticence of the participants, to discover from others.

That said, I must add that, on occasions, I do believe that the role of the Inter-Allied Commando has been somewhat underrated in the annals of the Second World War. The part the Polish Troop played in the crossing of the Garigliano, for instance, is not recorded in any English general history of the Italian campaign that I have ever come across; while the role of the Belgian and Norwegian Troops at Walcheren only rates a mention in any of the several books written about that crucial operation – which is itself vastly underrated as one of the critical battles of the war. And as for X-Troop! It is natural, I suppose, that the operational importance of such a small number of men, mostly acting alone or in small groups while always attached to other units, should be underplayed, especially as they were, to put it bluntly, both Germans and Jews. But their decorations totalled one MC, one MM, and a sprinkling of Mentions in Despatches, a derisory recognition of their extraordinary courage and accomplishments. Maybe, however, I am biased. The reader must judge for himself. At least those who fell in battle have a beautiful area of woodland in Northamptonshire dedicated to them, the idea of the Hon Mrs Miriam Lane (Miriam Rothschild), who was at one time married to George Lane.

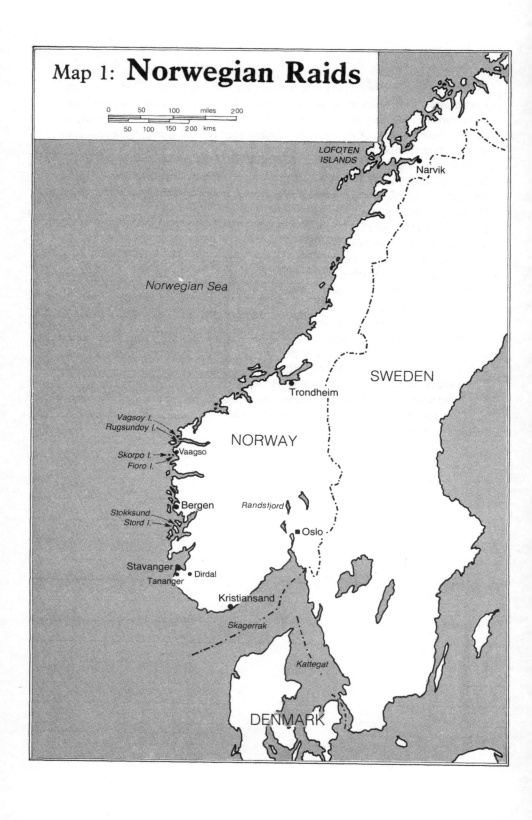

Map 1: **Norwegian Raids**

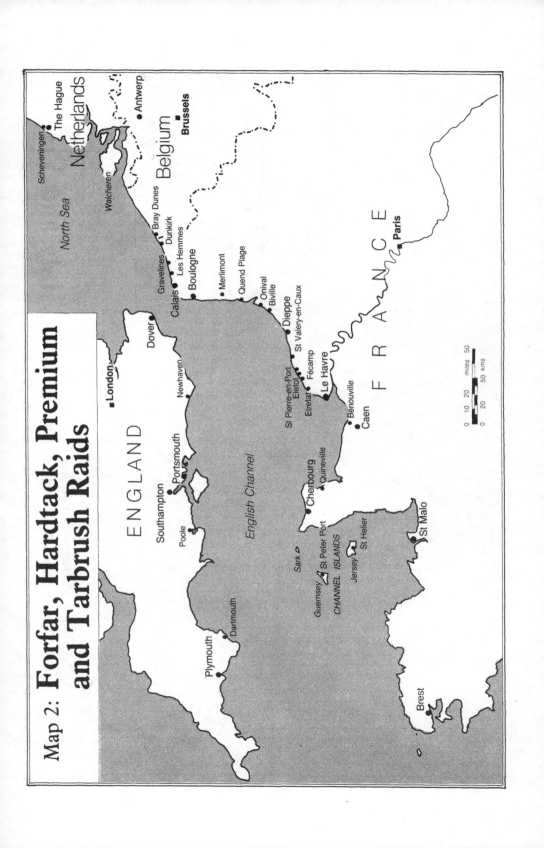

Map 2: **Forfar, Hardtack, Premium and Tarbrush Raids**

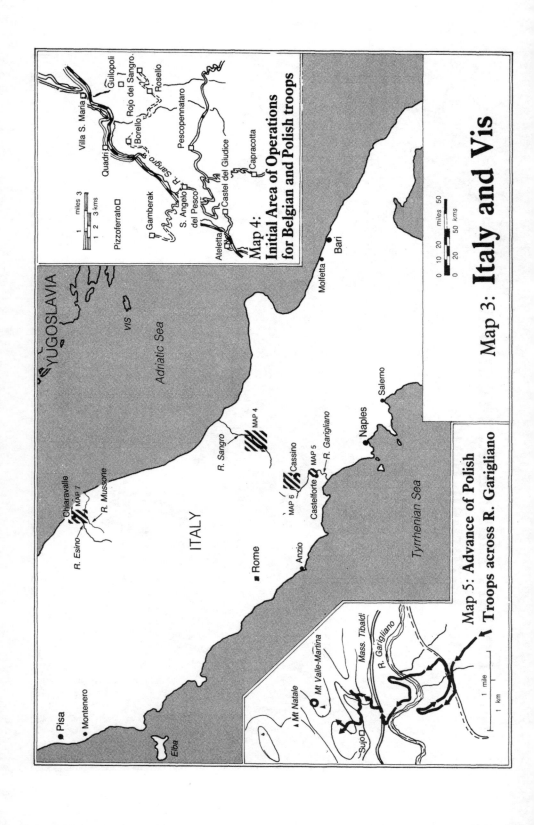

Map 4:
Initial Area of Operations
for Belgian and Polish troops

Guilopoli
Rosello
Rojo del Sangro.
Villa S. Maria
Borello
Quadri
Pescopennataro
Castel del Giudice
Capracotta
S. Angelo
del Pesco
Gamberak
Pizzoferrato
Atteletta

miles 3
1   2 3 kms

YUGOSLAVIA

VIS

Adriatic Sea

Molfetta
Bari

MAP 4

R. Sangro

Cassino
Castelforte
MAP 5
R. Garigliano
MAP 6
Salerno
Naples

Chiaravalle
MAP 7
R. Mussone
R. Esino

ITALY

Rome

Anzio

Tyrrhenian Sea

Pisa
Montenero

Elba

Map 3: **Italy and Vis**

0 10 20   miles 50
0   20   50 kms

Map 5: **Advance of Polish
Troops across R. Garigliano**

Mt Natale
Mt Valle-Martina
Mass. Tibaldi
R. Garigliano
Sujo

1 mile
1 km

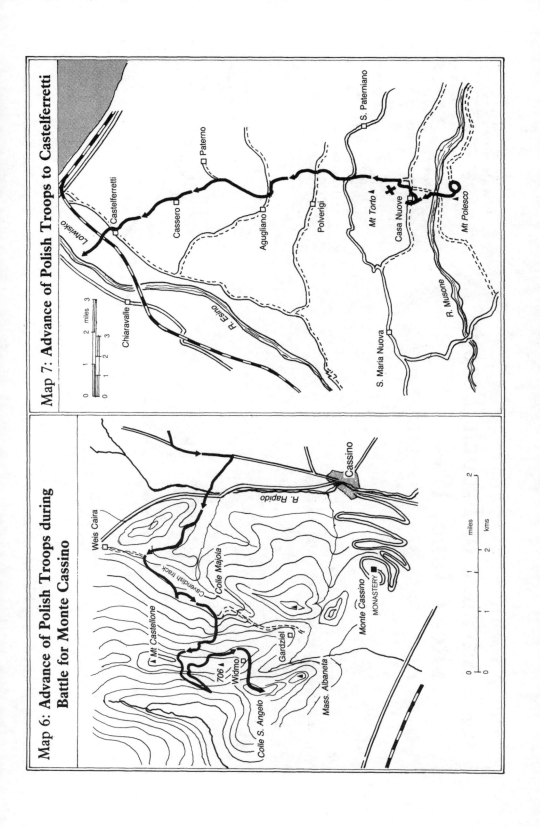

Map 6: Advance of Polish Troops during Battle for Monte Cassino

Weis Caira
Mt Castellone
Cavendish track
706
Widmo
Gardziel
Colle S. Angelo
Mass. Albaneta
Colle Majola
Monte Cassino
MONASTERY
R. Rapido
Cassino

Map 7: Advance of Polish Troops to Castelferretti

LORNISKO
Chiaravalle
R. Esino
Castelferretti
Paterno
Cassero
Agugliano
Polverigi
S. Paterniano
Mt Torto
Casa Nuove
S. Maria Nuova
Mt Polesco
R. Musone

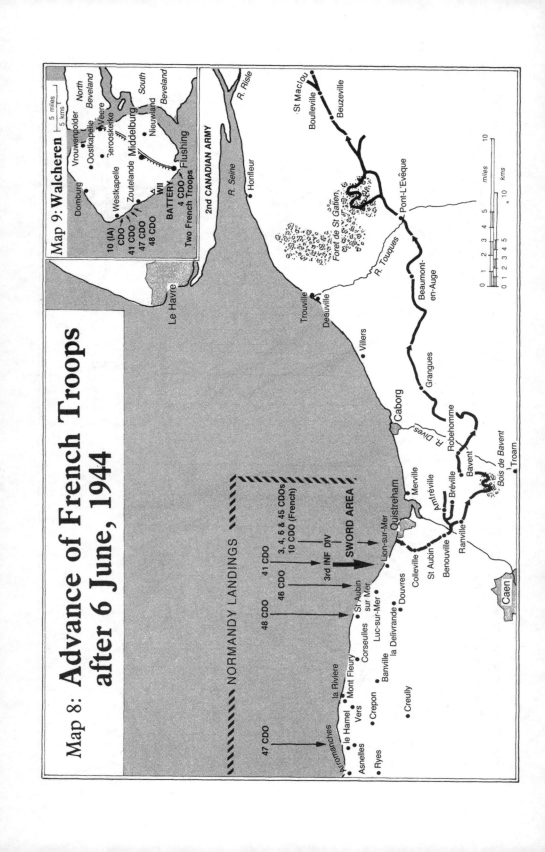

Map 8: **Advance of French Troops after 6 June, 1944**

NORMANDY LANDINGS

47 CDO

48 CDO

46 CDO

41 CDO

3, 4, 6 & 45 CDOs
10 CDO (French)

3rd INF DIV

SWORD AREA

Autromanches
le Hamel
Asnelles
Ryes
Vers
Mont Fleury
Crepon
Creully
Corseulles
Banville
la Delivrande
Luc-sur-Mer
Douvres
St Aubin sur Mer
Colleville
St Aubin
Benouville
Lion-sur-Mer
Quistreham
Ouistreham
Ranville
Merville
Amfréville
Bréville
Bavent
Troarn
Bois de Bavent
Robehomme
Caen
Caborg
Grangues
Beaumont-en-Auge
Pont-L'Evêque
Villers
Deauville
Trouville
Honfleur
Le Havre
St Maclou
Boulleville
Beuzeville

R. Dives
R. Touques
R. Seine
R. Risle
Forêt de St Gatien

2nd CANADIAN ARMY

miles
kms

0 1 2 3 4 5
0 1 2 3 4 5
5
10
10

Map 9: **Walcheren**

Domburg
Westkapelle
Zoutelande
Vrouwenpolder
Oostkapelle
Serooskerke
Middelburg
Nieuwland
Veere
Flushing

North Beveland
South Beveland

10 (IA) CDO
41 CDO
47 CDO
48 CDO

W11 BATTERY
4 CDO
Two French Troops

5 miles
5 kms

1

The International
Experiment

Like some of the work of one of its Troops, a certain amount of mystery surrounds the formation of the Inter-Allied Commando. In his book *The Unknown Warrior* James Leasor wrote that when "Mountbatten became Chief of Combined Operations in that year [1942], he decided to use the talents and abilities of young men who had come to Britain from countries occupied by the Nazis. Many were eager to join the Commandos, but no opportunity existed for foreign nationals* to do so. Mountbatten changed this by forming No 10 (Inter-Allied) Commando."[1] One of the officers in the Commando has stated that the idea "came to Mountbatten from a far Left adviser, prompted, of course, by the memory of the International Brigade in the Spanish Civil War".[2]

Though there is no documentary proof in either Mountbatten's archives at Broadlands[3] or in the Public Record Office that he was responsible for the formation of the unit – and despite the fact that, as his biographer, Philip Ziegler, commented[4], he was prone to taking over other people's ideas as his own – it is highly likely that it was Mountbatten who suggested that the Inter-Allied Commando be brought into being. Certainly it was very much his style to have done so.

The first Commando units were formed in the summer of 1940 soon after Churchill became Prime Minister. Churchill had served in the Boer War and knew how effective "irregular guerrillas" could be in tying down conventional forces. He therefore pressed for the formation of specially trained troops of the

* Foreign nationals serving in the Pioneer Corps were eventually allowed to join other regiments in the spring of 1943 and an Army Council Instruction was issued to that effect.

1

hunter class, who could create a reign of terror on the "butcher and bolt" policy.[5] Though the word "Commando" came into general use during the Boer War it was not Churchill who now proposed the word, but Lt-Colonel Dudley Clarke, then Military Assistant to the Chief of the Imperial General Staff, General Sir John Dill, who had succeeded General Ironside in this post on 10 June, 1940. Clarke told Dill he had some ideas, based on his time as Dill's GSOII during the Arab rebellion in Palestine, to put forward in response to Churchill's minute, and was told by Dill to put them on paper.

The result was the formation of the Commandos, initially called Special Service battalions, after the volunteers for special service in "mobile operations", which the War Office had already called for from the various Commands throughout the United Kingdom. No 1 Commando was to be formed from the Independent Companies which had fought in Norway, while Southern, Western and Scottish Commands were to provide two Commandos each; Eastern Command, the London District and the Household Division, one each. Northern Command was also meant to provide one, making a total of eleven. Then, in August, Northern Ireland Command provided an additional Commando, No 12, while No 14 came into being in October, 1942. By this latter date a volunteer Commando had been raised from the Royal Marines. At first this was simply called The Royal Marine Commando, but was then renamed 40 (Royal Marine) Commando, and it was later joined by eight other Royal Marine Commandos, Nos 41 to 48, none of which were volunteer units. In addition, a number of Commando units were raised in the Middle East and there were also a couple of units raised for special purposes.

The formation of No 1 Commando was delayed as the Independent Companies remained in existence for the time being, but all the others were formed with the exception of No 10, the number allotted to Northern Command, which failed to come up with sufficient volunteers. When, therefore, it was decided in the spring of 1942 to raise an Inter-Allied Commando the vacant number, 10, was the obvious number to give to it.

The formation of the Commando was, as one of its members commented after the war, "something of an experiment, embarked upon with some trepidation, for it involved the creation of an unknown quantity, bringing together men of all nationalities with, in some cases, conflicting points of view".[6]

The next two chapters explain in detail how these various nationalities, who were to make up this experimental unit, escaped the Nazis and arrived in England, so it is sufficient to say here that by 1941 there existed in Britain various units of the armed forces from Allied occupied countries which were directly controlled by their governments in exile. The fact that one or two of these governments seemed more concerned with protecting their legitimacy in representing the countrymen they had left behind than in the prosecution of

2

the war against the common enemy caused a great deal of bitterness among some units of these governments' armed forces. The army units, in particular, were frustrated, for, unlike the navy and air force, they had no immediate opportunity to strike back at those who had taken over their homelands. So great was the agitation in one Belgian unit "to stop this attitude of neutrality" that it culminated in fourteen soldiers being court-martialled for waging a propaganda campaign against the Prime Minister in exile, M. Pierlot[7]; on another occasion, a Belgian unit being addressed by the Minister of War simply booed him down.

When those most anxious to see active service read that the Commandos had been formed it must have seemed to them the ideal method of obtaining the revenge they so eagerly sought. The French and the Dutch were particularly quick to pick up on the idea of having their own Commando troops, and the first to take action was a tall, rugged-looking French Naval officer, Lieutenant Philippe Kieffer.

Kieffer, born in Haiti, had worked before the war in the US, so he spoke good English. When war broke out he returned to France, volunteered for the Navy and was later commissioned. At the time of Dunkirk he was sent to Britain and after the Armistice joined the Free French Forces, and was posted to an old French battleship, *L'Amiral Courbet*, lying in Portsmouth harbour where her anti-aircraft guns were particularly useful in defending the city against air attack. The ship shot down the occasional enemy plane but Kieffer and a number of his fellow officers found the life monotonous. Some volunteered to become agents but Kieffer wanted to fight the enemy directly. Then in March, 1941, he read about the Commando raids on the Lofoten Islands and decided to try and form a similar unit composed of Frenchmen who, because of their knowledge of the French coast, would be capable of raiding it to destroy enemy installations and personnel. He propounded his ideas to officers at the French Naval Surcouf barracks on Clapham Common, who received them with indifference. However, Kieffer was not one to give up easily and after months of badgering all concerned Admiral Muselier agreed to listen to what he had to say. Muselier liked what he heard but explained that all his resources were tied up in keeping the Free French naval units at sea and fighting. So if Kieffer really wanted to raise a French Commando unit he would have to find his arms, equipment and training from the British, which, he added, would be very hard to do as they were themselves stretched to the limit.

As a result of his interview with Muselier Kieffer obtained, at the end of March, 1941, a meeting with Brigadier J. C. Haydon,* then commanding the Special Service Brigade. Haydon and his advisers listened to Kieffer

* Later, as a major-general, Haydon became Mountbatten's Chief of Staff at Combined Operations Headquarters (COHQ), quartered at Richmond Terrace in London, after Mountbatten took over from Admiral Keyes as Chief of Combined Operations in October, 1942.

sympathetically, but the young French officer felt he had not really got the Britishers' full attention until he emphasized that his men would consist of those who knew the French coast from Dunkirk to Bayonne like the back of their hands. When he had finished Haydon thanked him politely and told him he would receive an answer in due course. Kieffer must have been sorely disappointed at the non-committal attitude of the British, but two weeks later he was delighted to receive the go-ahead to form his Commando unit.

Kieffer's first volunteer recruits were Sergeant-Major Francis Vourch, who came from Brittany (and should not be confused with Lieutenant Guy Vourc'h who joined later), and sixteen French Marines. They were, according to Kieffer, a motley bunch. Five were in detention, but were given their release when they volunteered.* Despite their sojourn in prison they made, Kieffer said, excellent soldiers.

In April Keiffer took this nucleus to a training camp at Camberley. Without arms, their uniforms creased, the French, Kieffer felt, were looked upon with derision by the British, but they trained hard and by July their numbers had swollen to about forty and they became known as the 1st Marine Company. They then underwent further training and in March, 1942, were sent to the Commando training centre at Achnacarry, the first foreign troops to train there. Only one man dropped out and at the end of the course the unit's name was changed to "1er Compagnie Fusilier Marin Commando". At first they continued to wear the blue beret and red pompon of the French navy but later, when stationed at Criccieth, changed to the much vaunted green beret. On this was sewn a hexagonal badge, incorporating the Cross of Lorraine, designed by one of their number. After Achnacarry the French were attached to No 2 Commando at Ayr for futher training, and in July 1942 they formed No 1 Troop of the Inter-Allied Commando.[8]

In the spring of 1943, a second group of Frenchmen, under Lieutenant Charles Trepel, who was later to form a second French Troop, No 8, arrived at Achnacarry for training, a moment well remembered by one of the centre's instructors. "There can be no more melancholy sight in the world than a group of lugubrious Frenchmen. They huddled together on the platform, misery written all over their expressive Gallic faces, shoulders hunched, chins tucked down into their collars. These were the men who had listened to the strokes of Big Ben – the symbol of freedom – as they were preparing to run the gauntlet of the escape route to Britain. Now another Big Ben was glowering down at them – big Ben Nevis!

"A dark, burly Frenchman stepped out from their midst and ceremoniously surveyed the scenery. The others murmured encouragingly, calling him Lofi.

---

* Several later members of the French Commandos had also volunteered in preference to serving out their prison sentences. One, called Boulanger, had "Pas de Chance" tattoed on his forehead, and answered to that when on parade.

4

He was obviously the wit of the company. His comrades waited expectantly for his pronouncements. It came. '*C'est formidable,*' he said, lifting his hands in supplication. '*Nous retournerons maintenant à Londres!*' "[9]

While the French were training at Achnacarry, a number of young Dutchmen serving with the Princess Irene Brigade were given the opportunity to volunteer for training with British Commando units then stationed in Scotland. Two officers and forty other ranks came forward and they were divided between No 3 Commando, stationed near Largs, No 4 Commando near Troon, No 9 Commando on the Island of Bute, and No 12 Commando near Dunoon. In May this nucleus, now joined by others, underwent the Commando training course at Achnacarry. Then on 29 June those who had passed were attached to No 4 Commando near Troon where the Dutch Commando Troop was formed under the command of Captain P. J. Mulders, and on 16 July it officially became No 2 Troop of the Inter-Allied Commando.

The gathering of the Inter-Allied Commando's two most senior Troops in Scotland does not seem to be have been a coincidence, for their future Commanding Officer, Lt-Colonel Dudley Lister, was at that time commanding No 4 Commando. On 26 June, 1942, he attended an Establishment Committee meeting at the War Office when approval was given to the forming of the Headquarters Troop – composed entirely of British personnel – for the new Commando, which itself officially came into being on 2 July.[10]

Though the two most senior Troops started their official existence in Scotland the decision had already been taken to station the new Commando in North Wales. The decision had also been made that it was better to billet the Troops in different towns in the area and not attempt to have them together, a wise one considering the volatile mix of so many different nationalities. Billets were found by the local police who at first found the inhabitants less than co-operative as they thought at first they were having English soldiers billeted on them. However, once it was explained to them who the Commandos were and where they came from, they were treated with the greatest generosity and kindness. On one occasion, or so the story goes, a policeman in Wales found one local particularly reluctant to have anyone billeted on her. As a final plea to her better nature the policeman said: "Oh, come on, Mrs Jones, these lads are all foreigners, away from their homes and their loved ones." "Foreigners they may be," said the stubborn lady, "but they can go and stay in their own homes." "Of course they can't, Mrs Jones. All their countries have been taken by Jerry." A look of comprehension dawned on the woman's face. "You mean they're real foreigners? I thought you were talking about English soldiers. I'd be only too glad to help, of course I will."

Another amusing example of the Welsh attitude to the English was recorded by one of the Norwegian Troop stationed at Nevin. When he attended divine service one Sunday the preacher ended his sermon with the words, "God bless Wales, Scotland and Norway", and did not mention England at all!

All the men from the Commando seemed to have thoroughly enjoyed their stay in North Wales, and many continued to return after the war to see their landladies. Quite a few married local girls and after the war either settled in the area or took their brides back to the Continent. So popular were the foreigners that it is alleged that the few British troops in the area adopted broken accents in the hope that they would get noticed more.

On 14 July the French Troop paraded before General de Gaulle and it was then sent to Criccieth where it was settled into billets. The same day the Dutch Troop arrived at Portmadoc and the Headquarters Troop at Harlech.

By this time discussions were already under way with the relevant authorities about recruiting a Belgian and Polish Troop, but before either of these arrived X-Troop was formed.

At the beginning X-Troop was also called, rather confusingly, the "English" Troop. Confusingly, because none of the Troop, except for its Commanding Officer, Captain Bryan Hilton Jones, and one or two of its other officers, was British. Its other nomenclature derived, according to one source, from the Prime Minister himself. "Because they will be unknown warriors," Churchill is alleged to have said, "they must perforce be considered an unknown quantity. Since the algebraic symbol for the unknown is X, let us call them X-Troop."[11]

Whatever it was called, the Troop was undoubtedly one of the strangest, if not the strangest, sub-unit to serve in the British Army during the Second World War. Behind its formation was, without much doubt, the fertile mind of Mountbatten, though, again, there is no absolute proof of this. It was certainly Mountbatten who first revealed the existence of the Troop to the press and the public during a speech at the dinner of the Commando Benevolent Fund at the Mansion House, London, in 1946. It consisted, he said, of volunteer refugees "who believed in democracy and liberty in their own country, men who left Germany because they hated the Nazis. The position was frankly explained to these Germans that they would face torture if captured. Not a man said no – and none of them let us down. It is to men like these we must look for the building of a new Germany. They were fine soldiers and I was proud to command them."[12]

In *The Unknown Warrior* James Leasor wrote that Mountbatten, whom he interviewed for his book, wanted to form X-Troop because he did not want anti-Nazi German speakers to be victimized as his German-born father had been during the 1914–18 war when he had been forced to resign as First Sea Lord. If this is so – and there is little reason to doubt it – Mountbatten showed commendable foresight, for X-Troop members were to serve with an unswerving loyalty to their adopted country, and with a courage and

6

usefulness totally disproportionate to their numbers. By the end of the war nineteen of them had become officers, some having been commissioned in the field for specific acts of gallantry. Their casualties were also high, sixteen being killed and twenty-two wounded or disabled.

All the future members of X-Troop volunteered from the Alien Companies of the Pioneer Corps. But seven of the first eight privates Hilton Jones and his Hungarian-born sergeant, George Lanyi, brought to Wales on 24 July, after initial training with No 1 Commando, were ex-Pioneer Corps who had been working with Military Intelligence at the War Office. "None of them really had the foggiest notion where they were being sent nor why," Hilton Jones wrote after the war. "Most had had previous parachute and special training but were woefully ignorant of elementary drill and weapon-training."[13]

Nothing much is known about these eight privates who formed the nucleus of X-Troop except that they were probably German-speaking Czechs and had had previous operational experience. Five of them went on the Dieppe raid, so the adopted English names of these are known. Only two of them came back: one, known as Platt, was wounded and became the Troop's storekeeper for the remainder of the war. He is now believed to be in South America. The other, who had taken the name of Latimer, served, as will be seen, with distinction, both in the Normandy campaign and at Walcheren, but is now dead.

Sergeant Lanyi, who later became George Lane, was an Hungarian Olympic water-polo player who had come to England as a student. He went up to Christ Church, Oxford, but left there to read English literature at London University. He then became a journalist, and when war broke out was accepted as an Officer Cadet in the Grenadier Guards. Although Hungary was not at war with Britain at the time, the authorities objected to him being recruited into the British Army and instead he was issued with a deportation order. Lanyi, however, had some powerful friends; the deportation order was withdrawn and he joined one of the newly formed Alien Companies of the Pioneer Corps as a private. After agitating, unsuccessfully, to serve in a more active regiment, he was recruited into the newly formed SOE – Special Operations Executive, an organization raised to carry on subversive operations in enemy-held territory – and was given extensive training. He soon found, however, that undercover work was not for him and he asked for a transfer to the Commandos. This was granted and he was sent to No 4 Commando at Troon where he joined Hilton Jones' Troop as a sergeant. He was commissioned in 1943 and was the first member of X-Troop to become an officer.

Hilton Jones was the son of a doctor from Caernarvon. He had taken a First Class degree in the Modern Languages Tripos at Cambridge not long before the war started and spoke perfect German. He was a brilliant rock climber and his youthful cherubic face belied a toughness of character and physique that was the admiration, envy – and sometimes the despair – of those he trained on the rocky slopes of Bethesda and elsewhere. He was quiet to the point of being monosyllabic, with a dry, understated sense of humour that only the British really appreciate. He drove his men with total ruthlessness, but today there are not many who do not thank him for the thoroughness with which he trained them. He was a totally dedicated officer, who, some say, had a touch of T. E. Lawrence about him. "He liked nothing better than talking in three or four languages at once," wrote one of his obituarists after he was killed in a car crash in 1970. "Out of business hours he was a Companion of All the Delights, consistently amusing, Welshly cynical, hard as nails."[14] His Troop called him "The Skipper", and most thought highly of him, though some remember him as being fanatical.

Though there were no stores or equipment when the Troop Commander and his handful of men arrived in Wales, Hilton Jones pitched them straightaway into a most vigorous training programme, which included scaling the walls of Harlech Castle at night – "to the slight uneasiness of the Home Guard who were then in occupation" – and a 53-mile march from Harlech to the summit of Snowdon and back in light battle order ("borrowed"), in 17½ hours, including three hours' rest on the summit.

So secret was the formation of X-Troop that even the man who had been selected to lead it had a hard time finding out what was going on. The birth of the Troop, Hilton Jones wrote after the war, occurred "in an atmosphere of considerable vagueness and tremendous secrecy . . . When the Troop Leader came to form the unit he could find very few people indeed who knew anything at all about it, and it was only by dint of rummaging boldly and sacrilegiously inside the War Office that the correct department for the recruiting of the 'bodies' could be found."[15] So though the nucleus of the Troop arrived in July, the main body of forty-three men did not reach their billets in Aberdovey until 26 October, as their recruitment – described in Chapter Three – and clearance by MI5 took longer than had been anticipated. On 13 February, 1943, a second intake of sixteen men arrived, and a third intake of thirteen men on 16 April, 1943, brought it up to War Establishment strength. They had been chosen from a total of over 350 applicants.

While the earlier Troops were assembling in Wales volunteers from the Belgian army for the Belgian Troop were called for, and on 14 August four officers and seventy-one other ranks, accompanied by additional recruits for the Dutch and French Troops, were sent to Achnacarry for the basic Commando training. When this was completed the Inter-Allied Commando's No 4, or Belgian, Troop was sent to billets in Abersoch with its headquarters based in the local yacht club. The Belgians were followed by the Norwegians and their Troop, No 5, consisting of six officers and eighty-nine other ranks, was billeted at Nevin. Lastly, the Poles arrived two days later. This Troop,

No 6, consisted of five officers and eighty-seven other ranks and was stationed initially at Fairbourne and from 13 February, 1943, at Caernarvon.

Very little documentation now exists about the founding of the Inter-Allied Commando, but there is a letter to General Sikorski, the officer commanding the Polish Free Forces, from Mountbatten in the Sikorski Museum in London which throws some light on how it was organized. It is dated 13 August, 1942, and reflects the diplomacy with which Mountbatten had to approach governments in exile when discussing the subject of their nationals serving in the British army.

"I am delighted and honoured to think that you will be forming a Polish Commando Troop.

"I am writing to confirm that your soldiers will be commanded by Polish officers during their training and in action, but the organization of the Inter-Allied Commando as a whole will come under direct command of a British officer, Colonel Lister. I shall be glad to send him round to see you, or any of your staff, whenever you like.

"It is agreed that they will be available to go on any other duties you might desire, provided you inform me in sufficient time.

"The Commando Troop will, of course, remain open to your inspection or to inspection by any of your officers whom you may wish to nominate at any time.

"I hope that you will agree that the Troop may wear the word 'Commando' on their shoulders as is the case of all other soldiers in the Commandos. This will, of course, be in addition to your own national badges, etc.

"The war establishment of the Troop is attached. At least one of the officers should speak English.

"The troops will be paid by the Polish Government and will be governed by Polish Military Law. They will be equipped with British equipment but will be permitted to wear their national dress as desired."

Sikorski agreed to this, but asked that a Polish Liaison Officer also be appointed as a link between the Troop and the Polish Government. Mountbatten readily concurred with this request, and later all the national Troops of the Commando almost certainly had their own Liaison Officers for this purpose.

Similar agreements for the raising of the Norwegian, French, Belgian and Dutch Troops were probably made, and it can be seen that by allowing such a degree of autonomy in dress and command, Mountbatten was opening a veritable Pandora's box. Throwing such a heterogeneous, polyglot group of highly motivated individuals into one unit could have been disastrous, and there was probably no shortage of doubters willing to voice their opinions about what would happen. Yet the worst never did happen. Because everyone wanted it to work it did work, though the Commando's first Administrative

Officer, Captain Connolly, remarked many years later that administration of the Commando in those early days was a "damned headache", an opinion born out by others.

"The French and Belgian names had been difficult enough, the Dutch a little more so, and with the arrival of the Norwegians it seemed that the ultimate limit in this respect had been reached. But the Polish Troop! Nominal rolls were the order of the day, and such things as Guard Orders had to be typed in all languages, so the state of the HQ typists may well be imagined. Three or four consonants in a row were quite common, and unpronounceable, and we found ourselves addressed in countless languages."[16]

The problems of so many different languages being used, and the misunderstandings caused by those trying to speak English, were of course not confined to the Inter-Allied Commando.*

At least the majority of the Inter-Allied Commando were recognizable as being foreigners, but members of X-Troop caused genuine bewilderment. Unlike the other Troops they wore the uniforms of the British army, but while they all spoke English, many still had strong accents. These were variously accounted for – they had lived with their parents abroad for many years, they had been educated on the Continent, and so on – and their Welsh landladies were very discreet and never asked questions. But once, while a group of X-Troopers was at Achnacarry one of them was asked who they were. "You vill laff," he was told, "but vee are British."

A number of X-Troopers had difficulty in understanding the Welsh. Lane was billeted in a house where the landlady had a young teenage daughter who one day entered the bathroom while he was in the bath and studied his reclining body with interest. "Surely," he said to the mother, "a man's bathroom should be a private place?" "Oh, don't worry about her," said the mother in her strong Welsh accent, "she's only a little tart." It took Lane some time to unravel that the woman had said "tot" not "tart".

Near the end of the war while some of X-Troop were fighting in Germany itself an incident occurred which showed just how easily misunderstandings arose. It is best described by the man who witnessed it, Brigadier Derek Mills-Roberts, commanding No 1 Commando Brigade. "We suddenly received an order to move up to a place called Helsdorf near the River Aller. We halted late that night in the area of a large farmhouse which we used as a Brigade Headquarters . . . Suddenly the door opened and in came the daughter

---

* One of the most amusing stories concerning the misuse of English to come out of the Second World War was when the Dutch Prime Minister, Professor Gerbrandy, first met Churchill on official business. Gerbrandy was a brilliant politician who, despite strong internal dissensions, held his government-in-exile together throughout the war, but his knowledge of the English language was limited. After crossing the lobby towards the British Prime Minister, he put out his hand and said cordially: "Good-bye." "Sir," Churchill is alleged to have replied, "I wish that all political meetings were as short and to the point."

of the house – a large handsome girl with flaxen hair – reluctantly followed by one of the members of our German Troop. She seemed distressed and hysterical and, pointing to the man, said in a voice ringing with emotion, 'This man! Is it that he must have my flesh?' 'Certainly not,' I said. 'Come,' she said, 'and I will show you.' 'You'd better come too, Joe,' I said firmly to my Intelligence Officer. Joe and I had the keen, self-conscious looks of those who imagine that they are unshockable. We followed the girl into the kitchen and waited for the tense moment when she would support her claim by some terrible evidence. Walking over to the kitchen table, she pointed dramatically. 'My flesh,' she declared, 'I tell him no, but he insists.' And there on the table was a pile of cold, sliced meat which she had been making into sandwiches. Our German soldier explained: 'I only wished to take one of the flesh sandwiches'."[17]

Confusion was also caused by the varying badges of rank among the different troops. The French officers had straight gold bars across their shoulders instead of the pips used by British commissioned officers. They also had a rank called a "*Aspirant*" which, broadly translated, meant "aspiring to the rank of officer". Though not commissioned, an *Aspirant* was treated as a 2/Lt. The highest non-commissioned rank with the French was their sergeant-major, whose gold braid was so lavish that he could easily have been mistaken for a Rear-Admiral, and probably was. The other French NCOs, however, simply had a piece of red tape sewn on the front of their battledress blouse, between the second and third button. The Dutch and the Belgian Troop, on the other hand, adopted the British system of rank insignia, though the Dutch officers carried their pips on the collars of their blouses instead of on their epaulettes. The Norwegian officers also showed their commissioned rank on their collars, whilst their NCOs had tapes on their cuffs. To make things even more confusing the Norwegians had, in addition to the normal ranks, Lance-Corporal Cadet Officers, Corporal Cadet Officers, and Sergeant and Sergeant-Major Cadet Officers. These ranks, in addition to their gold bars on their cuffs, had epaulettes surrounded with silver braid, which made them look like quite senior officers. Apparently it was not uncommon to see personnel from another Troop, and even from the HQ Troop, throwing up a smart salute to a very junior Norwegian NCO.[18]

Despite all the inherent difficulties of running a unit like the Inter-Allied Commando, the Troops settled in well and when they worked together on training exercises seemed to get on together. Soon a unit club, appropriately called "The Melting Pot", was opened in Harlech, where men from various nationalities all gathered in the evenings. It was there as much as on duty that the difference in behaviour and attitude of men from such different backgrounds was really revealed. When going out for the evening many of the men assumed an unmilitary stylishness, "somewhat reminiscent of musical comedy". Berets, despite repeated orders about how to wear them which included a laboriously printed sketch, assumed alarming angles during the evening and strange badges would appear on the left breast of blouses, while trouser legs became something like "Oxford Bags" with huge inverted V-shaped insertions in the inner leg, this last being a speciality of the French.

Some of the men seemed quite oblivious of rank. When "The Melting Pot" was opened by a famous General he was approached after the ceremony by a jovial member of the Dutch Troop who hailed from Canada. This individual was naturally cheeful and friendly, and his sunny disposition had doubtless been reinforced by liquid refreshment. He gave the General a resounding slap on the back and then shook his hand with vigour, and asked him how he was. This display of democratic friendliness was watched with some apprehension by his comrades, but the General merely grasped the private's hand and said he was very well thank you. The same Dutchman repeated this performance when Prince Bernhardt came to the club, though in a more restrained manner, and again remained unscathed.

The Poles, too, were extremely friendly and entertaining. Beside their habit of lavishing their vodka – which was "guaranteed to take the enamel off the best of baths" – on any visitor, they had a custom of showing their affection and welcome by catching hold of any guest and throwing him in the air, catching him again and throwing him up a second time before allowing him back on terra firma. They did this to Colonel Lister when he first came to inspect them and he seemed rather to enjoy the experience. But the Adjutant who was with him was wearing a kilt, and though he tried to leave before being spotted, he too sailed into the air watched by the other visitors who were amused to see him desperately clasping his arms around his knees in an effort to keep his kilt in a dignified position.

Encounters with the various nationalities were not always of a friendly nature, with the French in particular not much liking to take orders from anyone except their own officers. On one occasion when it was the turn of the French to provide the weekly guard for the Headquarters at Harlech Colonel Lister was a few minutes late in arriving to inspect it before dismissing it to its quarters, as was the daily routine. The corporal in charge waited a few minutes and when the Colonel did not appear dismissed the guard. Soon afterwards the Colonel arrived and voiced his displeasure at not finding the guard lined up as usual. The Corporal said he was sure his watch was correct and that the men had paraded at the appointed time, and that if the Colonel thought that he had not carried out his duties to the satisfaction of all concerned then he proposed marching the guard back to Criccieth then and there.

In those early days, before they had been honed by battle experience, the French seem to have been a touchy lot. On one occasion, after they had been involved in a fight with some French Canadians because of a political difference of opinion, Lister carpeted those involved. "His command of expletives was well known, and he berated them with strings of four-letter words. He was in great form. The gist of his raving was, not unreasonably, to save it for the Germans, and that was underscored with threats of RTU-ing* the whole unit. The interpreter, a young Ensign or Cadet, decided that his tough and aroused charges were not ready for this kind of sermon, so he took a certain amount of artistic licence when translating, saying something to the effect that 'Monsieur le Colonel wishes, to begin with, to congratulate you upon your victory. You have fought with exemplary courage, and he is proud of how you have acquitted yourselves, and what honour you have brought to this unit. But just one minute detail: save a little for the enemy. I know you will do even better against them, when the time comes.' The culprits beamed so broadly that Lister did a double-take. 'I must say, they are taking it very well,' he muttered, having just called them fucking bastards. 'Dismiss!' "[19]

On the whole, though, discipline was excellent which was just as well as Lister was a stickler for it. He seems, in fact, to have been rather a curious choice to command such an unusual unit, for he was no linguist, and had a rather rigid, authoritarian outlook. But there was no doubt that he looked every inch the kind of soldier a Commando was supposed to be. He had won the Military Cross in the First World War and had commanded No 4 Commando during the raid on the Lofoten Islands. He was an amateur boxer of some renown and possessed an imposing physique. Yet his temperament must be a matter for doubt as Lord Lovat, his second-in-command at No 4 Commando for a while, revealed in his memoirs when he wrote a vignette of him during Lister's time as Commanding Officer of No 4 Commando.

"Dudley Lister suffered from wife trouble (the old story), with a girl in every port, and it preyed upon his mind. The violent moods – never predictable – began to make inroads on his health and credibility. We were friends, which made the outbursts more embarrassing when I got promoted; a tactful second-in-command should help to leaven the loaf, but Dudley was an officer who never climbed down or apologized.

"Charles Vaughan's posting to the depot hastened these withdrawal symptoms. The dependable old soldier had a soothing influence on a man who admitted he lacked self-confidence. Lister proceeded to quarrel, for no good reason, with Mark Kerr; then, in turn, with three out of the six Troop leaders – Emett, Montgomerie and John Hunter – all good men who returned to their regiments. Then came a scene with Mr Pettigrew, the urbane manager of the Marine Hotel, over the disappearance of a teapot in which Lister's batman presented the early morning cuppa. This tiff brought about a curious

---

* Return to unit. Army Commandos were all formed from volunteers and were just on attachment to them from their normal army regiments. To be RTU'd, as it was called, was the biggest disgrace a Commando could suffer.

persecution complex: nobody loved him any more! So he took to the wild wood.

"Weather in the Firth of Clyde is cold at the best of times, and more so with winter fast approaching. Dudley retreated to a bunker on the golf course, where he pitched his tent beside the fairway, to live in defiance of convention – cooking on a Primus, sleeping in a flea-bag, and freshening up with a plunge into the sea. The golfers naturally complained, and the harassed colonel, moving closer to shore, dug himself into a sand dune which provided shelter from the winter blast. Here he was joined by his shivering batman. It was all very well for Dudley, with his passion for physical fitness, but poor Smith, a well-educated Yorkshire lad whose youthful appearance belied a serious soldier, had a lot to put up with.

"The colonel liked to be called 'with hot, sweet tea': Smith's day began early. His next duty: standing by in gumboots with sponge, towel and a torch in case things got lost as his master snorted naked in the waves. That was not all. When they waded ashore the frying pan came out: Dudley expected a big breakfast.

"The CO took proper pride in his appearance: he made an imposing figure on parade – which was why he got chosen in the first place. How Smith turned him out so well – working on boots, buttons and Sam Browne by the light of a hurricane lamp before daybreak – remains a mystery."[20]

Despite his peculiarities, Lister made a good job of training the Inter-Allied Commando; and though he once RTU'd one of X-Troop's best men because of some minor dress irregularity others remember him as generous to the point of eccentricity when brought before him for a misdemeanour – one X-Trooper, for example, shot another in the face with his tommy gun, luckily not badly, and received only a mild rebuke.

As his second-in-command Lister had Major Peter Laycock, the younger brother of Robert Laycock, one of the Commandos' most successful wartime leaders who succeeded Mountbatten as Chief of Combined Operations in September, 1943. In May, 1944, Peter Laycock took over from Lister as Commanding Officer and Hilton Jones was promoted to major and made the second-in-command. When Hilton Jones was wounded in Normandy his place was taken by Major Godfrey Franks who had been attached to the Inter-Allied Commando training some of the French in the Commando for cross-Channel reconnaissance raids. Laycock took part in the Walcheren operation but otherwise was obliged to run his disparate unit from his HQ at Eastbourne.

Though the Commando had training exercises together, most of the training was undertaken by each Troop on its own. Nevertheless it was Lister's ambition to see his Commando in action as a unit which, perhaps, was at least partly the reason why it was moved to Eastbourne at the end of May, 1943.

Here, at last, he could have the whole Commando "under one roof" and on 2 June the War Diary noted triumphantly: "No 10 (IA) Commando on parade as a whole for the first time in its history." This must have presented a very strange sight indeed, for, of course, not only were the men all dressed differently but they held their rifles at different angles. The parade-ground drill of each Troop was quite different too and Lister's orders had to be translated by the Troop Commanders and passed on to the men in their own language.

Soon after the arrival of the Commando in Eastbourne Lister had every man gathered in a cinema in the town and delivered a rousing speech to them. As he only spoke in English, he had interpreters at the end of each row who translated to those nearby the theme of his remarks which was that the Commando was now 200 miles nearer to the enemy – a fact which did not over-impress his audience as the Channel still remained between them and the Germans!

Though Lister would have liked the Commando to go into action as one unit, some of his Troop Commanders, and Hilton Jones in particular, was totally opposed to this idea. Discussions took place about the Commando's future role and in September most of the Troops were posted elsewhere: the Belgian and Polish Troops, along with part of the Yugoslavian Troop – of which more in a minute – and a few members of X-Troop, went to Italy; the Marines in the Dutch Troop were temporarily returned to the Dutch Government and then the whole Troop went to Glen Dye Camp in Aberdeenshire to await its posting to the Far East; the French were put on standby for an operation to invade Corsica, and were later detached along the south coast for reconnaissance raids across the Channel; the Norwegians, when the days became shorter, went to the Shetlands to take part in raids on their homeland, as some of them had done the previous winter; and the balance of X-Troop set up its base at Littlehampton, where, after a parachute course, it took over the role of preparing for small-scale parachute raids into France which up to then had been assigned to No 4 Troop of No 12 Commando under Captain O. B. Rooney.

"The training at this period was exemplified by load-carrying when parachuting, dory and dinghy landings, the use of silenced weapons, shooting at night, lying up and concealed bivouacing, abseiling on cliffs, practice parachute jumps, the use of homing pigeons, the use of the S-phone, etc. etc. Amongst the occasions which may be mentioned are: abseiling down the 'Seven Sisters' between Cuckmore Haven and Birling Gap near Seaford (an exhilarating experience), a night reconnaissance of Arundel Castle with a reward for anyone who brought back the Duchess of Norfolk's night cap (no one did!), marching from the Black Rabbit Cliff near Arundel to Littlehampton in 39 minutes, a week of night work in the country around Petworth, Midhurst, Arundel, and Steyning, and guest voyages on MGBs patrolling the

Channel and the French coast from Newhaven."[21] Though such intensive training caused injuries – some serious – no one was ever killed.

Soon after the Inter-Allied Commando's arrival in Eastbourne a second French Troop, called No 8, was formed under Lieutenant – soon to be Captain – Charles Trepel, which was made up from forty-five French marines who had returned from Lebanon after the dissolution of the 2nd Marine Battalion, and from about the same number of soldiers recently repatriated from Spain where they had been interned. All were volunteers. These two groups were put through a series of physical tests in Eastbourne, and a number were RTU'd, with the rest being sent to Achnacarry. After the basic Commando course had been completed the new Troop returned to Eastbourne where it consisted of a total of seventy-five all ranks. With the founding of a second French Troop, Lieutenant Lofi took over command of No 1 Troop while Kieffer, now with his own Headquarters, remained in overall command.

The new French Troop was not called No 7 because another new Troop was also in the process of being formed at around the same time which was allotted that number. Indeed, discussions about it had been going on for months, but it was not until 20 August that the Commando's Intelligence Officer, Captain J. G. Coates, whose job it had been to found the new Troop, and X-Troop's Intelligence Officer, Lieutenant James Monahan, who had recently joined the Inter-Allied Commando, went to London where, with General M. N. Radovitch, the Yugoslavian Military Attaché, they reviewed the first contingent for No 7 (Yugoslavian) Troop, which consisted of two officers and twenty-five other ranks.

This first contingent turned out to be the only one, though it is not known why no more volunteers were forthcoming. Monahan became their Commanding Officer temporarily and the group was put through Achnacarry in two batches. One batch was then posted to the Mediterranean to work with No 2 SS Brigade and the second batch followed early in 1944. Apparently they were all volunteers from the Royal Yugoslavian Army, but very little else is known about them. Many years later Monahan commented that he did "not have a happy time with them" and the Commando's medical officer, Dr Hodges, remembers having to stitch up several of them after they had fought each other in a pub. It is reasonable to assume that in the two batches were followers of both Mihailovich and Tito who at that time were fighting both the Germans and each other in Yugoslavia, and eventually, as will be seen, the Troop had to be disbanded.

The Yugoslavian Troop was apparently formed not only for possible use in its own country, but because of its members' ability to speak Italian – though from comments made by those who worked with them in Italy it seems that some could speak it only very badly. An attempt had been made to raise an Italian Troop from Italian citizens living in England but this had failed. A number of volunteers – most of them waiters and chefs – came forward to be interviewed by Coates, and he vividly recalls the look of horror on their faces when he explained that they were being asked to join the Commandos, and the idea was shelved.[22]

When the war in Europe ended there was also talk of raising a Japanese Troop, but the war against Japan ended before this could be taken any further. The only other Troops to be raised for the Inter-Allied Commando occurred after Belgium had been liberated, when a sufficient number of young men from the resistance, 327 in all, came forward as volunteers to reinforce the original Belgian Troop and to form Nos 9 and 10 Troops, though by the time they had been trained the war in Europe was practically over. As soon as the two new Belgian Troops had been raised and trained, the Commanding Officer of the existing Belgian Troop, Major Danloy, set up, as had Kieffer,* his own headquarters with each Troop having its own Troop Leader. The Dutch Troop, practically wiped out after Arnhem and Walcheren, was reinforced in a similar way by 107 volunteers who had come forward when two officers from the Troop held recruiting drives in liberated Dutch towns. At its largest the Commando consisted of as many as a thousand all ranks, nearly twice the size of a normal Commando.

Though the above Troops were the major additions to the Inter-Allied Commando, the very nature of the unit attracted to it individuals and small groups who were temporarily attached for special duties. A small number of No 12 Commando, for example, were attached to the Inter-Allied Commando when No 12 was disbanded in November, 1943, and No 10 was about to carry out raids on the French coast. They included highly experienced and courageous individuals like McGonigal, I. D. C. Smith, Brodison, Nash, and Barry, all veterans of many cross-Channel raids.

While men were often attached to the Inter-Allied Commando for short periods, so were men from the Commando also detached from the unit for special duties. Some were routine detachments, like the Norwegians to the Shetlands, while others were for special operations organized by SOE, Naval Intelligence, or by Combined Operations Headquarters (COHQ). Towards the end of the war some of the Dutch Troop, as will be seen, were also used by the Dutch equivalent of SOE, the BBO (Bureau voor Byzondere Opdrachten), while at least two members of this Troop, Zembsch-Schreve and Peter Tazelaar, were employed in clandestine operations, Zembsch-Schreve working for the French section of SOE and Tazelaar for "Contact Holland", which came under the control of SIS (Special Intelligence Service), and for the BBO.

Tazelaar escaped from his country for the first time by masquerading as a

---

* A third French Troop was also formed in the last months of the war, but this was numbered, as by that time were the two existing French Troops, to fit in with the other Troops of No 4 Commando to which they were attached.

member of the crew of a Swiss merchantman – in all thirty-one Dutchmen got away in this ship, the single largest escape from occupied Holland during the whole war – and was then taken to England by a British warship. When it was learnt that the British had no contact with the Dutch Resistance Tazelaar volunteered to return and in a most daring operation was dropped onto a Dutch beach with a radio operator on the night of 22/23 November, 1941. The mission went wrong, but Tazelaar managed to escape back to England via France, Switzerland, Spain and Portugal, with the knowledge that the Dutch resistance network had been split wide open by the Germans. Differences of opinion over this with his superiors led Tazelaar to resign as a midshipman in the Dutch Navy and it was then that he joined the Inter-Allied Commando as a corporal. But his conviction that the Dutch network was disastrously compromised led him to continue to argue for something to be done, and by the end of 1942 his position in England had become impossible. He therefore requested to be transferred to the Dutch army training camp in Canada as an instructor in the hope that once there he would be allowed to leave the Dutch army and cross the border and join the American forces who were fighting in the Far East – where Tazelaar had been born. His request to go to Canada was granted, but he was not allowed to leave the army so he returned once more to England where, totally at odds with those he had previously worked for, he enrolled in the National Fire Service in London. He remained there until a very senior member of the Dutch resistance arrived in London and took up the position of Minister of Justice in the government-in-exile. He asked where Tazelaar was and was astounded to hear he was a fireman. He ordered that Tazelaar be more gainfully employed and on the night of 22 November, 1944, the BBO parachuted him back into his country as contact man for other members of the Dutch Troop who had been dropped into occupied Holland the previous month. For his wartime work Tazelaar was awarded the Military Wilhelms Order, the Dutch equivalent of the Victoria Cross.[23]

Zembsch-Schreve had an equally hazardous wartime career. A Dutch national who was born in Switzerland, Zembsch-Schreve was working in Brussels when the Germans invaded Belgium. He managed to escape to Portugal and from there made his way to the United States where he enlisted in the Dutch army. After training in Canada he was sent to join the Dutch army contingent in Britain and was earmarked for an officers' training course. However, it seemed to him there were far too many officers already in the unit and he requested to be allowed to undertake more active operations. He was therefore transferred to No 12 Commando and after training with them and at Achnacarry joined the Inter-Allied Commando when it was formed in July, 1942. He again became restless and in February, 1943, was interviewed by SOE and asked if he would be willing to return to occupied territory to organize escape routes for agents operating in Denmark, Holland, Belgium and France. After training he was dropped in July, 1943, near Fleury-en-Bière with a wireless operator and worked successfully until the spring of the following year when, as the official historian of the SOE in France wrote, his luck ran out:

"The importance of luck in clandestine war can be taken for granted. But what happened to the agent whose luck ran out? If arrested, he did his best to tell his cover story; but seldom with success. Arrest usually meant discovery; discovery usually meant torture, followed by deportation; deportation in turn usually meant death. There were exceptions: a very few absolutely first-class operators stuck to their cover stories firmly and lucidly, and outwitted their interrogators. Zembsch-Schreve (Pierre), the organizer of DF's (SOE's escape section) Pierre-Jacques line, vanished in April, 1944, in Paris; his friends got to his flat before the Germans did, and removed the only compromising thing in it – a list of all the circuit's contact addresses and telephone numbers, in an easily broken Playfair code; at first they thought he had been picked up in a street rafle collecting men for forced labour, and when they discovered no one of his cover name had been arrested, they assumed he had disappeared for private reasons, with a girl he was fond of. In fact his security precautions had been so elaborate that he concealed even from his own second-in-command another cover name he was using; he had been caught passing a wireless transmitter to an agent of another section, in accordance with 'decipher yourself' orders from London in his personal code, but managed to convince the Germans that he knew nothing of the contents of a case he had handed over, at an unknown third party's request, to a business acquaintance."[24]

He was interrogated and beaten up in Fresnes prison, but revealed nothing. In August, 1944, the Germans then transferred him to Buchenwald, and later to a labour camp. With the advance of the Allies in March, 1944, he was marched to Ravensbrück concentration camp, but later managed to escape to the American lines. After the war he led the war crimes investigation department of the BBO and was subsequently awarded the OBE as well as Dutch, French and Belgian decorations.

2

These glimpses into the shadowy world of the secret services are, however, an exception in the story of the men who belonged to the Inter-Allied Commando. Almost without exception their war was fought in uniform.

There was one Troop, though, X-Troop, whose training made it specially suitable for clandestine operations. For not only did Hilton Jones train its members physically to a very high standard, but they became specialists in parachuting, small boat handling, explosives, cliff climbing, German weapons, and so on, as well as being versed in some more exotic skills like driving a train, picking locks, and identifying every known German army unit and rank. They were by far the most highly trained group in the British army, but then, as will be gathered, they were almost all men of extremely high intelligence and education.

Yet how many members of X-Troop were used in undercover operations, and which those operations were, remains something of a mystery. The stories of those who have been identified as taking part in raids by being named in reports in the Public Record Office or elsewhere, are recorded in later chapters. But there still remain an unsatisfying number of question marks over the activities of some other members of the Troop. Occasionally names and dates are mentioned in the Inter-Allied Commando's War Diary, but no further information is given. For example there is an entry under 30 March, 1943, which says that two men from the Troop, Corporals Bentley and Miles, reported back from No 62 Commando, to which they had been attached since 4 December, 1942. No 62 Commando was the cover name for the Small Scale Raiding Force (SSRF) run jointly by SOE and COHQ, but there is no further information about what these two did during these months either in the unit's War Diary or elsewhere.* The SSRF was not particularly active during this time, but they did undertake Operation Huckaback, a raid on the island of Herm in the Channel Islands, on 27/28 February, 1943, and it could well be that Bentley and Miles were part of the raiding force. Two other members of the Troop, Terry and Webster, were also probably attached to the SSRF for a time as the former recalls both being stationed at Anderson Manor, the unit's HQ, and crossing the Channel with Webster to rendezvous with a group of Frenchmen and bring back a suitcase.

Names of men detached for special training also appear in the War Diary. X-Troop was involved in several of these. One operation, codenamed Coughdrop, involved parachuting a party into the interior of France, near the Blavet River, after which the plan was to descend the river in rubber dinghies and destroy the German U-boat pens at Lorient. In another a party of X-Troop, as part of Operation Crossbow, was to be dropped near the V1 sites in the Pas de Calais with the object of bringing back information about them. Both these operations were nearly launched, but were cancelled at the last minute.

Often, however, the War Diary does not mention an operation at all, much less who took part in it. The Public Record Office does have a considerable amount of detailed reports on most COHQ operations, but the SOE files are still closed. Where there is no collaborative evidence on whether or not a member of X-Troop took part in a certain operation, it has seemed better not to name individuals who say they were on them, though this is not intended to cast any doubt on the veracity of their stories. One member of X-Troop, for

* The SOE archivist has confirmed that no recruitment list for the SSRF has survived in the SOE archives.

example, has detailed how he took part in Operation Freshman, when a group of Royal Engineer parachutists were dropped by glider into Norway to destroy the German heavy-water plant at Vemork in November, 1942. The records say there were no survivors, but the work of X-Troop was so secret, especially in those early days, that it is logical that his name would not appear on the nominal role of all those who took part in that tragic operation.

Occasionally, too, a name cropped up during interviews with surviving members of the Troop of which there is now no trace. Peter Giles was one such person. His original name was Otto Hess and he had taken his new one from a farming family who had "adopted" him when he first came to Britain. Some time in 1943 he was detached from X-Troop and was apparently dropped into Yugoslavia to work with the Partisans, but was caught, tortured and then shot by the Germans.[25]

Another story which is not possible to verify is the account of the activities of Stephen Rigby which James Leasor described in his book. The main witnesses of Rigby's activities were Lord Louis Mountbatten, Maj-General Sir Leslie Hollis, who was Senior Military Assistant Secretary to the War Cabinet and Chiefs of Staff Committee, and Sir Ronald Wingate Bt, all now dead. It was from them that Leasor gleaned Rigby's story of how he was dropped into France and pretended to be a German agent returning to report on the British plans to invade at the Pas de Calais. The trouble is that not one surviving member of X-Troop can remember Rigby, or can even think of anyone who left the Troop at that time who could have been him. This does not mean that Rigby did not exist, but as a number of enemy aliens served in the British armed forces – several also worked for SOE – even as illustrious a trio as those named above could have been mistaken when they thought that Rigby came from X-Troop, when he was actually recruited from another source.

3

The first action seen by men from the Inter-Allied Commando was the raid on Dieppe that took place on 19 August, 1942. Fifteen members of the French Troop, led by Francis Vourch, by now a lieutenant, were attached to the two army Commando units attacking the flanks and to 40 (RM) Commando, whose task it was to reinforce the centre.

Also on the raid were five of the early members of X-Troop: Platt, Rice, Latimer, Bate and Smith. As far as can be ascertained their role was to go with the troops that were to break into the town hall and the German Headquarters, and find and remove any documents of value from it. Bate was killed, and Rice and Smith were captured and never heard of again. None of them ever got anywhere near their objectives.

Platt, who was wounded in the left leg during the operation, was aboard TLC 124, the headquarters boat of the 4th Canadian Armoured Brigade. After the operation he wrote a report. "The first landing took place about 0605 under heavy machine-gun and artillery fire. As I was about to land just behind the first tank ashore we were given orders by shouting to come back owing to very heavy fire. We made a second try at landing at about 0900 at a different place. Another tank was landed. During this landing we were surprised by German mobile artillery. Nobody could land because the ramp was down and fire was directed right into the TLC. Whilst trying to land under cover of a tank at about 0945 I was wounded in the leg. I made no more attempts to land and after being transferred to another boat which towed TLC 124 I arrived back in Newhaven soon after 12 o'clock midnight."[26]

Platt only says that he was with two Canadian sergeants and had four tasks to undertake with them, without saying what these were. But Latimer in his report states that his orders were to proceed independently to German General Headquarters in Dieppe to pick up all documents, etc. of value, as well as, if possible, a new German respirator, and it can be presumed that Platt had a similar task.

In the same TLC as Latimer and the two Canadian Field Security sergeants who were to accompany him were a section of Sappers, three Churchill tanks and their crews, a jeep and a motor cycle. "Shortly after 0600 a landing was attempted. There appeared to be three TLCs with tanks. Two wire cutters and three tanks were landed. One I saw hit by a direct shot. It blew up. MG and howitzer fire was intense (cross and frontal fire). The other two tanks advanced a short distance, firing at pillboxes. Of the two wire cutters one came back injured. The other Sappers did not go on shore. Our small detachment waited its chance. We swam round from the galley of the TLC. We came onto the stony shore, lay in a hollow and looked around. The Germans were waiting for us on the beach. We could see some of them behind rocks and sand about 120 yards away. It was impossible to go forward. We swam back to another TLC. The steering gear and main door were broken. The TLC was tugged home by gunboats. No tanks re-embarked. Several buildings in Dieppe were ablaze. Over the radio of the TLC we heard that one of the tanks which had landed had succeeded in overrunning one of the pillboxes. We reached Newhaven about 2130."[27]

These two stark reports, which have lain unpublished in the Public Record Office for decades, are further eyewitness accounts of the slaughter that took place of Canadian troops that day. The Frenchmen attached to the two Commandos that attacked the flanks, and to the Canadians in the middle of the assault, fared no better.

Sergeant de Wandelaer, Sergeant-Major Montailler, Corporal César, Ropert and Errard were attached to No 3 Commando on the left of the assault; Lieutenant Francis Vourch, Sergeant Dumanoir, and Privates Loverini, Simon, Jean, Borettini and Tanniou were attached to 40 (RM) Commando;

and Corporals Balloche, Robouhans and Taverne were attached to No 4 Commando on the right. Their general mission was liaison with the civilian population with the object of reassuring them and of obtaining information. They were also given permission to recruit a small number of suitable local Frenchmen who were to be taken back to England.

Only the Inter-Allied Commando detachment with No 4 Commando succeeded in remaining ashore and accomplishing its task of contacting the local inhabitants. In doing so it obtained valuable information about enemy dispositions in the Dieppe area.

Orders were given that the word "France" was to be unstitched from under the word "Commando" on the Frenchmen's shoulders, and that they were to wear, as did everyone else, steel helmets. These orders were apparently ignored and all the Frenchmen wore their French naval berets with its distinguishing red pompon and retained their "France" flashes. If this is correct – and Lord Lovat, for one, said, many years later, that certainly all the Frenchmen under his command obeyed the order – it proved to be, in one case, a flamboyant but fatal gesture.

The detachment with 40 (RM) Commando did not get ashore at all, but all returned safely to Newhaven that evening. Most of those with No 3 Commando on the left flank were also unable to land but one of the very few who did manage to, on the beach codenamed Yellow 1, was Sergeant-Major Montailler. He was one of a small party who succeeded in climbing the Ciseaux and the Morval Gorge at Berneval Le Grand to reach the last villa, which belonged to a baker. But then they were spotted and in the fighting that followed Montailler was wounded and captured.[28]

Another of the French Commandos to be captured was César who had been trapped under the cliffs with a group of French Canadians, having landed with a small party of No 3 Commando at around 0530. They were made prisoner about noon and marched off with their hands on their heads. As they were being searched, César slipped off his wedding ring and let it fall into the grass, "rather than let them take it".[29] He had already taken off his battle blouse and thrown away his sailor's beret, so that he could not be identified as a French Commando. This no doubt saved his life for when the Germans captured Montailler they saw his "Commando" and "France" flashes and his beret and promptly shot him.*

Questions were being asked of the English officers whether there were any Free French fighting with them, and this made César realize that he must try and escape before he was questioned. At about 1400 the prisoners were marched towards Enverneu and spent the night in a half-built building. The

---

* According to Rear-Admiral Lepotier, who wrote a book called *Raiders from the Sea*, César returned to Dieppe in 1950, found Montailler's grave, and was told that he had been shot while trying to escape.

next afternoon he was taken to the station with other prisoners and put in a waggon with wooden slats across the windows. Once the train had started César, with the help of some French Canadians, levered off a wooden slat and managed to squeeze through and climb on to the buffers of the waggon. The train was travelling at about 25–30km an hour and when it passed through a wood César jumped. As he fell three rifle shots rang out and then, as he ran through the woods, a machine gun opened up, but he was not hit.

After resting, César began walking in the direction of Aufay and was then taken in by a French family who gave him some civilian clothes, three cigarettes and two boiled eggs. César now started to walk south towards the Spanish border but after several days was exhausted and had to ask for help. He was lucky, and was sheltered for several weeks on a farm where he looked after the sheep, but eventually found his way to St Quentin where his family lived. His brother equipped him with false papers and ration books, and for some months he lived a hazardous existence while trying to find a means of returning to England. Eventually he and some Allied airmen were taken south to St Pierre-sur-Mer, near Perpignan, where they were picked up by an SOE-operated fishing boat flying a Portuguese flag, which took them to Gibraltar.

4

While disaster was overtaking the rest of the Dieppe beachhead, No 4 Commando managed to land, unnoticed by the enemy, at the beach codenamed Orange 1. Their target was the Hess battery near Varengeville. The detachment of three French Commandos was attached to C Troop led by Major Mills-Roberts, whose task was to make a frontal assault on the battery while the rest of the Commando, under its Commanding Officer, Lord Lovat, landed at Quiberville on Orange 2 and attacked it from the rear.

Balloche and Mills-Roberts led C Troop off the beach while Rabouhans and Taverne became part of a defensive perimeter to guard the Troop's retreat – a task they performed so effectively that on 12 November, 1942, they were both decorated with the Croix de Guerre "avec étoile" by the Commander-in-Chief of the Free French Naval Forces, Rear-Admiral Auboyneau.

As C Troop moved cautiously forward towards their objective a peasant appeared out of nowhere with a basket of eggs and offered them to the Commandos. "They tell us you're starving in England." Balloche thanked the man but said they did not need eggs right then, though on their way back the Commandos did get given some and carried them carefully back to England.

In the final assault on the battery Balloche was one of the first. The British officer in charge of that last assault said he saw a small French Commando – Balloche was only 1m 60cm tall – trying to climb up the parapet of the battery with British Commandos all around him. When he got to the top he fell down the other side and apparently came face-to-face with a German and killed him before the man could move. Balloche was equally active after the battery had been destroyed for while under fire he carried a wounded British Commando across the beach to the waiting landing craft, and was later awarded the Military Medal for his part in the operation,[30] Lovat's recommendation stating that "He was attached to one of my Troops and played a conspicuous part in the searching and occupation of the village of Le Haut, which lies in close proximity to the German Heavy Battery at Varengeville. He proved of great assistance to the Troop Leader, who could not speak French, and having gained the information required, he subsequently went into action and, with the rest of the Troop, inflicted heavy casualties on the enemy." It was to be the first of many British decorations awarded to men of the Inter-Allied Commando.

2

Escape and
Evasion

We have seen that the Inter-Allied Commando was a most unusual unit, made up of most unusual men. As refugees, albeit many of them military personnel at the time, the men who were later to form the Commando did not simply catch a cross-Channel ferry when war started and report at the nearest recruiting office once in Britain. How they did arrive must be a book in itself and is certainly part of the story of the formation of the Commando. If they had not been determined to fight National Socialism actively by escaping from their homelands, or by returning voluntarily from neutral countries, there would never have been an Inter-Allied unit. A number suffered terribly in the process and quite a few took many months to make it from occupied territory to freedom. One, at least, took years.

Many of the Norwegians came across the North Sea in small boats and arrived in the Shetlands, the Orkneys or the Hebrides. Most of these perilous voyages were undertaken in small groups with inadequate navigational equipment. Normally it took only a few days to sail across, but one group of thirteen men got caught in a storm and were at sea nine days before being rescued by a Scottish fishing boat and towed in to harbour. Daniel Rommetvedt, a future officer in the Norwegian Troop, was luckier. With a group of seventeen other young men and one woman, he escaped from Tanager in a 45-foot fishing boat and crossed in remarkably quick time. It was not easy, for the Germans overflew the area frequently and fishing boats were restricted as to the hours they were allowed to be out of harbour. They all knew that if they were caught trying to escape they would be executed. "All the participants met in the darkness in Tanager and went on board the fishing boat

*Sjøleik** during the night of 10 October, 1941, and at first light we left harbour. Everyone except three stayed below deck. During the day we fished on the fishing place close to the coast. When the sun went down we steered a course towards the harbour, but at very low speed. After some time it became dark enough for us to take the chance to turn around and set a course westward for Scotland. This was the most critical time. Had the Germans seen us changing our course to the westward? But we were lucky and the next day we had a strong wind blowing from the west and low clouds which suited us very well. We landed in Aberdeen 54 hours later after a successful journey and went by train to London the next day escorted by two friendly Scottish policemen."[1]

Some future members of the Norwegian Troop served as crews, or were passengers on, two of the three Norwegian merchant ships which managed to evade the German blockade when they steamed out of neutral Gothenburg in the autumn of 1942. A total of ten Norwegian merchantmen were being held there by the Swedish Government, but as they were all loaded with special steel and ball bearings, essential cargo for the British war effort, the British Government put pressure on the Swedes to have them released. This was at last done and on the night of 1 April, 1942, all the ships sailed, knowing that the Germans were waiting for them. Five of the ships were sunk by their own crews, two returned to Gothenburg, while the remaining three escaped to England. Arne Sørbye, later a sergeant in the Norwegian Troop, was boatswain on one of the merchantmen and he, along with the rest of the crew of his ship and the other two which reached England, were subsequently awarded the Royal Norwegian War Medal for their bravery in bringing the ships safely to an English port. Three of the passengers on two of the merchantmen which made it to England also joined the Norwegian Troop after serving for a time with the small Norwegian army contingent stationed at Tain in Scotland.[2]

A few future members of the Norwegian Troop came back on British ships after the raids on Vaagso and Lofoten; others had served in the crews of the Norwegian whaling fleet. Two future members were ski instructors for the American forces in Iceland. Rolf Hauge, the Norwegians' Troop Commander, arrived after a most circuitous journey: he escaped into Sweden and then to Russia. He travelled across Russia, then neutral, to the Bosporus. From there he went to Cairo by train and ship before finding a berth on a ship filled with refugees and Italian prisoners of war which arrived at Glasgow on 9 September, 1941.[3]

Olav Gausland, who lived on a farm outside Stavanger and later became Hauge's second-in-command, also entered Britain in an unusual way. When the Germans invaded, he was a reserve infantry officer. His company made a

* *Sjøleik* and her owner spent the rest of the war fishing out of Buckie and after the German surrender returned to Norway.

stand against the Germans at Dirdal but was outflanked by Austrian mountain troops and forced to surrender. Gausland, however, refused and he and two friends escaped by boat across the fjord to Frafjord and tried to join the Norwegian army, who, they thought, were still fighting to the east; but they found Germans everywhere and were forced to return. Gausland now joined the police and was sent to the police college at Oslo. This soon lost its appeal when he was continually getting into trouble for not giving the Nazi salute, so one day in the summer of 1941 he took a train to the border and crossed into Sweden. He was interned but was asked by the Norwegian Embassy in Stockholm to go back into Norway on a mission. This he agreed to do and, though at the time he had no idea what it was about, he later learnt that he had gathered information about the massacre of some Norwegian resistance fighters at Trondheim.

Shortly after this he was allotted a seat on a small courier plane which flew him to Leuchars in Fife. After being cleared at the Patriotic School, he volunteered for the Commandos.[4]

By contrast, the Polish Commando Troop was almost entirely drawn from the 2nd Battalion of the Polish Grenadiers which had fought in France in 1940. Its Commander, Capt. W. Smrokowski, a 31-year-old professional soldier, had been involved in the bitter fighting when the Germans invaded Poland, but after the collapse of his country he had escaped to Hungary. From there he made his way to France where he joined the 1st Grenadier Division of the Polish army. He was wounded in France and by the time he had recovered the armistice had been signed, so he made his way across the Pyrenees into Spain and managed to get to Gibraltar without being caught, and from there went to Britain.[5]

The Dutch were among the most active escapers, but often they had the most difficult task for they were surrounded by water on one side and by occupied territory on the others. The French and the Norwegians, on the other hand, at least had border with neutral countries which, though it certainly didn't make escape easy, did at least make it conceivable. The Dutch had an even more severe handicap. Theirs is an open, flat country, which is small and highly populated. Unlike in France, it simply was not possible to organize armed resistance along the lines of the Maquis. Men, eager to fight the Nazis, had nowhere to hide, nowhere to go – except to Britain.

Most of the volunteers for the Dutch Troop came from the Princess Irene Brigade, which was formed from the remnants of the Dutch army which managed to escape across the Channel before the collapse of France. Others were trapped in Holland, and were demobilized by the Germans and sent home. A few started to work for the Dutch underground, but others, when they found what Nazi rule was like, were determined to escape. Some tried to get across the North Sea and de Waard was one of the few who succeeded.* He had been in the Dutch army, but after it was disbanded he failed to settle down and soon he and two friends were plotting to escape: they decided to try and get to England by the most direct route – across the North Sea.

They found a rowing boat in an outer harbour at Ymuiden, which belonged to the local blast-furnace works where de Waard had worked before the war. They then found an outboard motor, repaired it, tested it in a rainbutt, "borrowed" petrol from the works through a friend who worked there, and at the beginning of March, 1941, started to gather information on the whereabouts of German observation posts and patrols, and to collect the necessary food. Another friend owned a ship's chandlery so they bought a compass, but none of them knew how to read it, and they had to be taught the rudiments of navigation by an old trawler skipper.

The night they chose to leave was a moonless one in the middle of March. A few days before, they hid the outboard motor, extra petrol, and their food and compass in a huge pile of coke outside the furnace works. They dug it all out the night of the escape and successfully loaded the boat without being detected. Then with rags wrapped around the oars to muffle the sound they cautiously paddled their way out of the harbour. They had to pass a German strongpoint and some piers which were patrolled, but the night was dark and they were not detected.

Once in the open sea they started the engine, but were forced to stop it when they saw a searchlight and heard a German patrol boat approaching. It came within 150 feet of them but then veered off. When it had gone they restarted the engine and began to steer the course given to them by the trawler skipper. One steered, while another called out the compass course. When day broke there was nothing to see but grey water all around. They ate their meagre rations, were seasick, and once were nearly swamped, but they kept going and the next morning saw driftwood and seagulls and knew they must be near land. Then in the distance they saw a destroyer coming towards them, and they knew they were safe.

They were picked up and after an initial interrogation by the ship's officers were given their first introduction to British mild and bitter while their clothes were dried in the engine room. When the destroyer docked at Harwich they were put in a prison cell and the next day were transferred to the Patriotic School just outside London, through which every unofficial arrival passed for

---

* In his book *Soldier of Orange*, Eric Hazelhoff Roelfzema states, on page 58, that though more than a hundred Dutchmen set out for freedom across the North Sea less than a dozen actually made it. The Germans caught some, but most of those who reached the open sea were never heard of again. Roelfzema himself twice tried to take a small boat across and failed each time. All Dutchmen who escaped to Britain were called *Engelandvaarders* and were decorated for doing so. Those who escaped overland were awarded the Cross of Merit and those who escaped by sea were given, because it was so hazardous, a higher decoration, the Bronze Cross.

vetting. They spent a week there and were then released. De Waard decided to join the Princess Irene Brigade, then stationed at Congleton outside Wolverhampton, but both his friends opted for Intelligence work. Then in March, 1942, de Waard volunteered to be trained with the British Commandos and later became one of the original members of the Dutch Troop when it was formed.[7]

Another successful escape by sea was carried out by Jan Linzel who was later to command the Dutch Troop. After two failed attempts he and seven friends were given a small motorboat which they painted up to look like a German patrol boat. In September, 1941, they left at night from a small island near Rotterdam, but were soon challenged by a German patrol. The Dutchmen said they belonged to the German army and were on special duties, and when they were asked for the password demanded it from the patrol. The Germans hesitated, then said they were going to report to their command post. This gave the Dutchmen the opportunity they needed and they slipped away in the night. After nearly 14 hours at sea in thick fog they landed near Ipswich, guided ashore through the minefields by some British airmen.[8]

By no means all the members of the Dutch Troop, however, came from Holland during the war years, and several had no idea even how to speak Dutch. Westerling was born in Turkey and knew no Dutch when he first joined the Troop. Beckmeijer and Baggerman hardly knew any either as they had both come from China where they had been working in a bank, and Roozeboom only knew English as he, like Knijff and Offerman, came from Canada.

Others came from even further away. Van Gelderen was born in Holland but since 1936 had been living in South Africa. At the start of the war he joined the South African Air Force, but later volunteered to go to England. De Koning was a ranch manager in the Argentine who arrived in England in April, 1941.

Michels had volunteered for the French Foreign Legion in 1936, being unable to find a job in Holland. The Legion formed part of what was known as the 13½ Brigade which fought at Narvik before eventually ending up in England. "We were given the alternative of joining the Free French Forces or be returned to North Africa which was Vichy controlled. I did not want to do either so I joined the Pioneer Corps." From the Pioneer Corps Michels joined the Royal Engineers, and then volunteered for the Commandos.

A few, like Knottenbelt, were already in England when war started. He had been brought to England as a baby by his parents and was at Oxford University in 1940 when he left to join the nucleus of the Princess Irene Brigade. Like other volunteers for the Commandos he found it "was not an exciting unit" and was one of the first volunteers to be picked to train with British Commando units.

2

The Belgian Troop consisted almost entirely of volunteers from the remains of the Belgian army that managed to escape across the English Channel after

30

Dunkirk. Some of the future members of the Troop were unable to escape immediately, and had to find a more roundabout route. Noel Dedeken, for example, helped to defend Dunkirk, but was wounded there and repatriated to a Bruges hospital. He escaped from there and went into hiding, and then set off with a friend to bicycle to Paris, managing to avoid or bluff their way through German road blocks. They then crossed into unoccupied France, and after a spell in a refugee prison they escaped into Spain and eventually into Portugal. They were then put into the care of the Belgian Embassy and were eventually taken at night in a motorboat to join a British cargo ship bound for Gibraltar. From Gibraltar Dedeken was sent to Greenock, arriving there in March, 1942, exactly a year after starting out from Bruges.[9]

Although many of the Belgian Commando Troop came direct from the Belgian army, some of its members were civilians when Germany invaded Belgium in 1940. Carlo Segers was a young student and his story is a good example of the chaos and suffering that occurred in those last days before the Nazis overran what remained of free Europe. He escaped on his bicycle and on 21 May, 1940, found himself on the outskirts of Calais. After spending a night at a farmhouse in the company of a dead farmer and his dead son he made his way into the town and boarded a Norwegian ship called the *Leka*. With 1100 refugees and soldiers aboard, the ship left Calais and made for Cap Gris Nez where the Captain asked for instruction as to which route to take across the English Channel. He was told to halt immediately, an order he ignored as it was obvious that Cap Gris Nez was already in German hands. Instead, he steamed straight across the Channel.

In his book[10] about the exploits of the Belgian Troop, Segers vividly describes that nightmare passage with the ship full of abandoned children, deaf-mutes, drunken soldiers and invalids. The next morning a woman tried to jump overboard with her baby and on the crowded decks people fainted with hunger and thirst. In protest against the way the refugees were being treated, a Frenchman undressed and leapt into the sea and another went mad. Later, the soldiers started pilfering what food the refugees possessed and the Captain was forced to appoint a military commander. He confiscated all weapons and all military personnel were sent below in case German aircraft might mistake it for a troopship. When it changed course rumours spread like wildfire among the refugees, one of them being that the Captain was a German sympathizer and that he intended taking the ship to a German port. Another was that he was heading for Gibraltar.

Eventually the Captain explained that he had been diverted to Southampton by the authorities at Dover, and when the *Leka* arrived there, on 24 May, 1940, the passengers were greeted by a detachment of British soldiers with fixed bayonets, lining the quay. No one was allowed ashore, but a doctor and two nurses came aboard to take care of the children. Later, some milk and bread was brought aboard. Then came the amazing news: the ship was only allowed to stay until 0600 the following morning and would then have to leave with all its passengers.

The Captain refused to accept these orders and a British official went on board to discuss the matter with him. As the man left, Segers overheard him say to the Captain, "Well, you didn't have to bring these people here! You could have landed them somewhere in the southern part of France."

The next morning a pilot came aboard with orders for the *Leka* to sail to St Malo, but the Captain refused to leave without written instructions as to what he should do with the sick, the women and the children. He requested that the pilot ask for supplies and life jackets, and for a doctor and nurses. This did the trick for, after the pilot had delivered the Captain's message, the authorities relented and in the afternoon a large barge came alongside the ship and the refugees began to disembark. They were housed in a hangar and interviewed by immigration authorities before being allowed to go on to a refugee camp. Segers was lucky and found lodgings with an Anglican priest. He had to report twice weekly to the police and was not allowed to work or to be on the streets after 10pm. "By some miracle" he was allowed to use the local library and spent his time reading newspapers there. On 23 June he was delighted to hear the only Belgian minister at that time to reach London, Marcel-Henri Jaspar, proclaim that Belgium intended to fight on, and soon afterwards he joined the nucleus of the Belgian army which was at that time at Tenby under the command of Lt-General Van Strijdonck de Burkel.

3

Like the Dutch, the French Commando Troop was made up of men from all over the world. Pinelli, for example, came from New Caledonia, and César and de Wandelaer had both served in the Foreign Legion in North Africa, while Jean Zivohlava had come from Mexico.

An Austrian living in Paris, he had changed his name to Jean Gautier to avoid Gestapo interrogation. He went south and when the Germans eventually reached where he was living at Angers, he got out immediately and managed to get aboard a ship bound for Canada, but it was bombed and sank in mid-Atlantic. Another ship in the convoy picked him up but it was later torpedoed and Zivohlava found himself in the water again. This time he was picked up, dressed only in his shirttails, by a merchantman whose convoy was going back to Britain and he was finally dropped at Oban – still in his shirttails.

"He had nothing. He was handed over to the police and locked up in gaol. An unknown picked up out of the sea in wartime had to be checked. The police were thorough but treated him well. Before being passed on to the Special Branch in London, a constable took him shopping.

"In London, the Special Branch were thorough. They had to be as this was wartime. A meticulous process began but finally Jean Gautier was cleared and sent to the Free French Forces."[11]

Another member of the French Commandos took an astonishing length of time to reach England. This was Maurice Chauvet who, aged 20, had been a gunlayer on a French cruiser which was in Algiers harbour when the armistice was signed. The captain was in tears when he made the announcement but many of the crew were only too glad that the fighting, for them, was over. Chauvet, however, was determined to continue fighting. The cruiser sailed for Toulon the next day and was then ordered to Dakar, but as Chauvet had finished his tour of duty he refused to sign on again and was demobilized. He returned to his family in Paris where he soon found others who wanted to continue the fight against the Nazis, and when the BBC announced that anyone who wanted to join de Gaulle in England should make their way to a port and find the Gaullist representatives there, Chauvet, in January, 1941, set off for Marseilles. He escaped being arrested because whenever he was interrogated he said he was going to Marseilles to re-enlist. When he got there he became involved with the Gaullists and after a couple of months had to find work aboard a steamer bound for Dahomey in order to escape being arrested. He worked as a deckhand and when the steamer was on its return voyage to Europe he changed ships at Port Lyautey (now Kenitra). Then on the night of 13 October, 1941, he and two Norwegian sailors took a small dinghy and started rowing for Gibraltar. It took them several days to reach the Straits; frozen and starving, they were picked up by a Spanish patrol boat and taken to Algeciras.

After interrogation, Chauvet and his two companions were taken to a military prison in Seville and then, at the end of November, to Madrid where the two Norwegians were liberated by their Consul. Chauvet, however, remained a guest of the Spanish Government who transferred him to the notorious Miranda de Ebro camp in the department of Burgos. Here were incarcerated the remnants of the International Brigade, some 600 or 700 men of many nationalities, as well as men who had been picked up while trying to escape from France to Gibraltar.

Conditions in the camp were appalling. It was bitterly cold and there was only one tap to serve the whole camp. When the Germans occupied Vichy France the numbers were swelled to around 5000 as Frenchmen fled across the Pyrenees. There was nothing Chauvet could do except sit and wait.

Eventually, it became plain to the Spaniards that the Allies were going to win the war and their policy of neutrality became less hostile. In March, 1943, Chauvet was released from the camp and the following month he boarded a steamer leaving Setubal in Portugal for Casablanca, now in Allied hands.

But Chauvet's problems were not over yet, for when he reached Casablanca he was again imprisoned, this time by the Allies. His stay, however, was short for he was released when he volunteered to join the Free French Forces in

Britain. He was put aboard a troopship and on 6 June, 1943, arrived at Greenock. From the time he had started out from his home in Paris to the time he arrived in London, the morning after he landed, had taken an incredible 882 days![12]

Another member of the French Commandos who suffered at the hands of the Spanish authorities was Charles Trepel. Trepel, who was probably of Czechoslovakian origin, was born in Odessa, but his family moved to Germany during the Russian Revolution. When the Nazis came to power in 1933 Trepel moved to Paris and when war was declared he joined the artillery. The following year he was commissioned as a lieutenant and was demobilized after the armistice. But, instead of returning home, he chose to escape to Spain, which he did in July, 1941, but was caught and interned at a camp called Barbastro. Unlike Chauvet, however, he managed to escape after a short time, found his way to Barcelona, signed up aboard a neutral cargo ship as a stoker, and in September, 1941, arrived in Gibraltar from where he made his way to England.[13]

Gwenn-ael Bolloré, who joined the French Commandos under the name of Bollinger, did not take as long as Chauvet to reach England, but the dangers he faced in order to get there were equally real. Bolloré was only 14 in 1940, but he never forgot the sight of groups of French soldiers hanging around his town, Quimper, in August of that year. Though the Armistice had not been signed, the soldiers had done nothing to prevent a handful of German motor cyclists from occupying the town. Bolloré was appalled by their behaviour and swore that as soon as he could he would fight for a free France.

For three years Bolloré and his young friends plotted how they could get to England to fight. When he had just turned 17 Bolloré met someone in the Resistance who arranged for him to buy a small boat off a boat-builder at Carentec, and Bolloré sold his horse to find the money for it. On 5 March, 1943, he was guided by a local Resistance leader to the boat-builder's home where he found eight other Frenchmen who were to accompany him across the Channel.

The boat that Bolloré had bought was old and rotten, and was only just over 20 feet long, but it had an engine and some old sails and Bolloré was confident he and his crew would be able to take her across. They left on a moonless night just as a storm was beginning to blow up. They could not use the sails for fear of being seen by a German blockhouse near the harbour entrance, but good friends had given the German sentries a case of wine and they crept out by using the oars. Once beyond the harbour, they hoisted the sails and headed north. Later, they tried to start the engine, but it had been swamped during the storm and would not start. The wind continued to rise and soon it was blowing almost at gale force. Bolloré was violently seasick and while bailing the boat out he lost a glove and his hand became frostbitten.

When daybreak came the nine men were in a sorry state, soaked to the skin and frozen. The boat, too, was in a terrible condition: the mainsail had been ripped and they could only use the foresail. However, the wind was so strong at first that they surged on at about 7 knots. Later it moderated and that evening they saw the English coast. When light came the next morning, however, it had disappeared. The wind was now very light and the boat just drifted. Things did not look too good, but in the middle of the morning they saw a small convoy approaching, escorted by a Norwegian warship, which drew close and opened fire on them. They began waving and shouting and it came alongside and picked them up. They were then transferred to a British destroyer which took them to Plymouth. After the usual vetting process, Bolloré signed on as a member of the *Forces Navales Française Libre* and went to the French barracks, Bir-Hakeim, near Portsmouth. From there he volunteered to serve under Kieffer and trained as a medical orderly.[14]

Another member of the French Commandos, Lt Guy Vourc'h, also escaped from occupied France. At 18 he had left his home in Finisterre to go to Paris to study medicine. When war broke out he joined the Medical Services but later transferred to the infantry and became a cadet officer. When France was overrun he tried to catch a ship from Rochefort, but the last one had left. He made his way to Nantes, where he exchanged his uniform for civilian clothes. Then he returned to his home in the village of Plomodiern and for the next month tried unsuccessfully to bribe fishermen to take him to England.

Despairing of finding anyone who would agree to sail him across the Channel, in August he bought a 30 ft fishing boat and began to prepare it for the voyage he now planned to undertake without the help of local fishermen. This took him two months and on 21 October, 1940, he set out from Douarnenez with five others, including his young brother, Jean, to make his way to England. At first all went well, but on the second day they ran out of petrol and lay becalmed. Then the wind came from the wrong direction and blew them south, before another gale sprang up and blew them back north again. For ten days and nights they were driven north, huddled together to survive the freezing conditions, having run out of both food and water. By now they had no idea where they were and had very nearly given up hope when they were picked up by a steamer somewhere off Milford Haven.

All six volunteered for the Free French Forces. Vourc'h was sent to a camp at Camberley and was commissioned. He then volunteered to be sent as an agent into France, but, having completed a parachute course, his mission was cancelled and for a year he was attached to the Political Intelligence Department in London before joining the French Commandos.[15]

There is not space to catalogue the adventures each member of the Inter-Allied Commando encountered in reaching freedom, but these examples show that there is little doubt that most of them had to use their courage and resourcefulness to the utmost before they even became Commandos.

3

The King's Own
Enemy Aliens

The rise of Nazism in western Europe during the 1930s caused a refugee problem of considerable magnitude, with Jews and those with left-wing sympathies fleeing from their homelands. It was from these exiles, either enforced or self-imposed, that the men who were to make up X-Troop were eventually chosen. The majority were Germans and Austrians, and nearly all were Jews. Broadman had to escape from Vienna because of his known left-wing views as did Gordon's family, while other Austrians in the Troop included Masters, Streets and Tennant. Latimer and Platt came from the Sudetenland; Lane, Sayers, Swinton and Kershaw were Hungarian, Watson Rumanian, Davies Danish, while Jones, it seems, was of Russian extraction. Barnes was technically a Pole because that was the nationality his parents chose when the Austro-Hungarian Empire was divided, but they lived in Austria and Barnes knew only German until he came to boarding school in England and then on to Manchester University. McGregor was probably the only one who spoke no German, though a member of the Troop has said that Davies "spoke no language I understood". McGregor was born in Germany of German parents called Kury who had been married in England and had lived there for many years. They returned to England when McGregor was three, but though he was brought up in England, he was never naturalized and was technically a stateless person and was interned with other enemy aliens in June, 1940.

Many of those who escaped suffered humiliating experiences. One man was made to scrub the streets of Vienna by Nazi stormtroopers, another was forced to help pull down his local synagogue. Several lost relatives in the concentration camps, and a few were incarcerated there themselves. Turner was in both

Dachau and Buchenwald, and was only released because the British Labour Party arranged for him to enter England as a refugee. He left only just in time, arriving in England in August, 1939. Watson, whose father was Rumanian and mother Czechoslovakian, lived in Berlin. After *Kristalnacht* in November, 1938, Watson, his brother, and two friends decided to get out of Germany as quickly as possible. With just one suitcase each they walked to the Dutch border but were caught crossing it and were handed over to the German police. After four days in the local prison they were put aboard a lorry with the words, "Here is the lorry which will take you to the railway station."

"We thought we were on our way to Berlin! There were already ten or twelve men on the lorry when we climbed onto it. They too had no idea what was to happen. On the way we collected perhaps another dozen men and when we arrived at the railway station, the lorry was surrounded by SS men and guard dogs. After we had been virtually chased into the trains, most of us were quite bewildered. In every town we passed through, more people were being bundled into the train. It was not until we had been under way for about eight or ten hours that we began to realize that our destination could well be some kind of prison camp. Finally the train drew to a halt and, looking about, we saw the name Dachau-Bavaria on large sign posts. I had never heard of Dachau and was not aware of the existence of the place till then. They hauled us off the train, with dogs harassing us and the SS men wielding sticks. We were marched to what appeared to be a prison camp and had to assemble in the compounds. There we were made to stand for several hours whilst being divided into groups according to age, fitness, etc. Next we had to have a haircut – a very simple procedure, each one of us had his hair shorn off completely. Then followed a session with the photographer, who made us hold a plate with numbers in front of us, before taking the picture. Obviously we were going to be treated like criminals. The photos were taken in a cubicle which we had to enter one by one. At the end of the session the photographer pressed a button which released a steel pin through the seat which we had to occupy and the pin penetrated our posteriors. Naturally everyone jumped with shock and left the cubicle as fast as he could. Had things not been so terrible, one could perhaps have laughed it all off in time. As it was, no one had known what to expect and our tormentors had their perverse pleasure at our discomfiture.

"All this took place in the middle of November and it was bitterly cold. We were also very very hungry. After they allocated us to our blocks, we just had to lie down on the floor without any covering, only wearing our clothing. We slept like sardines, as close to one another as possible to keep warm. That state of affairs lasted for a whole week, when at long last we were given one blanket each.

"During my time in the concentration camp, I saw many terrible happenings. I cannot relate them all except the ones which have left an indelible mark in my memory of their exceptional brutality.

37

"On several occasions men could be seen hurling themselves against electrified wire fencing. They would rather meet a terrible but instant death, than face any more of the heinousness meted out by the SS. Sometimes these diabolic guards would chase a man whose face they did not like, shouting at him to run fast. When their victim had run across an area which was 'forbidden' to prisoners, they would draw their pistols and shoot him in cold blood. They shot to kill and were without mercy. One captive managed to escape. When the SS found out, their fury was terrible and they called each one of us onto the parade ground. We had by then been issued with our 'uniforms', striped prison garb like pyjamas made of very very thin material. It was bitterly cold and we had to stand to attention all night long from 6pm until 12 noon the next day. We were not allowed to move from the spot, not able to use the toilets and if anyone dared to shift from one foot to another he would immediately be hit with a rifle butt. The year was then 1939 and all 20,000 of us had to go through that trial of endurance.

"Eventually the man was caught and we could return to our huts. At 11am the next morning, we had to assemble again on the parade ground and the prisoner was brought out. He was carrying a large drum in front of him which he had to beat whilst marching. As he marched and beat the drum, his tormentors attacked him with butts, sticks, anything they wanted to use. This went on for a while until he could not stand it any longer and collapsed. After that they just beat him to death like an animal before our eyes. The Commandant then dismissed us after saying that if anyone tried something like that again, he could expect the same treatment.

"That fateful day and night when we had to stand exposed to the bitter cold must have been the beginning of my brother's illness. Amongst hundreds of others, Bruno caught pneumonia of which he died four weeks later. I had tried so hard to get him into hospital, but was refused by the guard who thought my brother was fit enough to go out and work. I remember, he was in the bed next to mine and could not breathe. He asked me to open the window and I did not dare do that. The guards in the watchtower would have shot at us if they had spotted anyone trying to open a window. My brother died the next day and I am certain that he was in terrible pain. At the time of his death he was 22 years old."[1]

After four and a half months Watson's wife managed to buy two tickets for China, which was one of the most generous countries in accepting refugees. With this guarantee that he would be leaving Germany, Watson was released. He rejoined his wife and two children in Berlin and worked illegally to keep them all alive. At the same time he contacted an uncle who lived in America and he eventually sent the necessary affidavit that stated he would be responsible for Watson when he reached the United States.

At that time the tactic was for one member of a family to get out of Germany to a safe place and then arrange for the rest of the family to follow. Watson, therefore, left on his own for America. He went via Britain where he planned his family would join him before they crossed the Atlantic. He was housed in Richborough refugee camp and he eventually found someone who would employ his wife. The work permit and affidavit were sent to Berlin but the following week war broke out. He never saw or heard of his family again.

2

Not all future members of X-Troop suffered the barbarities of the Nazi regime. Indeed one, Saunders, was able to leave with his family and most of their worldly goods. Saunders' original name was Saloschin and in due course he became a Count on his father's side and a vicomte on his mother's. They lived in some style in Munich where Saunders' maternal grandfather owned a liberal newspaper. When the Nazis came to power they took over the running of the paper, but otherwise left the family alone. It was not until 1937 that they started to weed out part-Jewish families and aristocrats in the Munich area, and the Saloschins qualified on both counts. By this time Saunders was at Gordonstoun – he was in the same class as Prince Philip for two years – as its principal, Kurt Hahn, was a family friend. One day there was a knock on the door and outside was an SS General in a black Mercedes requesting an interview with Saunders' mother. With some reluctance they allowed him in. The General clicked his heels and said that Saunders' mother had always been very kind to him and that he had came to warn them that an order for their arrest was about to be issued. "It took a moment for my mother to realize who the man was. It was her old groom! He had, he said, three railway trucks which he would put at our disposal. The next day he would send round packers and anything that we could put in those three trucks we could take with us out of Germany. Sure enough, the next day they came and the SS carefully packed all our belongings and took them to the trucks. We went straight to Gordonstoun where all the family furniture was scattered about the school, and my parents started teaching there until they were both interned in 1940. My mother spent some time in Holloway gaol, while I was sent to Canada."[2]

Some future members of X-Troop had even less contact with the Nazis for they had been brought to England by their parents and were thoroughly anglicized, while others had come to Britain under the various forms of sponsorship run by the Quakers, religious organizations and political committees and were already at school or University in England. Many of them volunteered for the army immediately the war started, but were either too young or were deemed ineligible because they were not Btitish subjects. And because the parents of some had neglected to become naturalized, or because they had not lived in England the statutory five years, they were deemed enemy aliens at the start of the war.

Others, of course, had only recently fled from Nazi oppression when war broke out, and many of these, like Watson, were housed in Richborough camp near Sandwich, organized by the Council for German Jewry, while waiting for visas to the United States and elsewhere. When war was declared half of those in Richborough volunteered for the army and formed the first five "alien" companies of the Pioneer Corps. They swore allegiance to the King, received the King's shilling, and called themselves, with ironic wit, the "King's Own Enemy Aliens". Some of these early volunteers, like Watson, Merton and Turner, were future X-Troop members. In 1940 several Alien Pioneer Companies were sent to France. Though non-combatants, they had been armed on the spot during the last days of fighting in France and had fought with the rest of the British Expeditionary Force during the evacuation from Dunkirk, acquitting themselves, in the words of one MP, "in a manner worthy of the best traditions of the British Army".[3]

All enemy aliens not in uniform had to appear before a tribunal. Those put in Category A, some six hundred or so, were considered a danger to the state and were interned immediately; those put in Category B, 6800 of them, were allowed restricted freedom; while those in Category C, 64,200, were not restricted in any way. From November, 1939, a few of those in Category C were even allowed to volunteer for the armed forces. It seemed that, although the tribunals often worked on different criteria and no one quite knew why they were in one category instead of another, a typical pragmatic British compromise had been achieved.[4]

But when the "phoney war" ended all this was swept aside. On 9 April the Germans invaded Denmark and Norway and soon the papers were demanding that the police round up every alien in the country. Then on 10 May, 1940, Holland and Belgium were invaded and that evening Churchill became Prime Minister. Amid the rumours of fifth columnists and invasion, the pressure on the Government to act against the aliens became irresistible and nearly all of those not in the armed forces were arrested, even though most had done everything in their power to enlist. Swept up in the net were academics, musicians, writers, lawyers and scientists, and all were bundled into camps. By one of life's little ironies a future Circuit Judge and a future Judge of the Court of Appeal of Jersey and Guernsey, Brian Grant and John Wilmers – both future members of X-Troop – first met in the back of a police car which arrived to fetch them from their Cambridge digs.

In fact the whole policy of internment was carried out in an atmosphere of panic, almost, at times, of farce. It was also extremely haphazard. The father of one future member of X-Troop, Kingsley, had fled the Nazis in the mid-thirties and now held an important position in the Manchester textile industry. It might have been thought that as his job was vital to the war effort it also made him vulnerable to arrest. But not at all. He was exempted, but his son, a teenager at university, was interned.

Many of the detainees ended up on the Isle of Man from where a number were sent abroad. Some 2000 were sent on the notorious troopship *Dunera* to Australia while others were shipped to Canada. Recently published books show that these refugees from Nazi persecution were themselves persecuted by the authorities from whom they sought protection.[5] It was, as the Conservative MP, Major Victor Cazalet, said in the House of Commons on 22 August, 1940, "a bespattered page in our history".

One member of X-Troop described how he came to leave his own country, Germany, and the manner in which he was subsequently treated on the *Dunera*. "After *Kristalnacht* we had our first visit from the Gestapo. I was given a choice between going to a concentration camp and pulling down the local synagogue. I chose the latter, as it was in ruins anyway. When that was done I had to do other work for the Nazis, but one day I was just given two weeks to leave Germany. I took the train, but was taken off it at the border by the Gestapo. They took my suitcase and threw the contents all over the platform. Then they made me wait until the train had gone so that I had to walk across the border. I arrived in England in August, 1939, and was interned in June, 1940, on the Isle of Man. Then I was put aboard the *Dunera*. They kept us behind barbed wire, and did not even separate us from pro-Nazi prisoners-of-war who were also on board. Not surprisingly, there were some bad fights. For six or seven weeks we never had a real wash, nor did we have the use of a proper toilet. The guards opened my suitcase, took what they wanted and threw the rest into the sea. There didn't seem to be much difference between their behaviour and the Gestapo's."

At Sydney the ship was met by armed guards with bayonets fixed and the refugees were sent by train, which had its windows boarded up, to a camp at Hay in New South Wales. It took some months for the treatment of the refugees to filter back to England and it was then explained to the Australian authorities who they really were. The young men were then given the opportunity either to go to an open camp in Tasmania or to return to England and volunteer for the Pioneer Corps.

It mustn't be thought, however, that the camp at Hay was as terrible an experience as the *Dunera*, for the refugees were adequately housed and fed, and, as there were a lot of talented people amongst them, there was some very good entertainment. Anthony Firth, who later became a member of X-Troop, felt in retrospect that he benefited from those months in Australia. A German engineer graduate who had turned to being a film extra in England in 1939, as he could not obtain a work permit, Firth became involved in all aspects of show business in the camp which, as will be seen, proved very useful to him after the war.

Those who were sent to Canada fared little better and were equally bitter about being treated as enemy prisoners-of-war. One of those who was sent across the Atlantic was Eric Howarth who rose to become X-Troop's sergeant-major, and in many ways his story is typical of those who joined X-Troop. Born Eric Nathan at Ulm in Württemberg in 1922, Howarth was the son of a Jewish lawyer in the town. In 1938 his father was sent to Dachau concentration camp – though he later managed to get to England – and his mother, who came from a Protestant family, fled with Eric and his sister to England. Howarth learnt English at the London Polytechnic and then went to King's College, Canterbury, where he excelled at sports and music. On Whit Sunday, 1940, he was interned and went first to a camp at Huyton, then to the Isle of Man and finally he was shipped to Canada. He languished there for some months, frustrated at not being able to join in the fight against the Nazis. Then, when the British Government was forced to revise its policy towards enemy aliens by the public outcry which internment had caused, an official from the Home Office, Alec Paterson (later Sir Alec), a Prison Commissioner with a great reputation for humanity, was sent to Canada to sort out those suitable for serving the Allied cause and rescued Howarth and others like him.[6]

"The one ambition that consumed him," Paterson wrote after the war of Howarth, "was to join the British army at the earliest moment. It was impossible without his parents' consent. But among the thousands in these camps, he was so exceptional in his promise and personality that I wrote that night to his father in Streatham and secured his consent."

Paterson's intervention enabled Howarth to return to England where he volunteered first of all for the Pioneer Corps and then for the Commandos. He quickly rose to the rank of sergeant and took part in the Normandy landings where he was seriously wounded on the beaches by mortar fire. He managed to get hold of two German prisoners and ordered them to give him morphine periodically, telling them that this was the only way they would get to England alive. As he had to wait for over a day before being evacuated this probably saved his life. He underwent surgery several times and could have been invalided out of the army had he wanted to be. However, he was determined to return to the front line and made such a nuisance of himself to the medical authorities that they eventually allowed him to return to active duty.[7]

"Just before he returned to the front," wrote Paterson, "he spent several evenings with me, and on the last of these agreed that after the war the best service he could render was to go back to Germany as a headmaster in a school, where he might teach young Germany something better than they had learned in their Nazi training. In such a task he would have been unique."[8]

At least one member of X-Troop did, in fact, do exactly that, but tragically Howarth was killed in Germany during the last weeks of the war. "The last time I saw him," Hilton Jones told Paterson after the war, "was here in Eastbourne when he came back to get his 'immediate commission' – as you may know he got the commission, but I don't know if he ever knew that he had. It was typical of him – and I think one of the many reasons why the men liked him so very much – that he'd always refused a commission unless he could get an 'immediate' one. I'd talked about it with him several times (I remember particularly talking about that and other things once when we were rock-climbing in North Wales) – and his point of view was always the same: he wasn't prepared to leave the troop and any danger it might incur in order to spend months at an OCTU. There was no sort of arrogance about it; on the contrary I think it was the extraordinary integrity and forthrightness of his attitude which won me – and all the rest of us."[9]

Another future member of X-Troop, Paul Streeten, was sent to Canada during those grim months in 1940. A Viennese by birth and upbringing, Streeten was raised in an atmosphere of intellectual stimulation which must have sat oddly with a future Commando private but which was by no means uncommon amongst the enemy aliens who volunteered for hazardous duty. Wilhelm Reich was his adviser on sexual matters – advice that Streeten by no means always followed – and Karl Popper was one of those who joined in the Sunday games of handball in the Vienna woods, though he was not regarded as one of the brightest of the family's circle of psychologists, composers and journalists. It must have been an idyllic life, but it was not to last. In 1933 the activities of the socialist group to which Streeten belonged, the *Roten Falken*, were declared illegal. The young Streeten continued to be actively involved in the movement even after it had been driven underground, but he was in constant danger of being arrested and imprisoned. He was studying law at Vienna University at the time of the *Anschlüss*, and his position became quite untenable for he was a Jew as well as a socialist, an impossible combination in Nazi Austria. Luckily, Streeten's family had changed addresses only the previous month and by the time the Gestapo had found their new home the family had fled.

Through English friends Streeten was provided with the necessary visa and affidavits for him to go to England where he was looked after by a group who called themselves the Knighthood of the Blue Pilgrims who helped Jews and others to escape to Britain. The International Student Service then found him a place at Aberdeen University to read political economy, and when war came he volunteered for the air force. He was put in Category C by a tribunal, but was arrested and interned in June, 1940. Ironically, his call-up papers arrived soon afterwards and were forwarded to him in the internment camp.

"We were shunted from Banff outside Aberdeen to a housing estate in Huyton near Liverpool, to a seaside hotel on the Isle of Man, and eventually to Canada. I remember one man who already had become a lecturer at Aberdeen University, crying on the train from Banff to Liverpool. In the camp in Banff, which was run on a combination of friendliness and muddle, I was allowed to sit a University exam, supervised by the crying lecturer, on the strength of which I was awarded in 1944 an ordinary MA . . .

"The voyage to Canada on the *Ettrick* was one of the most horrible experiences in my life. We were herded together, behind barbed wire on the ship (so that escape would have been difficult if the ship had been torpedoed), and slept in three layers: hammocks, beneath which were tables, and under the tables. There was only one meagre meal a day. The sanitary conditions were appalling. Many suffered from dysentery and there was no medical help. In another part of the ship were German prisoners of war who were treated much better because they had Red Cross protection.* The ship ahead of us was torpedoed, and many interned refugees perished, including the famous writer Rudolf Olden.

"On arrival in Quebec we were driven through the town to our first camp, with police sirens wailing from the Black Marias. The camp was strongly guarded by layers of barbed wire and towers with armed sentries and searchlights. One poor elderly disturbed refugee who wandered about after curfew was promptly shot.

"Physical conditions in Canada were better than they had been in England. Food was plentiful, the huts were well heated, and we were provided with prison uniforms, including jackets with large red spots on the back. The Canadians seemed very pleased that they could contribute to the war effort by at last having got hold of some real and particularly dangerous enemies, disguised as civilian fifth columnists, and were correspondingly nasty to us.

"We started a successful camp university. We slept in double-decker beds and in the bed next to me was Klaus Fuchs, later famous for being a Soviet spy. Other friends were the scientist (now Sir) Hermann Bondi (whom I had known well in Vienna) who tried to teach me mathematics, Tommy Gold the astronomer, and a wonderful art historian named Wilde."

After being shunted around for five months or so in various camps in Canada Streeten was selected by Paterson to return to England. He landed in Liverpool during the Christmas holidays in the middle of an air raid, but, instead of being free, as he had supposed, he was again interned at Huyton. He was kept there for a few months and was then released on condition that he joined the Pioneer Corps.

"The Pioneer Corps was much better than internment, but it had some similarities. It was recruited from mental defectives, criminals, conscientious objectors and enemy aliens; some of the best and worst human material."

During his time in the Pioneer Corps Streeten was joined by Arthur Koestler. "His ideas of the alternations between *la vie tragique* and *la vie trivial* were illuminating of much of our experience, both in internment and, later, in action, and I admired him for refusing the privilege of a private room and exemption from duties of manual labour in return for writing a complimentary

---

* Actually the British Government told the German Government in a communiqué which was sent via the Swiss Legation in London on 15 June, 1940, that "Civilian internees will be treated in general, as at present, in accordance with the principles of the [Geneva] Convention". There's little doubt that this was ignored by those in charge of the *Ettrick*.

history of 251 Company. But he was a bully: selfish, anti-social, always jumping meal queues."[10]

3

Most of the future X-Troopers ended up in either 77 Company or 87 Company of the Pioneer Corps. Peter Terry joined 77 Company. His exit from Vienna had been aided by a powerful benefactor, but his story is not untypical of many of those who were to join X-Troop.

"On the night of the *Anschlüss*, we received a 'phone call from the Duke of Windsor, who was then in the South of France, asking whether he could help as my father knew him. My father thanked him and declined, as he felt that, after the initial excesses of the Nazis, matters would calm down. It was only after we were both arrested by the Gestapo (I was not yet fourteen) and released (again on account of my father's connections – Seyss-Inquart, the new Nazi Chancellor, was one of his patients) that he contacted the Duke who first arranged for a British Embassy car flying the Union Jack to be at our disposal in Vienna and subsequently became our sponsor in England.

"Some unkind things have been written about the Duke, but I only remember his concern and considerable efforts to save my family. It was primarily his action which caused me to feel that he saved our lives and to do something more active for Britain than rolling tar barrels in the Pioneer Corps. Thus, the circumstances of our arrival in England were very different from those less fortunate and the Duke's secretary, Sir Geoffrey Thomas, awaited us at Victoria. It was also largely due to our illustrious sponsor that neither my father or I were interned as enemy aliens. I went to boarding school at Frensham, then to Oxford, and joined the Pioneer Corps as soon as I was of age."[11]

Terry joined 77 Company in February, 1943, with two friends, one of whom, Farago,* consequently joined X-Troop with Terry. The company was stationed at Long Marston camp on the edge of the Cotswolds. At first glance it appeared to Terry to be a prisoner-of-war camp for it was completely surrounded by barbed wire and watch towers. It was, in fact, one of the secret staging grounds for the warehousing of equipment needed for the coming invasion of Europe, which then must have seemed remote indeed.

Terry and his friends were billeted in a windowless Nissen hut which was fifteen minutes' walk from the bath house. This consisted of a tin roof supported at the sides, but otherwise open to the weather. Along its centre ran a pipe from which cold water poured between 6am and 6.30am every morning.

---

* Farago was an Hungarian communist who changed his name to Ford when he became a member of X-Troop. He was RTU'd after collapsing during a particularly gruelling route march in North Wales. When the war ended he returned to his own country and is now, apparently, an important functionary in Budapest.

From the first moment he saw the camp Terry's thoughts were engaged in finding ways to get out.

77 Company consisted of some two hundred men of varied backgrounds but all had, of course, one thing in common: none was a British citizen. The majority were refugees from Germany who had arrived in England penniless and had gone through a series of refugee camps before being interned. They had then been given the choice of staying interned or enlisting in the Pioneer Corps. They had been used to communal life for years and some were apparently content to sit out the war as they were. Terry's English was better than his German, but he soon found that everyone only conversed in German and even the sergeants shouted their commands in German Army style. Because of the low health and intelligence classification of most of the British members of the company they were known by their German colleagues as "Rachiten", which derived from the German word "Rachitis" meaning "rickets" and non-alien companies were known as "Rachiten Kompanien".

After Terry had been put to work rolling barrels, he applied to the Colonel for a posting to an army unit which was likely to see action. He also asked his father, who had Lord Beaverbrook as one of his patients, to ask Beaverbrook if he could use his influence to have his son transferred to a fighting unit. His father agreed and the upshot was that Beaverbrook asked the young Pioneer Corps private to Cherkeley for an interview. This was interrupted by an urgent telephone call but Beaverbrook's last words were, "We need young men like you and I will see what I can do."

If Terry expected to be posted to a fighting unit as a result of his meeting with Beaverbrook he was to be disappointed. It would have been strange if he had been, but what happened was stranger still, and though his story is certainly not typical of how potential members of X-Troop were selected for interviewing, it is an interesting insight into War Office recruitment methods for those volunteering for hazardous duties.*

Some weeks after the interview a private by the name of Hartmann was assigned to Terry's hut. He stood out from the rest of its members if only because he was thirty years older than most of them, spoke German with a flowery phraseology that had gone out of fashion with Kaiser Wilhelm, and, most unusual of all, was extremely polite. He befriended Terry and Ford by offering them some of his sandwiches one lunchtime, and the next day invited them to tea in Stratford-upon-Avon.

At first Terry thought he was joking, but when shortly afterwards they were ordered to put on their best uniforms and to report to the CO's office he knew that something unusual was happening. He was right, for Private Hartmann

* George Clare, in his book, *Last Waltz in Vienna* (p.4), makes it clear that he at any rate was simply sent by his CO to be interviewed. But Clare wanted to join an ordinary fighting unit, believing that the Inter-Allied Commando was "just another ghetto"

was waiting for Terry and Ford outside the CO's office with a staff car and an ATS driver. When he saw them coming he opened the back door and asked them to get in. This they did, and with Hartmann sitting in the front drove out of camp.

The journey to Stratford passed in total silence. Then, when they reached the Stratford Arms Hotel Hartmann led the way up to a private room and asked his guests to sit down. He then opened a briefcase and took out a document which he asked Terry and Ford to read. It was a letter on War Office letterhead which stated that its purpose was to introduce Lt-Colonel R. Hartmann of Military Intelligence, Section 5, who was acting for Special Operations Executive.* It also stated that before Terry or Ford carried out any further instructions from Colonel Hartmann they were to ask for other means of identification. There was then a space for their signatures above which was a paragraph which stated that the undersigned had read the relevant passages of the Official Secrets Act and that they agreed not to discuss any disclosures made by Colonel Hartmann with anyone except officers of MI5 or SOE.

After the two men had read the letter Colonel Hartmann produced a War Office identity card with his photograph on it and then asked them, in English, to read relevant parts of the Official Secrets Act. They did and signed the letter. Hartmann then explained that he was head of the War Office Special Services recruiting section and began asking them questions about their backgrounds. After he had asked if they were both willing, if necessary, to be dropped in German-occupied territory, and they had replied that they were, Hartmann explained what their rights would be.

"The War Office will provide you with false documents showing the United Kingdom as the country of your birth. You will also be provided with a British cover name. While this would serve to mislead the enemy in the eventuality that you are captured, the British Government is unable to accept any responsibility for further enemy action in such cases. You must understand that your activities would not be governed by the rules of the Geneva Convention. Under these rules, the German authorities would be empowered to convict you for treason or subversive activities. In recognition of your services, the Home Office has agreed under a special arrangement with the War Office to give you full British citizenship on a priority basis as soon as the Emergency Powers Act has been lifted after the War, and naturalization

* The SOE archivist confirms that SOE did help recruit for the Inter-Allied Commando and that this is recorded in an SOE paper summarizing the wartime history of the liaison between SOE and COHQ. In this paper under the heading "Provision of Allied and Alien Personnel" it states that "The provision of German speakers to accompany a raiding force, either to act as interpreters, or to shout conflicting commands to the German troops, was another of the personnel tasks undertaken by SOE. Many of the men were Sudeten Germans already in this country, and their inclusion in a raiding force presented many security difficulties; these were ultimately solved by the formation of a unit known as No 10 Commando, under the command of the SS Brigade, which was composed of foreign nationals."[12]

again becomes legal. In the meantime any restrictions imposed upon aliens in this country will not apply to you and all identity documents issued to you will, in fact, state that you are a British citizen, although de facto you are not. You may refuse to have any futher discussion concerning these matters, in which case you will merely be bound by the Official Secrets Act in the matter of today's conversation. If you do not refuse now, however, you will have further opportunity to decide upon your actions during later interviews at the War Office."*

Terry was to hear this speech several times in the following weeks for he and Ford told Hartmann that they did wish to pursue the matter further, and Hartmann said they would be hearing from his department in a short while. He then took them back to the camp, but did not rejoin them in their hut. They never saw him again.

Some days later both men were interviewed by a major wearing Intelligence Corps insignia. They were again asked to sign the Official Secrets Act statement and the Major then produced a street map and asked Terry where it was. Terry told him it was Vienna and the Major then asked him to point out where he had lived and had gone to school. This apparently satisfied the Major as the following week they were both told to report to an address in Marylebone Road where they met a group of other German speakers who said that they, too, had been recruited by Hartmann, though few of them, apparently, had any serious intention of volunteering for hazardous duties.

Terry was now interviewed by a captain, who had a group of officers with him. The captain told Terry that if he accepted to undertake secret work, he would have to undergo parachute training. He was also told that this was his final interview and that he would now have to make an immediate commitment without having a further chance to refuse. Terry agreed at once and, when his turn came, so did Ford. Terry later recognized the captain as Hilton Jones.

Terry and Ford returned to Long Marston, but shortly afterwards were ordered to report to the same building in Bradford in which Terry had spent his first few miserable nights in the army. During the next few days they and the other volunteers with them were given brand-new uniforms with plain War Office General Service Corps insignia, and every single piece of equipment that had their names on it was replaced.

All future members of X-Troop when they arrived at Bradford were told by Hilton Jones that because of their future roles they were going to have to change their names to English-sounding ones. They were advised to keep the same initials and to choose names they could pronounce. Telephone directories were available for those who lacked ideas, but most came up with their own though a few had to be discouraged from adopting high-sounding aristocratic ones like Beaufort. Ascher chose Anson, because a plane of that name was

* In the early days when aliens from the Pioneer Corps volunteered for duty overseas they signed a declaration which began: "I hereby certify that I understand the risks . . ."

flying overhead at the time; Sauer had bought a book by Dorothy L. Sayers to read on the train so he opted for Sayers; Wilmersdoerffer simply shortened his to Wilmers; while Lane at first chose Smith. "Don't be a bloody fool," Hilton Jones said briskly, "you can't even pronounce it properly." "I thought my English was pretty good, sir," Lane replied stiffly. "It is, but not your accent. Your real name is Lanyi, so why not be Lane? But not English – Welsh." Lane accepted this idea and later, under interrogation by the Germans, his "Welsh" accent prove invaluable.

One man noted down in his diary his feeling on so precipitous a change as altering one's name and assuming a different personality. "It took less than one minute to become Brian Groves.* I was not amongst the first in the queue. By the time I was near the door rumour had spread that we were getting new pay books and that we had to choose different names. Perfectly reasonable, I thought. I should not like to be caught with a pay book in the name of Goldschmidt, although I had come prepared to chance it. My confidence in my English was considerable. I might get away with it. But why should I be captured anyway? Like a prospective burglar I was not concerned with capture and punishment. I was dreaming of triumph, not failure.

"Occupied with these thoughts, I had not even begun to choose a name for myself when I found myself facing the Captain sitting at a table laden with a pile of brand-new pay books and an alphabetical list of names to help the timid ones with their choice. To my utter amazement the Captain remembered my name. Was he a wizard after all? He had only seen me for a few minutes, and that was weeks ago.

" 'And what name would you like, Goldschmidt?' He seemed to be enjoying himself; but his amusement was subdued as if he was ashamed. Did he perhaps realize the enormity of the moment for myself and the others? These thoughts occurred to me later. At the time I was myself amused, excited and fascinated by what was going on: chaps copying particulars from their original pay books, and the Sgt-Major forging 'officers'' signatures. His apparent aptitude surprised me then, but no longer.

"This is how I became Brian Groves and added Hubert as a tribute to my cousin Bertie."[13]

Besides new names and pay books the men were issued with army numbers which made them members of one of four regiments – the Royal Sussex, the Buffs, the Royal West Kent and the Hampshires, and later they wore the regimental cap badges of these regiments in their green berets. They were also told by Hilton Jones to make up a complete cover story of their backgrounds

---

* He chose Brian Groves because a great friend of his at Cambridge by this name had just been killed and Goldschmidt wanted to have it in memory of him. But when the parents heard their son's name had been taken by a German they had been horrified, so Groves later changed his name to Grant.

which would stand up to interrogation, and were aided in this by being provided with false next-of-kin, false mail facilities and so on, which involved "a tortuous procedure whereby all of it was kept secret from the normal army pay and record offices without disturbing the normal administrative channels".[14]

The origins of the Troop was in fact such a closely kept secret that their new and original names were known only to a handful of people outside the Inter-Allied Commando. One of them was a senior civil servant from the Casualty Department at the War Office named Dawkins who apparently kept a parallel list of their original and their assumed names along with their true next-of-kin. When the department was evacuated to Liverpool Dawkins was billeted with the same family, the Clelands, who had shown great kindness to one of the Troop, Ascher. Because Ascher – or Anson as he had become known – had no relations in Britain he had given the Clelands' daughter, Pat, as his true next-of-kin. Dawkins – the Clelands nicknamed him "Blossom" for some reason – of course knew when Anson was wounded in Italy, but the security surrounding the Troop was so strict that he was unable to tell Pat and had to affect surprise when she heard the news.[15]

After vetting by MI5, a process that took time and which took place for some in a converted mill house near Bradford, Terry and the others with him were given railway passes and told to go to Shrewsbury where they would be met by an escort. On the train the group was approached by an officer who told them that at Shrewsbury station they were to look for a sergeant-major who would be waiting on No 2 platform and that he would be wearing Tank Corps insignia. When contact was made the group was to follow him without speaking to him and without showing any signs of recognition. The officer then got off at the next station and Terry never saw him again.

The men were all rather apprehensive about this turn of events and one suggested it was all a joke and that the group was actually being abducted by enemy agents. But the sergeant-major was on the platform at Shrewsbury and when he boarded another train the others followed. The carriage was empty and had "reserved" stuck on the windows. The men sat apart from the sergeant-major who made no attempt to speak to them.

After the train had been going for some time one of the group realized they were heading into North Wales. At one point the train stopped at a small station just before entering a tunnel and it was then that the group noticed that the sergeant-major had changed his forage cap for a green beret. Minutes later, a group of Commandos who had climbed on the train at the station came into the carriage to greet the newcomers. Among them were faces who had mysteriously disappeared from Long Marston.

Terry, although he still did not know it, was now a member of X-Troop, 10 (Inter-Allied) Commando.[16]

4

Early Small-Scale
Raids

After the abortive Dieppe raid, the next members of the Inter-Allied Commando to see action were members of the Norwegian Troop. They were sent to Lerwick to operate with the Norwegian-manned MTB Flotilla which, with elements from No 12 Commando, were based there in order to launch small-scale raids and reconnaissance missions on the Norwegian coastline.

The idea for this raiding force – codenamed North Force – came from the fertile mind of the Chief of Combined Operations, Lord Louis Mountbatten, who considered that specialist forces trained in fighting and acclimatized to the sub-zero temperatures of a Norwegian winter were essential if Norwegian raids were to be successful. A small force from No 12 Commando, commanded by a South African, Captain F. W. Fynn, and codenamed Fynn Force, was therefore sent north under the cover of being Royal Marines engaged in hardening training and was joined by Lieutenant Harald Risnes and his men on 16 November.[1]

The men from the Norwegian Troop, Sergeant Rostøen and ten other ranks under the command of Lieutenant Risnes, were all chosen because they came from the areas to be raided and because they were mostly seamen who understood the sea. The Inter-Allied Commando's War Diary records that the first reconnaissance mission in which the Norwegians were involved had to be aborted. Three MTBs, with Risnes and three other Norwegian Commandos aboard them, left Lerwick on 22 November, but were spotted by a German patrol. With the element of surprise lost, the MTBs were forced to return to base. However, four days later they had better luck and Risnes and three of his men, now all in one MTB, arrived off the Norwegian coast near Bergen that evening without having been spotted by the enemy. In the early hours of the morning of 27 November the MTB anchored in a small fjord and two of the Norwegian Commandos were sent ashore to make certain that no one left a house that overlooked the anchorage.

During that day several fishing boats passed in and out of the fjord. All were stopped and the crews taken aboard and questioned by Risnes. They were then detained on the MTB but were later released when "all proved to be patriots". A fisherman's motor boat was then requisitioned and a sortie was made up the fjord by Risnes, but nothing was found. The MTB stayed throughout that day and the next because of bad weather, but returned safely to Lerwick on 29 November.

Bad weather now kept the MTBs and the Commandos in harbour until 27 December, but even then the sortie that sailed on that night had to be abandoned when high seas prevented the MTB, with five Norwegian Commandos aboard, from finding shelter in a suitable fjord. However, the next attempt resulted in one of the most successful small-scale raids of the Second World War.

The object of this operation, codenamed Cartoon, was to destroy the pyrite mines at Lillebo on the island of Stord along with a silo and other installations near Sagvaag quay. The force involved in this consisted of Fynn, with Risnes, now an acting captain, as his second-in-command, forty men from No 12 Commando and ten men from the Norwegian Troop.

Risnes was anxious that his men should be able to retain their Norwegian flashes as he must have known how heartening it was for the Norwegian civilian population to know that their own countrymen were in action against the Germans. His request was refused.

"Dear Risnes," wrote Captain Tronstadt of the Norwegian General Staff in a letter dated 8 January, 1943, which underlined only too well the appalling severity with which the Nazis dealt with the people of Norway. "I have been asked about this question of wearing Norwegian insignia. We understand your desire to do so and would very much like to have supported it if it had been possible. But unfortunately the situation as regards reprisals at home is such that it is safer to operate in British uniforms with British marks of identity . . . Once the Germans know that Norwegian soldiers have been at work they will naturally conclude that the Norwegian authorities with the King at their head have given it their blessing. Great propaganda use will be made of this and will lead to greater hurt and the Germans will without any doubt take most drastic measures against our loyal countrymen at home. There is to be no present taking to the civilian population since capital punishment is in force for failure to hand over all articles of British origin brought into Norway in any way whatsoever. The civilian population must be told to keep away from the operational area and will not be allowed to come to UK with the force. One can reckon that for every man who leaves at least as many will be taken hostage and their houses and property burned or confiscated."[2]

This order, unlike the one to the French at Dieppe, was strictly enforced. Also, the Norwegians were given false identity papers and these, along with escape maps and Norwegian money, were sewn into their clothing in case they became separated from the force and had to make their own way back to Britain via Sweden.

At 0730 on the morning of 23 January the Norwegians embarked with the men from No 12 Commando aboard four of the seven Norwegian-manned MTBs which were to take part in the operation. When the force left Lerwick half-an-hour later the weather was good: force 3 or 4 wind, 6/10ths cloud and a visibility of 15–20 miles. No doubt these conditions were welcomed by the Commandos crowded aboard the small MTBs, but the excellent visibility and patches of clear sky nearly caused the cancellation of the raid for at 1115 Scapa Flow signalled that the force had probably been sighted by enemy air patrols. This was soon confirmed when German aircraft started to shadow the MTB flotilla and though the Senior Officer in charge tried to throw them off by turning round on several occasions it was quite obvious to them that the enemy shore defences in the direction they were heading would be fully alerted.

Worse, the evasive action taken by the flotilla delayed its arrival, and made a very tight schedule even tighter. The Norwegian coast was not approached until about 2100 and the force was at that time well north of its objective, Selbjørn Fjord. When the coast was sighted the Senior Officer came alongside Fynn's MTB and explained that they were still an hour and a quarter from the fjord. With so much time lost and the German defences aware they were somewhere in the area, did Fynn wish to proceed? Fynn replied that if the time of departure could be delayed for an hour he would like to carry on. The Senior Officer agreed, and now luck – favouring, as it so often does, the brave – took a hand. A warning message transmitted by a German defence post which had spotted the flotilla was relayed to the garrison on Stord but was misunderstood. The garrison not only stood down, but they nearly all went to bed.[3]

At 2245 four of the MTBs entered Selbjørn Fjord. The others veered off to attack enemy shipping in Leirvik harbour, but none was found, though on the way back they came across a 2000-ton enemy ship and sank her. They also shelled German defences in the area before returning to Lerwick a few hours ahead of the main force.

At 2325 the landing force was divided into two groups and each put aboard an MTB. Group I, commanded by Fynn, was made up of Force A, with eleven men and the Norwegian guide, commanded by Risnes, and Force B, with eleven men under the command of Sergeant Metcalfe. Group II, which had an observer from COHQ (Combined Operations Headquarters) with it, consisted of Force C with eleven men, under the command of Lieutenant Hallett, and Force D with eleven men, under the command of Lieutenant Shaw who was also the Group's leader.

53

At 0100 on 24 January the two heavily loaded MTBs approached Sagvaag quay. When it was within range the leading MTB fired two torpedoes and opened fire with all weapons. One torpedo missed its target but the other detonated with a tremendous explosion. The Germans, however, were not deterred by this but opened fire with every weapon they could bring to bear and in this early exchange one of the Norwegian Commandos, Corporal Haga, was hit and killed, and two members of No 12 Commando were wounded.

Despite heavy small arms fire the skipper of the MTB with Group II aboard brought his ship alongside the quay. Some delay occurred because the quay was 20 to 30 feet above the deck of the MTB, but both Force C and Force D were soon ashore. Three men from Force C were sent to cut the communications while the rest cleared the quay of opposition. Three prisoners were taken. Force C then made for the village to establish road blocks while Force D prepared demolition charges for the silo and the quay.

While Group II were landing at the main quay at Sagvaag, the MTB with Group I on board headed for what was called the Boat House quay on the northern side of the fjord. They landed without opposition and both Force A and B then rapidly covered the three kilometres to the pyrite mine which was reached at 0058, just 33 minutes after landing.

As the mine did not work after midnight on Saturday, there were hardly any civilians about. Those that had left their beds to find out what was happening – four air-raid wardens and six mine officials – were told to go to their homes and stay there.

Time was now extremely short, so only the priority targets at the mine were blown up. An attempt was also made to open the large safe in the wall of the manager's office. "There was no time to find anyone who could open it," Fynn wrote in his official report, "so I tried to blow it up. The first charge buckled the door badly, but we could not open it and it is doubtful whether anyone else will for some time either." So as to leave no doubt as to who had been visiting the mine Fynn left a notice on the main door of the office: "Achtung – Commando – Aufwiedersehn" along with a drawing of D Troop, 12 Commando's crest.[4]

Working with Fynn in laying the charges was Corporal Trygve Sigvaldsen of the Norwegian Troop who was the leader of a demolition group in Force B. After the raid, Fynn recommended him to be awarded the Military Medal. "His leadership was of a high standard throughout," the citation stated. "He handled the local population tactfully, and his demolitions of Lillebo mine were quickly and accurately performed. His coolness, especially after the alarm had been given, was exemplary. During his two months' attachment to No 12 Commando Corporal Sigvaldsen accompanied the MTBs on two smaller raids on the Norwegian coast. His courage and leadership in action were an example to all, and his thoroughness and reliablity were a real asset in wielding the two Allied units into one force."

The sounds of the demolition led someone to ring the senior German officer on the island. He immediately commandeered one of the few private cars available – it belonged to a local doctor – and forced its owner to drive him and two German soldiers to the pyrite mine. At 0205 it was seen approaching one of the road blocks Force C had established by blowing up a tree and the bren gunner fired a warning burst of fire to make it stop. The car skidded to a halt and the doctor jumped out and ran towards the road block shouting that he was a Norwegian who had been forced to drive the Germans to the mine.

The road-block party now opened fire on the car. One soldier and the German officer jumped out and ran into some nearby woods, but the third was hit and fell by the car. One of the road-block party now managed to crawl up to it and took out a brief case, a small attaché case, a Norwegian rifle and a machine carbine, while all the time being sniped at by the two Germans in the wood. He then began to search the dead German but had to abandon this as the German fire was becoming too accurate, and the whole party retired to rendezvous in Sagvaag with the rest of the force, before they made their way back to the quay which was reached at 0300.[5]

The height of the quay above the MTB again made it difficult for the men to re-embark, but at 0320 the MTB slipped its mooring and headed out into the fjord to rendezvous with the other members of the flotilla. By 0340 all the forces had re-embarked on their original craft for the return voyage, and the four MTBs set off for Lerwick with three prisoners aboard. On the way back two of the MTBs shot down a Ju88 but otherwise port was reached that evening without incident. For the loss of one killed and two wounded a mine providing the Germans with 160,000 tons of iron pyrites a year had been put out of action for more than a year.[6]

The next raid, codenamed Operation Crackers, was less successful. It took place on 23 February, 1943, when a small party from No 12 and No 30 Commandos, and three NCOs from the Norwegian Troop, made a landing at Stokkevaag and set up an observation post at Gjeteroy with the idea of attacking two German posts. However, the attack had to be abandoned because of adverse weather conditions, but the force remained in the area for over a week, information being obtained on local fortifications and Quislings. German-controlled newspapers were collected and possible points for landing a future raiding party noted. The party then returned to Lerwick, arriving on 3 March.[7]

Risnes and his party were now relieved by Lieutenant (acting Captain) Daniel Rommetvedt and sixteen men from the Norwegian Troop, and it was members of this new group which took part in the next sortie. This took place on 12 March when Rommetvedt and six of his men left Lerwick aboard two MTBs, 619 and 631, to attack enemy shipping at Florø, an operation which was codenamed Operation Brandy. They arrived at 0150 and anchored in a small inlet at the north-west end of an island called Skorpa near Florø and camouflaged themselves. During the following day a number of fishermen were stopped and questioned, but all were later released. Two Norwegian Commandos then went ashore and established an observation post to watch Florø harbour. They soon found themselves in luck for on the following evening they were able to report that a convoy of three German merchant ships had just entered the harbour, escorted by an armed trawler.

At 2300 that night the two MTBs slipped out of their inlet and headed towards Florø. Before they entered the harbour they mined the main channel, and then slipped through a narrow channel into the harbour. Their targets lay at anchor and the two MTBs fired their torpedoes at a range of 400 metres. Two were sunk, and the third was mined as it tried to leave harbour. In making their escape, however, MTB 631 ran on to a rock and its crew and Commandos had to transfer to MTB 619. Attempts to sink the stranded MTB failed and as the armed trawler was now bearing down on the surviving MTB it turned for home. The return voyage was made in appalling conditions but 619 eventually reached Lerwick safely on the evening of 16 March.[8]

Three days later two of Rommetvedt's men were attached to a party of No 12 Commando which was taken across in MTBs to the Stadt area. Rommetvedt stated in his report of the raid that there was a fight with some Germans on a bridge between two islands, and that two of them were killed, one of them by one of the Norwegian Troop. The raid had to be abandoned because of this, but on 9 April a much larger raiding party, consisting of seventy men from No 12 Commando plus Rommetvedt and nine members of the Norwegian Troop, returned to the area.

The plan for this raid was to attack an anchorage up Nordfjord, at Rugsundøy, which was used by German convoys. In order to do this a German coastal battery on the western side of Bremanger, which protected the anchorage, had to be attacked and overrun. The force was to shelter overnight under the lee of a nearby island. Then at dawn the next day the Commandos were to be put ashore to attack the battery while the MTBs made their way up the fjord. It did not work out like that. Firstly, one of the MTBs had engine trouble and then, when the force finally found shelter for the night, at Skorpa, the local inhabitants told them that a German observation post had recently been set up on the island they had planned to use as the start for the attack. The operation was abandoned and the force was refused permission to attack an alternative target by ACOS (Admiral Commanding Orkneys and Shetlands).

This was the last raid to be undertaken on the Norwegian coast by members of the Norwegian Troop, for, though at first the raids may have boosted the morale of the local population German reprisals began to make them unpopular.

2

The following winter a larger detachment of the Norwegian Troop, consisting of one officer and twenty-three other ranks, under Lieutenant Gausland, returned to Lerwick and operated as part of what was known as Timberforce, and they were joined by the remainder of the Troop, seven officers and fifty-nine other ranks, on 9 February, 1944.

The idea behind Timberforce was for the Norwegian-manned MTBs to lie in wait for enemy shipping and to attack anything that was considered worth sinking.

"We went with the MTBs in order to defend them," said a Norwegian member of Timberforce. "There were usually two of them and they would lie up in fjords and observe enemy shipping. They would be well camouflaged and we – there were usually four or five of us – would go ashore and form a small perimeter to make sure the MTB was not surprised from landward. We sometimes also landed agents and picked them up."[9]

The War Diary for the Norwegian Troop for the period shows that these sorties into enemy-occupied territory were a regular occurrence.

"10 February: 1 sergeant and 5 men returned from operational work on Norwegian coast. Had to abandon MTB 625* which sank in shallow water at the Skerries (Shetland). Some equipment lost owing to this.

"11 February: 1 officer, 3 sergeants and 3 men detailed to MTB 653 and 627 and patrol ship *Molde*, all of the Royal Norwegian Navy, for operational work on Norwegian coast.

"14 February: 1 officer, 3 sergeants and 3 men returned from operation on Norwegian coast. Reported torpedoed: Norwegian mail steamer *Irma*, Norwegian steamer *Henry*, south of Kristiansand.

"17 February: 1 sergeant, 1 private detailed to Royal Norwegian Navy for operation work, Norwegian coast.

"23 February: 1 officer, 3 sergeants, 6 corporals detailed to Royal Norwegian Navy for operational work."

In the following month there is only one reference to any operations – "19 March: 6 other ranks returned from operational work on the Norwegian coast" – and in April and May there were none. The reason for this was because by now the German forces were really on the alert and the nights were no longer long enough to get over and return under cover of darkness. The Norwegian MTB Flotilla was then withdrawn for the D-Day operations and on 17 June the Troop returned to Eastbourne.

The weeks of incessant training in such a remote place as Lerwick – the Norwegians reckoned that the nearest railway station to their camp was Bergen – and in such a climate without seeing any action must have sapped the morale of the Troop. This is borne out by a memo written by Maj-General Sturges, the

---

* The MTB had been caught in a bad storm on the return voyage but had managed to anchor in a bay in the Skerries, but later sank while being salvaged. The CO of the MTB gave the ship's ensign to the Commandos in recognition of their help during the storm. One of them, Oivind Larum, landed with it at Walcheren wrapped around his chest.

Royal Marines officer commanding the Special Services Group, which included all Commando units. "I am most anxious that the Norwegian Troop not be banished to Lerwick for a second winter," he wrote on 15 August, 1944. "Both Lt-Colonel Laycock and o/c Norwegian Troop agree on this point. Discipline and morale suffer with long periods in the Shetlands. The Norwegian Troop is keen for battle anywhere. This they know is available for them in Normandy whilst lurking operations, while intensely interesting, give no guarantee of action. I suggest that the nomination of Commandos for Lerwick be the responsibility of COHQ and the following proposal is put forward: the Norwegian Troop relieve a Troop of Nos 1 or 4 SS Brigades in Normandy. The Troop that has been relieved to be allocated to ACOS for a period of three months. After this an exchange of sub-units should take place. The men are battle-trained and a proportion of the Troop are trained in cliff climbing and/or dory work."[10]

Before this idea could be translated into action the supply crisis that hit the Allied armies necessitated the clearance of the Germans from the banks of the Scheldt estuary so that Antwerp could be used to bring in essential supplies for the last drive into Germany. The Norwegians, late into the fray, certainly made up for their enforced abstention from battle when on 1 November, 1944, they landed on Walcheren to take part in what was to be one of the toughest Commando battles of the war.

3

Towards the end of April, 1943, a requirement from GHQ Home Forces (afterwards 21 Army Group), and later from their higher command, COSSAC (afterwards SHAEF), arose to implement a series of small-scale raids on the north coast of France between Fécamp and the Dutch/Belgian border. The purpose of these raids was laid out in a memo dated 28 July, 1943:

"1. The real object of Operation FORFAR is to help the STARKEY plan to convince the enemy that a large-scale landing in the PAS DE CALAIS area is imminent.

2. The Military Force Commanders of the FORFAR operations cannot be told of the real object; they are, therefore, being given a subsidiary object such as taking a prisoner.

3. As the Force Commanders would normally try to withdraw undetected if they failed to get a prisoner, they have been directed to leave evidence of their visit in the shape of black and white beach markers; they have been told that these are merely to mystify and annoy the Germans.

4. It is hoped to arrange for low-flying aircraft to circle the beach markers on the morning after each operation. The Germans will deduce that we are carrying out some kind of coast reconnaissance which required the use of these markers; it is thought that this will be less likely to make them suspicious than

if a different article is left behind on each occasion to ensure that the visit of the party is noticed."[11]

The planning of these raids was to be undertaken by COHQ and was to be carried out under the command of the C-in-C Portsmouth or Vice-Admiral Dover, depending on the area involved. There were no hard and fast rules for the Forfar raids – or for the ones that followed them – but the raiding parties were normally made up of one or two officers and eight to ten men, including a signaller. They were taken across the Channel in an MTB (occasionally, an MGB) which was escorted by MGBs one way and by a fighter escort the other. They were put ashore by powered dory manned by a coxswain and a signaller, who worked the S-phone* and kept in contact with the signaller with the landing party. If the landing place was known to be tricky an interceptor rubber dinghy was used to take the raiding party on to the beach while the dory anchored beyond the surf. A light line usually connected the dinghy to the dory so that it could be hauled off in an emergency. A signaller also remained aboard the MTB to work the S-phone and the radio, and there was sometimes a medical officer, or medical orderly, aboard as well. It was not unknown for officers, who had only a peripheral connection with the raid, to go along for the ride as observers.

The men used in the Forfar raids came mostly from No 12 Commando and they were organized into three groups: Fynn, now a major, was brought south with four officers and thirty-nine other ranks to form a new Fynn Force; Captain O. B. Rooney formed Rooney Force, made up of seven officers and sixty-two other ranks; and Lieutenant Hollins was in charge of Hollins Force, which consisted of three officers and nineteen other ranks.[12] A fourth group, consisting of about twenty Frenchmen of the Inter-Allied Commando, codenamed Frankforce after their English commanding officer, Major Godfrey Franks, were trained at Dover during the last two weeks in September, but were never used operationally. On 28 September they were returned to Eastbourne as both French Troops were expected to be sent to the Middle East theatre of operations for an invasion of Corsica (which never took place).

Though No 12 Commando provided most of the manpower, selected members of the Special Boat Service (SBS), and of X-Troop and the two French Troops of the Inter-Allied Commando, also took part in some of the raids. Combined, all these groups were known as Forfar Force.

The raids took place during the three dark periods between July and September, 1943. Eleven were mounted, but only seven actually landed. Each area to be raided was given an alphabetical codename, A for Able to P for Pound, and if one raid on a particular area had to be aborted it was repeated under the same codename. Harry Drew of X-Troop was certainly on at least

* A primitive homing device with a range of about three miles that enabled the dory to return to its mother ship.

one of the earlier – aborted – operations. He was chosen early on to train with Fynn Force on the Isle of Wight for he was a good cliff climber and an excellent athlete. He remembers that they were given an escape kit – local maps, a compass, French and Spanish money – as well as the very latest equipment such as walkie-talkies and lightweight American carbines. He went on some of the early raids but was then replaced by one of the Frenchmen when Fynn found he needed an interpreter more than an interrogator.[13]

The first operation to be mounted was Forfar Easy (at Onival, south of the River Somme) and it took place on the night of 3/4 July when two officers and eight men of Hollins Force, led by Hollins, made an unopposed landing. The beach was reconnoitred and some barbed wire was brought back, but the party was unable to make any contact with the enemy and returned without a prisoner. Two nights later Forfar Beer (at Elétot, east of Fécamp), Forfar Dog (at Biville, east of Dieppe), and Forfar How (at Quend Plage, north of the River Somme), were all mounted. The first and last had to be aborted, one because the MTB encountered an armed trawler, the other because of heavy surf, but the two officers and men of Forfar Dog managed to scale the cliffs though they then had to return when they found an impenetrable tangle of barbed wire at the top.

Forfar Easy and Forfar Beer were repeated on the night of 31 July/1 August, but both had to be aborted as was a repeat of Forfar How two nights later. A third Forfar Beer raid was mounted the same night as Forfar How and this had better luck for the party at least managed to land. But though they lay up in a fold in the cliffs all the next day they had no opportunity to take any prisoners before being picked up the following night.[14]

It might be supposed that the Forfar raids up to this point had been something of a failure both from the point of view of 21 Army Group, who were wanting the enemy alerted to the presence of reconnaissance raids on the coastline, and of those taking part in the raids, as they had neither managed to contact the Germans nor bring back a prisoner. However, the last two Forfar operations, while not being totally successful, at least showed the planners and those involved what could be achieved with luck and daring. Both included members of the Inter-Allied Commando.

These last two raids were launched within 24 hours of each other.* Forfar Beer was launched yet again, on the night of 1/2 September, while the first attempt at Forfar Item took place on the following night.

Fynn, the Military Commander of the Forfar Beer raids, had apparently argued with the planners that it might be necessary to stay ashore for more than

* A third raid, Forfar Pound, took place near Ushant at the same time as the other two. In his book, *The Green Beret*, Hilary St George Saunders says, on page 215, that a German sentry was "set on fire", but that no prisoner was taken. He was obviously quoting from the Force Commander's report, but this is not in the relevant files in the Public Record Office.

a few hours if a successful mission was to be accomplished. So it was planned that Fynn and Lieutenant I. D. C. Smith, and seven other ranks, including Corporal L. Casalonga of No 1 French Troop, should not be picked up until early on the morning of 4 September, unless Fynn was able to take a prisoner that same night.[15]

The party embarked on MTB 250 on the evening of 1 September. The sea was calm and without a swell, and by 2200 they were ten miles off the French coast. The dory was put into the water at 2305, and, towing an interceptor rubber dinghy heavily laden with stores, made its way to the beach. A strong tide was running and it did not put the party ashore, between Elétot and St Pierre-en-Port, until 0005.

It was Flynn's intention to climb the cliffs at once, take a prisoner from the observation post on the cliff top, and return the same night. But when the party was three-quarters of the way up the cliffs Fynn came across a cave with a big overhang which he found impossible to negotiate. At 0210 he abandoned the climb and gave orders for the dory, which was under the command of Lieutenant McGonigal, to return to the MTB with instructions for it to pick them up in the early hours of 4 September.

Fynn now sent Smith and Casalonga to reconnoitre along the beach towards St Pierre while the remainder of the party took the stores and equipment from the invader dinghy, and stacked them in a hideout which had been found at the foot of the cliffs. Smith and Casalonga returned at 0530 and reported that they had got as far as the Casino where there was a German sentry post.

The party rested in the hideout until the tide was high, at 1430, when there were no local fishermen in the area, and Fynn then sent three of his men to try and climb a nearby gully to see if it led to the top of the cliffs, while Smith, Casalonga and himself went to investigate another possible route off the beach, which Smith had seen on his return from St Pierre. The route looked promising and when Fynn heard that the other party had made no headway up the gully he decided to try and climb it that night. He also decided to risk interrogating one of the French fishermen who had reappeared on the beach when the tide had receded. So when the fishermen had finished with their nets Casalonga left the hideout, went down to the beach and whistled sharply at one who was walking by himself. The man turned and Casalonga waved him towards him. The man hesitated and then walked over to him.

"I told him that I was a French commando soldier," Casalonga wrote in his report, "and that my two comrades (Maj. Fynn and Lt. Smith were beside me at the time) were British officers. He held out his hand to us while he stared at our clothes and boots. Then I made up my mind that he was alright, for he told me that he was a good Frenchman and that we need not be afraid. I told him that we wanted to go to St Pierre and asked him what was the way across the beach there for the night before we had found barbed wire right along this beach. He told us, a little hesitant and agitated, that we had to find a green dory and that the way through the wire began there. Following the path that led from the green dory, we should arrive right in the centre of the Casino and there turn right to go into the village. He told us that there was no sentry at night; he was quite sure of this. We asked if there were mines; he did not know. We had now got a certain amount of information and he was anxious to get away because he was overstaying his time to get back to the village. We made an appointment with him for half past seven the following morning. After he had left it struck me, as I remembered that he had told me he had a wife and four children, that it was only on their account that he showed some distrust of us – a feeling that in any case turned later to complete confidence."

At 2000 Fynn sent Smith, Sgt-Major Brodison, and Casalonga along the beach towards St Pierre for a further reconnaissance while he took two of his men to try yet another climb. Again, the gully proved impossible to ascend for caked mud overlay the chalk which made it impossible for either their pitons or crampons to hold. At 2230 Fynn abandoned the climb and when the reconnaissance patrol had not returned at 0030 he went with one of his men to try and find another way up the cliffs. They had only gone 500 yards when they heard shooting from the direction of St Pierre, and soon afterwards Smith and the other two returned along the beach.

Smith reported that they had found the entrance where the Frenchman had indicated. "After reaching the green boat they watched the village for about an hour and heard a sentry moving to the west of the Casino below what Lt Smith thought was the tennis court. They were unable to get closer because the beach was dead white shingle between the gap in the wire and the wall at the end of the beach [and was] without any cover. As they were crawling back they were challenged by someone near the tennis court. They remained still for a while but when they went on they were challenged again and fired upon by a rifle and then by an LMG from the cliff top. The shooting was wild to start with but the third burst from the machine gun was very accurate."

The party now scattered – Smith jumped into the sea – but were eventually able to make their way back. The firing continued for five minutes after they had left the area which showed that the Germans had poor nerves.

When Fynn heard it was possible to get off the beach he decided to delay the pick-up party for 24 hours. He wrote out a full report of what had happened in duplicate and attached one copy to each of the two carrier pigeons which they had brought with them. These were then released and the party watched them circling upwards, but then saw to their horror that five peregrine falcons were attacking them. They drove the pigeons down on to a ledge, but when one tried to rise again the largest falcon grasped it and flew off with it into the cliffs. No one saw what happened to the other but they knew it would never survive.

The party was somewhat disturbed at seeing their only means of communication severed with such cruel swiftness, and they were further alarmed when later in the morning they saw two Focke-Wolfe aircraft flying over the beach in a westerly direction. The planes passed right over the hideout, turned back, circled over the area and then flew inland. It was unlikely that they had been seen, but they now knew the Germans were out hunting for them.

To add to their troubles the French fisherman did not keep his rendezvous on time, but he eventually turned up saying he had been interrogated by the Germans who had told him that a British landing had been made during the night but that the party had now left.

"We asked him if he had heard the firing during the previous night," Casalonga wrote. "He replied that he had not, because he lives not at St Pierre but at Elétot. We told him that a sentry had shot at us but that he had told us that there would not be a sentry. This distressed him and he then said that perhaps sentries did sometimes walk along the promenade . . .

"He asked us if we would like to have some photographs of St Pierre: we told him 'yes', so he explained that one of his friends would come during the afternoon with some postcards. This friend would be dressed in blue and would pass close by some fishing nets which were at the foot of the cliff. Then he left us and we saw him going back later.

"Fairly late in the afternoon (I do not remember the exact time) I saw with my glasses a fisherman in a blue coat coming in our direction staring at the cliff. I thought that this was the man we were expecting, and he did in fact go straight up to the fishing net and put down his basket there. I called him and went towards him with Lt Smith; he seemed pleased enough to see us. We greeted each other, and the first thing that he said was that as soon as he knew that we were there he wanted to come and shake our hands. From his pocket he produced some postcards which showed St Pierre very clearly as viewed from the sea. He was at pains to explain to us where the Boch machine guns were, where they had their guns, mines, billets and headquarters – in fact he gave us every scrap of information he could. There were 40 men, he said, who held the village. He showed us the path which we should follow and added, incidentally, that we should take care not to miss it! We asked him where there were sentries. He replied that there were not any, but that near the Casino there was a post with a guiding light for boats and that no doubt it was from there that we had been fired on the night before.

"We talked of all sorts of things for a while . . . [and then] we saw that two other fishermen were coming and Lt Smith and I made off to hide; but he told us that they were two of his comrades. They turned out to be the fishermen who we had first seen with another who was his brother. We said 'good day' and he gave us some more postcards; one of these was particularly clear. They each confirmed the information given by the other. They mentioned then that there was an AA/MG position on the cliffs, with an underground shelter, with ten men in it."

Casalonga told them that the party was trying to climb the cliffs so that they could attack the machine-gun post, and the fishermen gave him what information they could about where it was possible to ascend. Casalonga tried to persuade them to lay ropes down the cliff but this the fishermen refused to do, saying it would be too dangerous. They went on talking and the fishermen all said that the Germans were demoralized and that that very morning a German who had come back from leave in Berlin had told one of them, "Germany is *kaput*". They then asked Casalonga if he had any weapons he could give them, and seemed a good deal concerned about this; for they said they did not know how they were going to deal with the Boche and would prefer always to be ready to attack them. Casalonga told them that unfortunately they had nothing to spare. After some time the Frenchmen shook hands warmly with the raiders and departed after saying he hoped that soon they could talk freely once more over a good bottle of wine.*

After again failing to climb the muddy gully that had defeated them the previous day, Fynn decided to make another reconnaissance of St Pierre. He left two men behind at the rendezvous where the dory was to pick them up with instructions to let him know as soon as it arrived. Then, at 2300, he set off down the beach with five men.† On arriving at St Pierre he left a covering party behind some rocks and went forward with Brodison to the first row of barbed wire. He then saw a convoy of E-boats going east and soon learnt from the men he had left behind that because of this the pick-up would be delayed as the dory had had to be dropped five miles east of St Pierre and three miles off shore. As soon as he heard this, Fynn knew he still had time to take a prisoner, and he and Brodison tried to find a way through the wire. They got some way but then it defeated them. By now it was 0215 and Fynn decided that if he could not cut his way in to get at the Germans he would try and entice them out. They therefore retired about 40 yards, and laid a bangalore torpedo across some wire and exploded it. When this did not have the required effect they fired some shots with a silent weapon towards where they knew the sentry was, but the German neither returned the fire nor came out to see what was happening.

Time had now run out and Fynn was forced to return. Lieutenant McGonigal picked them up in the dory at 0230. It was near high tide and the swell prevented the dory from coming right into the beach, so that the exhausted party had to wade up to their necks to get aboard. The MTB was a

* They did, having many reunions during the postwar years.
† In his report Fynn states that by this, the third night, various members of the party were suffering from fatigue, which showed itself in somewhat curious illusions. One person saw a plane coming down in flames and another ran into the sea to look at what he described as a chequered object. Fynn thought this exhaustion was partly due to the very heavy exertion of continually walking along shingle silently and partly due to nervous strain.

long way out and it took them some time to find her. Eventually they did, at 0445, and arrived back in Newhaven at 0700.

4

While Fynn and his men were involved in Forfar Beer, Forfar Item, perhaps the most daring – in conception at least – of all the Forfar raids, was launched under the command of Captain O. B. Rooney. Unlike all the other Forfar raids, the men taking part in Forfar Item were dropped by parachute and retrieved by dory. Three elderly Whitley bombers, now only used for leaflet raids, were used for the operation. Two of the aircraft flying at two thousand feet attracted the enemy's attention, while the third flew in over the cliffs near St Valéry-en-Caux, climbed to seven hundred feet, and then dropped Rooney and seven men into the stubble fields some way inland. They then made their way to the coast to the rendezvous with the dory which had come in from an MTB to pick them up.

One of the men with Rooney on Forfar Item was Munich-born Corporal John Wilmers of X-Troop who later wrote a vivid account not only of the raid itself, but of the frustrations, anxiety and excitement that the party all suffered before it.[16]

"Officially, we went to Wherwell for a rest. Wherwell is a lovely, quiet, little country village on the Test; green as only England can be; with hills and woods and orchards and fields where the harvest was just being brought in. The people were friendly simple folk who took us into their homes and made it a very real rest for us.

"In Littlehampton with the Troop we had worked at night and slept in the morning, practising abseiling in all available quarries. Now we never started before ten. Officially we were here for a rest and no one knew any different.

"But every night we were standing by, despite the weather which seemed against us. It had to be just right for all three of us, the army, the air force, who were to take us there, and the navy who were to bring us back. We could only operate during the moonless period. The RAF had to have clear visibility and a wind of not more than 20 mph over the target to be able to drop us and preferably cloud higher up to get cover. The navy needed visibility at sea level and a calm sea without swell. Altogether a rare combination. On Saturday, 28th August we went up to Thruxton, where the aerodrome was, to have a joint party with the RAF at 'The Bell' near Andover, but the weather showed no sign of a change. Then at last Monday was a beautiful day. We all believed that this was it. In the afternoon we checked all equipment and went through the brief for the last time. At Wherwell all seemed quiet and peaceful, we were ready mentally and physically. At 6.30 we drove off in our lorry in the best of spirits. At Thruxton we drew 'chutes and fitted them over all our equipment. This took some doing: I remember I weighed over sixteen stone with it all.

Then all the air crews came in. The Air Liaison Officer was there and two important-looking Group Captains. Minnie, the Squadron Leader, pilot of our aircraft, finally briefed everybody; the Met. Officer gave us a last weather report and then we drove over to our Whitley. As we filed in the ground crews all wished us good luck and we felt thoroughly happy about it all. It was a clear and lovely evening. Vaguely one realized that it might be our last; that we might not see England again. After all this was it: a new experiment never tried before. But nevertheless we felt happy.

"Often you feel nervous before a drop. You think of all the things which might go wrong, from your 'chute not opening or breaking a leg on landing, to the flak which might hit you. But this time we all agreed that we felt just ready.

"We got in awkwardly with all our load and moved as far forward as possible to take off. All was prepared and the engines were just about to be started when Minnie stuck his head in and called out to our CO: 'You've had it'. We could hardly believe it. It seemed an ideal night. Apparently the sea hadn't calmed down enough for the navy and there was nothing to do but go back to Wherwell.

"We felt cheated. What an anti-climax. Here we had been waiting for days and then when we were all but in the air this had to happen. We could hardly believe it. Somehow we felt this had been the chance and that now we would never go. Months of training, weeks of preparation, all gone for nothing. Sadly we took our 'chutes back to the Ops. room and piled back into the lorry.

"The next night we stood by till six when the message came through: scrubbed. Yes, we felt, we had missed our chance. Yesterday was the one good night we were going to have during this moonless period. Then on Wednesday, 2 September, we were again told to stand by. The weather still seemed uncertain and doubtful, and I for one just didn't believe that we would go. Still no further message had come through and hopes began to rise again. Perhaps we would get a second chance after all.

"We left Wherwell at a quarter to seven and drove through Andover to Thruxton. There was no further briefing beyond a very short weather report and there were no group captains. In a short time we were air-borne . . .

"Time goes so quickly in the plane once you're told to get ready that it is hard to recollect anything beyond the normal routine. There we sat with our backs to the side of the aircraft facing each other with only one thought. When the green light follows the red we must shuffle and shift out of that hole quicker than ever before. As you had to do this sitting down and as you also had to concentrate on making a good exit you were fully occupied. The rear gunner stood by the hole to count us out and time us. Nine seconds for eight men fully equipped with tommy guns, ropes, wireless and other paraphernalia must have been something of a record.

"I dropped no. 5 from the Whitley at five minutes past ten. In the air I noticed several other 'chutes both in front and behind, great mushroom umbrellas floating down to earth very quietly. The DZ was a stubble field and I landed perfectly, lying down quietly for a second or two to listen and look around. The sky was lit up now by searchlights playing feverishly and there was some firing answered by the machine guns of the Whitleys going on inland. All was quiet on the ground except for dogs barking in the near-by village.

"I rolled up my 'chute, checked my gun and equipment and made contact with numbers six and seven, both within 20 yards of me. We orientated ourselves by compass and moved off carefully northward towards the village to find the remainder. The pre-arranged blue pin-point light on which we were to collect was nowhere to be seen, but after crossing some fields we heard whistles. They might have been ours, but again they might not, and it was not our object to make contact with the enemy. By then it was eleven o'clock and we had previously arranged to meet at the corner of a near-by wood at that time if we hadn't found each other before. So on we stalked, gingerly crossing wire fences, with our bundled 'chutes hanging over our backs . . .

"We skirted the village and its surrounding orchards to the east and dashed across the main road. Something was moving in a field but it turned out only to be a horse. The dogs were still barking and we heartily wished they wouldn't, particularly as we had been told that there were troops billeted in the village. Then we struck a path running to the coast and along this signal wires were laid going back to the village. Moving along the path was much more quiet than shuffling across stubble fields where it had seemed that we were bound to wake up the whole village sooner or later . . .

"The path led straight up to what we had been told was probably a searchlight under construction on the coast. The others thought they heard voices so we skirted out to the east and very shortly hit the coast itself after crossing a simple barbed wire fence. Below was the sea, our way back, and all was quiet. On we went eastward now to look for the rest of the party. From the air photos and maps it was quite easy to identify the coast and we soon came to Z point. All was deserted . . .

"It was nearly one o'clock and we had lost much precious time. Down below at sea we could see a small convoy moving along the coast, but could only hope that our people's luck would keep them clear. It was time now to return and bring in the dory. The others might have run into trouble and we might have to get them away quickly. At Z point we found another 'chute and a rope which clearly meant another member of the party had turned up. One of us had bruised his shoulder on landing so we left him now while we other two went to look for the newcomer. Soon we saw someone approach. Quickly we lay down and covered him with our tommy guns. Just as he had passed us I called out. It was one of our two officers, who had wandered about on his own since landing and we were mutually glad to see each other.

"As we now had two ropes and a piton and the only wireless in the party, we lowered the man with the bad shoulder down the cliff. If things went wrong our plan called for a walk right across France to Spain and in that case we would have to pull him up again. On the whole to cross the Channel seemed greatly preferable.

"I kept guard while the other two handled the rope. Something seemed to be moving about 50 yds to the east. As it came closer the officer came up to give me covering fire if necessary. Two figures approached and soon to our relief we found that it was the OC and his batman. They had found the remainder of the party on the DZ and had then made for the coast which they hit well to the east of us. Turning west they found another dip in which they also had established a bridgehead. With one rope and their parachutes and the second piton they also had let one man down to try and bring in the dory by torch signals . . .

"Through not meeting up earlier we had lost a great deal of time and it was now a question of getting the party off with a safety margin against the dawn. All we could afford to do now was for two of us to go back to the searchlight while the others got down the cliff. The second officer and I, each with a tommy gun and two hand grenades, set off as fast as we could go. As we got nearer we were careful to listen and strained our eyes to try and see. No noise whatever could we hear and we saw no sentry. Gently we moved on. Yes, here it was, an enormous new searchlight with barrows, concrete mixer, picks and shovels all lying about as the workmen must have left them. Dug in below ground level was a big hut, obviously the crews' living quarters, now empty, but showing signs of recent occupation. What a pity we had no explosives with us, but at any rate we could throw all their picks and shovels and barrows down the cliff into the sea and cut their telephone wires.

"By the side of the searchlight mounted on a heavy tripod and wired to the ground stood an obviously valuable optical instrument, some kind of special field glasses used with the searchlight. At least we could take these back. We couldn't in the dark get them off their tripod so we wrenched the whole thing away . . .

"Back at the rope the last man but one was just going down. We told him we'd pull the rope up after him to let our instrument down and then we'd follow. I was last but one down and I didn't envy the CO those few lonely minutes on top by himself. If a patrol should come along he hadn't much chance. With this in mind I got down pretty quickly, but a nasty surprise awaited us.

"It seemed that the man we'd let down first had been unable to make any contact with the dory, but had after much effort been told by the MTB that they had been washed ashore further east and urgently needed our help to push them off again. He had thereupon walked east for a mile or so but hadn't seen them and felt he couldn't go further as we might come down and not realize

68

what had happened. He had, however, found the second rope and lying below it unconscious the man the others had sent down it. What had happened was that he had fallen off where the rope had been tied to the parachutes and so must have fallen nearly a hundred feet. Three things saved him: he was wearing his parachute helmet, he landed on shingle and probably managed to reduce his speed by sliding down the parachutes. We couldn't tell if he was injured but anyway he managed to walk when he'd come to which at the moment was all that mattered.

"The first three people down, when they realized what had happened, had wisely gone on to find the dory. We now picked up our kit and carrying guns, parachute and my precious instrument we too set off east along the cliffs. This was tiring work. For every step forward you slipped back half a one in the mountains of shingle, and our loads were heavy and awkward to carry . . .

"At last after walking some three miles we found the dory and its crew. But it was at least 50 yards up on the dry shore. They told us that they had run into the enemy convoy that we had seen from above and had had to shut off their engine so as not to get noticed. This had caused them to get washed ashore here. The engine was smashed and we'd have to paddle but first we must all push her down into the sea. Nor was this all. It was getting lighter every moment and we were no more than a few hundred yards from the lighthouse at St Valéry harbour entrance.

"We worked hard then and with a purpose. We stripped naked and pushing for all we were worth finally got the dory back into the water and we kept right on pushing till we had to swim for it. She was leaking badly and to keep her from sinking we dumped chutes and all other unnecessary kit overboard and now stark naked we paddled for our lives. In, out, in out; yes, we were making progress. In the stern our bren gun faced back to the coast: at least it was a gesture. Meanwhile over the wireless we made contact with the MTB. 'Blokes very tired, boat slowly sinking' was the report we had to give and up in the bows stood one of the crew waving a torch in a slow semi-circle out to sea. 'Dory to MTB, dory to MTB, can you see us? Can you see us?' And back it came. Yes, they had picked us up, but would we go as hard as we could. They'd come to within a mile of the shore. It was the very utmost they could do. In, out, in, out; our timing may have been ragged but no boat race crew could ever be more intent on their rowing than we were, sitting there with our short paddles out over the side, peering before us in the grey dawn with the water slowly rising round our feet. And then we saw her dark shape and were clambering aboard helped by friendly sailors. The dory was hauled up and then the MTB showed us what she could do. There were the cliffs of France, white and quite clear now, but we were bound for Newhaven and going below there was tea and rum and cigarettes and blankets."

5

Later Small-Scale
Raids

On 11 September, 1943, the Chiefs of Staff ruled that in future all cross-Channel reconnaissance raids were to be co-ordinated with COSSAC, for, as will be seen, there was mounting opposition to any taking place at all. It took some months for the next ones to be planned and it was not until December that the first of the new series, codenamed Hardtack, was launched, though a preliminary raid, codenamed Hardtack Dog, was carried out on the night of 26/27 November.

The role of the Inter-Allied Commando in the Hardtack raids was far greater than in the Forfar operations. The unit's second-in-command, Major Peter Laycock, was put in overall charge of the force, called Layforce II, and he had at his disposal not only elements of 2 SBS and the now disbanded No 12 Commando, but both French Troops and X-Troop of the Inter-Allied Commando. It was official policy to give the French, in particular, leading roles in the raids to alleviate their disappointment at not being sent to the Mediterranean theatre of operations as had originally been planned.

At least one of the Hardtack raids, led by a Frenchman, provided essential information for the D-Day planners, but basically the series was obviously intended, like the Forfar operations, to confuse the Germans as to the Allies' intentions, though some were meant to be preliminary reconnaissances for larger raids (codenamed Manacle) which never materialized. About fourteen were planned in detail and a more extensive length of the continental shoreline, including some of the D-Day beaches, was raided. It is fair to assume, from the codename given to the preliminary raid, Hardtack Dog, that the Hardtack raids were going to be allotted the same codenames as the Forfar ones, but, apart from Hardtack Item,* they were eventually all given numbers, with most of the raids being mounted in the same areas as the Forfar operations.

On 9 December, 1943, the two French Troops were moved from Eastbourne and billeted in the Newhaven-Peacehaven-Seaford area and intensive training began for the new operations, the first of which were to be launched during the forthcoming lunar dark periods over Christmas and in January. The raids were planned by a syndicate at COHQ who then gave the outlines of them to Laycock for the detailed planning. Four of these, which were to take place in the January dark period, were cancelled. It is not known why Hardtack 14 (Berck Plage, Captain Trepel and six other ranks of Troop 8) and 19 (Le Touquet-Stella Plage, Lieutenant Lofi and five other ranks of Troop 8) were cancelled, but both Hardtack 24 (Varreville-La Madeleine, Lieutenant Guy Vourc'h and six other ranks of Troop 1) and 27 (Morsalines [La Belle Croix], Lieutenant Smith and six other ranks of Troop 1 or Troop 8) were both almost certainly vetoed by COSSAC which, as D-Day approached, became increasingly nervous about operating anywhere near Normandy.

In fact, the whole policy of small-scale raiding was brought into question when a request was made to draw up plans for a further ten raids of the Hardtack type during the February dark period. The request was made to the Chief of Combined Operations on 26 January, 1944, by the Naval Commander of the Allied Expeditionary Force, Admiral Ramsay, but even though these later raids were to take place nowhere near the invasion beaches they provoked a strong memo from Montgomery's Chief of Staff, Major-General de Guingand, who felt that "a policy of raiding anywhere on the Belgian/French coasts is wrong. We have told the enemy that we are going to invade the continent this spring. I feel that the best way to fox him as regards the sector which we have chosen for the invasion is to stop raiding altogether."[1] He then detailed his reasons for this attitude. They seemed to the Small Scale Raiding Committee who had to consider them fallacious and in parts contradictory, but when they were put before the SHAEF Raids and Reconnaissance Committee it agreed with them and all further raids, except COPP (Combined Operations Pilotage Parties) raids, were banned on the French and Belgian coasts.†[2]

As with the Forfar operations, several Hardtack raids were launched the same night. They left from Dover, Newhaven and Dartmouth, which were all coastal forces bases. The first to take place was Hardtack 11. This sailed from

---

* Hardtack Item was to be a repeat of Forfar Item. This time it was due to be mounted by members of X-Troop, led by Hilton Jones, with Lieutenant George Lane picking them up by dory. After intensive training the operation was delayed several times because of adverse weather conditions, and was eventually cancelled.

† Even Hardtack 35, which seems to have had the same objectives as Hardtack 36 (later Operation Premium), and which was to have taken place as far north as the Dutch-Belgian border, was cancelled, though there is no certainty that this was on the orders of COSSAC.

Dover on the night of 23/24 December, 1943, but the MTB's escorts had to be withdrawn to attack an enemy convoy and the raid was cancelled, but went ahead the following night. Hardtack 23, led by Captain Kieffer, was also due to be mounted on the night of 23/24 December but was cancelled, probably because of the weather.

The objective of Hardtack 11 was to make a reconnaissance of the beaches and dunes near Gravelines, situated between Calais and Dunkirk. The raiding party consisted of five members of No 1 French Troop and was commanded by Warrant Officer Wallerand. They embarked at 2200 on MTB 25 which left harbour an hour later. Also aboard the MTB was a French doctor, Captain Villiere, and the Layforce Signals Officer, Major A. J. Leahy, who later wrote a detailed report of the disaster which was to overtake Wallerand and his men.[3]

The landing place was reached at 0230 and the dory was launched. The sea was smooth, but the swell caused sufficient surf on the beach to drown the noise of the MTB's engines. The dory's coxswain was Sergeant Parks from 2 SBS and the dory signaller was a Russian-born member of X-Troop, Corporal Jones, and their job was to lie offshore until they received a wireless message from the raiding party that they were to be picked up. The signalman aboard the MTB had a 536 set on the same network and there was also an S-phone that guided the dory back to the MTB.

The party landed all right, but in the opinion of Corporal Jones at least, Wallerand ordered the dory to stand in rather too close to the shore, making it vulnerable to the surf. Worse, the party rushed ashore without pushing the dory back out, so that Parks and Jones could not stop it being swamped and washed ashore. They managed to refloat it, but could not restart the engine, so they began paddling towards the MTB whose outline could plainly be seen.* On the way back Jones sent the codeword "Donkey" which meant "Engine stopped, am using oars", but this was received aboard the MTB as "Sunk", which naturally caused some consternation, and the MTB signaller was still trying to establish contact with the dory when it appeared from astern and came alongside.

After the dory had been bailed out, the MTB moved out to sea a mile, reanchored, and then the dory was hoisted aboard. Strenuous efforts were now made to start its engine but without success. When it became obvious that the dory's engine would not work the MTB moved towards the shore again and at a depth of about two fathoms – about 400 yards from the beach – the dory was released and was paddled towards the shore by Parks, Jones and another signaller called Chapman.

As the dory was slowly paddled in to the beach the men on the MTB could

---

* Because of wartime shortages the dories were equipped with converted Austin motor car engines. They were vulnerable to water entering their exhaust pipes which stopped them and they could not then be restarted.

dimly see Wallerand and his party on what was perhaps a sandbank and moments later they began signalling the code sign X with a blue torch to bring the dory in to collect them. It had been planned that just outside the breakers Jones would swim ashore to collect Wallerand while the other two crew kept the dory out of danger. But at 0535 the dory suddenly disappeared from the view of those aboard the MTB and a few minutes later they received the codeword "Maroon" meaning that the dory had been sunk or wrecked.

The CO of the MTB now ordered that his ship be taken right to the shore and as it crept in a number of swimmers were seen in the water and shouts of help were heard. The MTB continued to edge in as near as it could, and only stopped when the leadsman in the bows called "Five feet". Scrambling nets were then lowered over the port side.

"The swimmers were making no progress at all," wrote Leahy in his report, "except one man who came right up to the side.* The crew threw ropes to him, but at this moment the MTB swung round. The skipper called out to know what had happened to the swimmer and was told he had drifted away aft. I do not know why he was not pulled on board. The skipper than ordered 'Out carley float'. This was unlashed from its carrying position and put over board but failed to float away from the MTB."

Those on the MTB now realized that they could no longer see any of the other swimmers, though the occasional shout was still heard. The MTB continued to wait in very shallow water, but no one appeared, and at 0600, when no more shouts had been heard for some time, the skipper decided to withdraw as he was drifting dangerously close to Gravelines, and Leahy concurred with his decision.

The MTB returned to the same spot the following night – it was a prearranged plan in all raids that this should be done if possible – and searched one mile east and west of the landing place, but without seeing any survivors or any of the prearranged signals. Shortly afterwards the Germans issued a communiqué saying that a Commando party had been landed at Gravelines but had been wiped out. This, however, was far from the truth.

What really happened to those Frenchmen who took part in Hardtack 11 can be pieced together from the reports of those who survived that night.[4] Their story is a classic example of how highly trained men can use their initiative in the face of seemingly impossible odds.

The initial landing was carried out without trouble and Wallerand, Navrault and Meunier set out to reconnoitre a nearby minefield while Caron, Madec and Pourcelot stayed in the dunes to cover them, after making sure a machine-gun emplacement in the vicinity was empty. At 0400 a two-man German patrol passed along the beach but saw nothing, and shortly afterwards Meunier appeared carrying part of a mine. Then at 0520 Wallerand and Navrault

* This must have been Wallerand.

returned carrying two French anti-tank mines and the party returned to the beach.

"I came back to the beach at 0520 with my other comrades and entered the water," Madec wrote in his report after he returned to his unit in September, 1944, "while WO Wallerand was calling the dory by an appropriate signal. The dory came to us rowing as the engine had been drowned, but it was at the same time taking a lot of water on board. We cleared the water out and then pushed the dory away, going in the water up to the neck so that the Germans could not detect us if it so happened that another patrol should pass through the beach. At about 100 yards into the sea we tried to embark on the dory, expecting to row to the MTB 400 yards away. During the embarkation a swell took us by the side and filled the dory."

The dory was now emptied of all its contents and an attempt was made to tip out the water, but without success. To prevent it being driven nearer the shore both Parks and Wallerand took grapnel anchors and swam out to sea. "I am going to see what is going on," Wallerand was reported as saying. He was never seen again.

"I then decided to try and join the MTB myself," wrote Madec. "I had reached some way when I noticed that the MTB was changing place. I was getting tired and as Sgt Parks, the dory's coxswain, was in the water asking for help, I tried to reach him. I did not succeed, being too tired, and I had to go back ashore. I found there the signalman of the dory and one sailor of the MTB who had embarked in the dory to help us.

"I saw at this time that the remainder of the party had crossed the minefield and I asked the two British personnel [Jones and Chapman] to follow me across it also. They did not do so, thinking it better to wait for some help on the next morning or the following night. I therefore went by myself and joined my comrades through the minefield. They all thought I had been drowned."

Pourcelot, Navrault and Madec made their way towards the first houses of Gravelines, while Caron and Meunier decided to continue inland. At 0830 they found a hut and went to sleep there, and then walked during the following three nights and hid during the daytime. On the evening of the fourth day they were taken in by a widow near St Omer who next day put them on a train for Fresnoy-le-Grand where Meunier lived, and Meunier's family put them in touch with the local Resistance. Arrangements were being made for their escape to England when the Gestapo struck and arrested several Resistance leaders. Caron left to try and find another Resistance group which could return him to England, but later, when Paris was liberated, he was able to rejoin his unit. Meunier, however, was arrested in Paris while trying to escape to Spain and was thrown into Fresnes prison where he was tortured and beaten. At the beginning of July he was told he had been condemned to death, but was liberated on 18 August by members of the Resistance.

The three other Commandos were taken in by a farmer who gave them some food and dried their clothes. The farmer told them that both Jones* and Chapman had been captured and had been seen passing through the town making V-signs from a German lorry.

Following the capture of Jones and Chapman, Gravelines and the surrounding country was searched by the Germans. They even searched the farmer's barn where the three Frenchmen were hiding but failed to look in the room above it. Madec and the other two stayed in the room that night and throughout the following day, then, in civilian clothes given to them by the farmer, they made their escape under cover of darkness with a guide taking them to another farmhouse nearby.

The next morning the three of them boarded a train to Hazebrouck and then another to St Omer. At St Omer it was decided that it was too dangerous for the three of them to travel together and they split up. Navrault and Pourcelot travelled to the former's home in Paris while Madec went to Amiens where his parents lived. Navrault's mother put them in touch with a local Resistance leader, but attempts to return them to England proved fruitless and they went to stay with Pourcelot's family at Lyons. Pourcelot then went to Besançon, where he joined the local Resistance, and Navrault went to Bellenaves, where he joined the Raphanel Resistance group which operated to the north of the Puy de Dôme. Pourcelot was eventually arrested on some minor charge and in September, 1944, was sent to Buchenwald concentration camp. As the Allies advanced Pourcelot was marched from one camp to another so that by the time he was liberated he weighed a mere 44kg. In the meantime Navrault had been involved in a full-scale battle with the Germans which nearly wiped out his Resistance group and had then taken charge of a sabotage unit. In September, 1944, he was able to get to Paris and then reported back to his unit.

After the other two left him, Madec began walking towards Paris to try and get to his sister who lived in the suburbs at Châtillon-sous-Bagneux. After one night on the road he was picked up by a civilian lorry and the driver took him to a railway station. From there he took a train to Paris. By this time the jacket the French farmer had given to him had fallen to pieces and he was forced to put his battledress top back on. He had of course stripped it of all insignia; one pocket had been ripped off and it was filthy dirty. Nevertheless it does seem extraordinarily audacious for him calmly to take the Métro – which was filled with German soldiers – from the Gard du Nord to Porte d'Orleans, but this is exactly what he did.

Madec's sister sheltered him for a few days and persuaded the local mayor to provide him with papers saying that he was a carpenter who had just

---

* Jones must have managed to hide his real identity for he survived imprisonment and returned to Britain after the war where he was seen by several members of his troop.

been released from Germany. From Châtillon-sous-Bagneux he made his way to Agen in the South of France, having been previously advised to go there by Wallerand who, before he had joined the Free French Forces in England, had worked with the underground movement there. However, when he reported at the address given him by Wallerand – Le Bar du Coin – the owners allowed him to sleep there but said they could not otherwise help him. After attempting several channels of escape which came to nothing Madec travelled to the village of Kernevel just outside Rosporden near Finisterre where the father-in-law of Lieutenant J. Mazeas, the French Commandos' Administrative Officer, had a farm, and here, at last, he found a safe refuge.

As soon as he could, Madec began to work with the local underground movement, and within weeks had started his own group with the son of the farmer. "In the beginning, having no arms with which to fight, we only did sabotage work on the roads, railway lines and telephone wires. We cut the underground cables joining Nantes to Brest through Vannes, Lorient and Quimper, in many places."

Arms for the Resistance fighters began to be dropped by parachute at the beginning of July, 1944, and Madec was then able to take the head of an armed section and several clashes with the Germans followed. In August Madec and his men took part in the fighting for the liberation of Rosporden. The fighting was very bitter with the town changing hands several times, but eventually the Germans were driven off. Following the liberation of Rosporden, Madec was involved in ambushing German convoys and then in the liberation of Concarneau after which he returned to Rosporden where he reported to Lieutenant Mazeas while the latter was on leave seeing his parents. Mazeas took Madec back with him to Arromanches where he was eventually reunited with his unit.

2

The débâcle of Hardtack 11 did not, of course, in any way alter the plans to mount the other raids and the following night Lieutenant McGonigal and five men from No 1 French Troop embarked on an MGB at Dartmouth for a reconnaissance raid on Sark, codenamed Hardtack 7. The same night another party consisting of Lieutenant L. Hulot of No 8 French Troop, one British Commando and three French Commandos, all under the command of Captain A. P. Ayton, a member of 2 SBS, embarked at the same place for a raid on Jersey, codenamed Hardtack 28.

McGonigal and his party were landed on rocks at Derrible Point, but after spending several hours in an unsuccessful attempt to climb the cliffs, they returned to the dory and re-embarked at 0300. McGonigal then ordered the dory to move westward to Derrible Bay where he and a member of No 1 French

Troop, Boccador,* carried out a reconnaissance of the beach area in the north-east corner of the bay. "With Sgt Boccador, I worked along the cliff edge to the beach moving slowly and carefully since Sgt Boccador had reported to me that he had seen a sentry patrolling the cliff over the bay." All they found was a box of fuses which they took back with them to the dory, re-embarking at 0410 and reaching the waiting MGB at 0425.[5]

Meanwhile, Ayton and his men had made a scramble landing on rocks just north of the cove at Petit Port, Jersey, and had then made their way inland. After reconnoitring a deserted village and an unmanned blockhouse they walked along a road till they came to an isolated farmhouse. They knocked on the door, but at first no one would come out. After about 20 minutes, however, a very frightened woman opened a first-floor window and asked them what they wanted. The Frenchmen asked if she knew where any German patrols were operating, but the woman said she knew nothing and advised them to go to another farm nearby where they might obtain the information they needed. This they did, but when a man opened the door and saw them he was too frightened to speak. His brother then came to the door but he too became very agitated when he saw who was there. Eventually the Commandos managed to calm both of them down and they were able to give Hulot detailed information on the whereabouts of the German garrison. "We were given a glass of milk each," Hulot wrote in his report, "and the farmers said that they were very glad to have met us and hoped we'd come again soon."[6]

The brothers then guided the party across country to the edge of a German strongpoint at Les Platons, but they could not find the entrance to it or a way across the minefield that surrounded it. They waited a while but could see no sign of movement. By now they only had three-quarters of an hour left before they were to be picked up, so it was reluctantly decided to abandon the search for a prisoner. At 0445 they reached the re-embarkation point at Petit Port, but as there was no sign of the dory they moved northward along the cliff looking for it and flashing a torch out to sea to catch its attention.

"We came to a three-strand cattle fence which extended down the cliff. Captain Ayton crawled under the fence and had proceeded about five yards on the other side by the time I was at the fence. Suddenly, there was a vivid red flash, which lit up the whole area, and a loud report, which sounded like the explosion of two 82 grenades. I first thought that a German patrol had found us and proceeded cautiously forward but saw no one and presumed that Captain Ayton had trodden on a mine. At first we could not find him and searched the cliff side. Then we heard a faint cry for help and I found him lying badly

* Boccador had been one of the two Frenchmen to join members of No 12 Commando mounting the Forfar raids, but Casalonga, by his participation in the raid near St Pierre-en-Port, was the only one to have landed in France up to that time.

wounded on the cliff side with his foot entangled in some brambles, which probably prevented him from falling down the cliff. This would not have been a normally exploded S-mine as only Captain Ayton was wounded by the explosion."

Soon after Ayton was found the party heard the MGB and then saw it about 400 yards from the shore. They signalled it and the MGB answered. By now the dory had returned to the MGB but it was sent back to the landing point and after great difficulty Ayton was brought down the cliff and the party re-embarked at 0520. Despite having to wait half-an-hour for its arrival, nothing was seen of the enemy nor did they react in any way. Ayton died before the MGB reached Dartmouth, but the rest arrived safely.

3

After the first two nights of Hardtack operations little had been achieved and casualties had been severe, but on the third night, that of 26/27 December, the raiders had better luck. Three raids, Hardtack 4, Hardtack 13 and Hardtack 21, were all mounted, from Newhaven, and though none was able to bring back a prisoner, they all managed to land and one came back with essential information on the German beach defences.

Hardtack 4, which had first been mounted on 24/25 December, but had been forced to return because of bad weather, was successfully launched the second time when Lieutenant I. D. C. Smith and his party of eight men, which included Lance-Corporal Félix Grinspin* of No 8 French Troop, landed in the area of Biville, between Dieppe and Le Tréport. The party reconnoitred the shoreline and then two of them climbed the cliffs and dropped down ropes for the others. Grinspin was chosen to ascend first as he was the lightest. Just as he was being hauled over the lip of the cliff the men at the top noticed a light, and one of them went to investigate. What he saw – fifteen Germans advancing towards him in line abreast their rifles at the ready – made him order a hurried retreat, and Grinspin went down the rope a lot faster than he had come up it.

The raiders crouched at the foot of the cliff while the German patrol passed above their heads, and then Smith and another man climbed three-quarters of the way back up the rope and lay there listening. When they were certain the patrol had moved on they came down and then, with the rest of the party, moved east along the beach, but found nothing of interest. As they were doing this their MTB was spotted by the Germans who opened fire on it from the direction of Creil-sur-Mer and it was forced to move further out to sea. When the time came for the Commandos to return they embarked in the dory and started the long trip back to the waiting MTB. When well offshore they saw flashing lights between the shore and the dory and then spotted a flotilla of

* A number of the French Troop altered their names for fear of reprisals against their families, so Grispin became Grinspin.

78

E-boats heading eastwards at high speed – another few minutes ashore and the dory would almost certainly have been spotted by the enemy.[7]

While the members of Hardtack 4 were having their series of narrow escapes, those belonging to Hardtack 13 – which had also been first mounted on 24/25 December but had also been cancelled because of the weather – were landing in the area of Benouville just east of Etretat. The party was led by Captain Kennard, a member of 2 SBS, and he had with him Lieutenant J. Pinelli and nine men from No 1 French Troop. Their objective was to try and scale the cliffs, but although strenuous efforts were made no way could be found up them and the party was forced to withdraw, and did so without incident.[8]

The most successful operation that night was undoubtedly Hardtack 21 – which had also had to be cancelled the previous night – when a party of five men from No 1 French Troop, under the command of Lieutenant Francis Vourch, extensively reconnoitred the beach at Quineville south of St Vaast and the ground inland of it. Their brief was to reconnoitre a stretch of coastline 500 yards in length that lay between two strongpoints, and to record the beach obstacles there as well as the inland inundations. What they found was of intense interest to the D-Day planners, for their landing place was in the area of what was later to be codenamed Utah Beach, where the 4th Division of the American army landed on 6 June.

Vourch and his men landed at 2350 on 26 December and after a fifteen-minute walk came to a marsh into which they sunk up to their knees. However, this was eventually negotiated and after cutting their way through some old barbed wire on the other side they reached hard ground and were able to continue. Then, halfway between a small bank of sand and a flooded inland area, they came across an anti-tank obstacle, details of which the Allies urgently needed. It had been detected in aerial photographs and labelled "Element C" but up to that time no one knew exactly what it looked like. Now Vourch was able to supply the details needed. "The height was 7ft 10in," he wrote briefly in his report, "and the width of one section 9ft 1in. This was followed in a southerly direction till the road at pt 363107 was reached."[9]

After collecting a sample of mud from the flooded area and measuring its depth accurately, the party lay up for half-an-hour in the hope of taking a prisoner, but at 0220 they were forced to start the return walk to the dory which was boarded at 0300. It took them four and a half hours to reach the MTB as a searchlight from the direction of Port St Marcouf swept the whole area at half-hourly intervals throughout the night.

For bringing back such valuable information Vourch was awarded the Military Cross, the first to be won by the Inter-Allied Commando. His citation read: "He was ordered to land on the east coast of the Cotentin Peninsula with a small force to carry out a reconnaissance to obtain information. The safe withdrawal of the force unobserved by the enemy was an important consideration. Despite the fact there was every indication that the presence of German patrols was suspected Lt Vourch meticulously carried out his orders and with determination accomplished a difficult task in enemy territory, a task which was carried out in the smallest detail. Through Lt Vourch's personal courage he was able to withdraw the whole force without loss or casualties and returned with the most valuable information."

Vourch did not receive his decoration until after D-Day as approval for it was delayed by French Government red tape. However, in August, 1944, Vourch was visited by the Chief of Combined Operations, Major-General Robert Laycock, while he was serving with the 1st Special Service Brigade in Normandy. "The investiture was a simple ceremony and took place in the dugout which served as the HQ for the 1st Service Brigade. Laycock pinned the medal on Vourch and said, 'I give you this in the name of the King', after which everyone sat down for a drink and Vourch handed back his medal to the General for safe keeping."[10]

On the night following Vourch's successful mission, 27/28 December, Hardtack 7 was remounted with the same men. This time they went ashore on the headland opposite Derrible Point at Sark and after climbing a 200-foot sheer rock face, and then a further very steep slope of about 100 feet, the party encountered a wire fence. This was cut and they then found a path with thick gorse on either side, which forced them to keep to it. Unfortunately it was mined and two members of No 1 French Troop were wounded, Bellamy dying almost immediately. The party continued to move forward but then two more mines exploded, wounding McGonigal and killing Dignac who had previously been wounded.

With the operation now compromised, McGonigal ordered his men to withdraw. In doing so, however, further mines were exploded, some possibly by remote control though the enemy did not otherwise react. These explosions slightly wounded another member of the party, Private Joseph Nicot, leaving Boccador the only one uninjured. He helped his wounded commanding officer back to the beach while Le Floc'h and Nicot made their own way down as best they could. Though quite badly hurt, McGonigal retained command and all four were eventually taken off without any further incident. For their part in this operation McGonigal was awarded the Military Cross and Boccador was Mentioned in Despatches.

On the same night as Hardtack 7 was remounted, another attempt was made to mount Kieffer's operation, Hardtack 23, but the MTB ran aground and the raid was abandoned. It was not tried again.

With the exception of Operation Premium only one other Hardtack raid, 26, was launched. It was mounted from Dover on the night of 20/21 January, 1944. The objective for Warrant Officer P. Chausse and six other Frenchmen from No 8 Troop was Middelkerke near Ostend. The dory was launched but the

Gobetz (*right*), a Dutch Commando, talking to Dutch resistance fighters at the rear of the Hartenstein Hotel in Oosterbeek, 18 or 19 September, 1944. This shot is a clip from a cine-film taken by a British Army Film Unit.

Walcheren, 1 November, 1944, taken from the landing craft carrying the Norwegian Troop ashore.

D-Day, 6 June 1944: A Commando bicycle Troop – probably from No. 6 Commando – stumble ashore. In the foreground is Cpl. Sayers of X-Troop.

Norwegian Commandos struggling ashore at Walcheren after their landing craft had been hit. Behind them is an LVT (Buffalo).

The Headquarters of 10(IA) Commando ashore at Walcheren, 1 November, 1944. Lieutenant-Colonel Peter Laycock, cigarette in hand, is with his radio operator. Behind the operator is the Commando's second-in-command, Major Franks.

4 November, 1944. Belgian Commandos arrive to take over positions of Norwegian Troop in woods north of Domburg.

Grispin (*right*) and Cabanella, two members of the French Troop who took part in the ill-fated Operation Premium, February 1944. The Frenchmen wore French naval uniform during training for the operation for security reasons.

George Lane's identity card issued when he was made a POW after a Tarbrush raid, May 1944.

Belgian Commandos with Partisans on Vis, 1944.

The two French Troops embarked on their landing craft, 5 June, 1944.

Sergeant Messanot leading his section, Ouistreham, 6 June, 1944.

Prince Bernhard decorates d
Koning with the Dutch Bron
Cross, Eastbourne, 17 August
1944.

(*Below*) Paris, 31 August, 19
Meunier in civilian clothes,
re-united with some of the
French Troop after release
from Fresnes prison. On his
right is Bolloré, the Medical
Orderly for No. 8 Troop. O
the extreme right, also in
civilian clothes, is another
member of the disastrous
Hardtack 11 raid, Caron.

engine gave continuous trouble and as Chausse approached the shore he spotted an unknown vessel. By now the party was running well behind schedule and the sea was rising. Chausse therefore decided to withdraw. The raid was not remounted.

4

Between Hardtack 26 and the vital Tarbrush raids of May, 1944, the ill-fated Operation Premium was undertaken by Captain Charles Trepel and five men from No 8 Troop just north of Scheveningen on the Dutch coast.*

Originally Trepel and members of his Troop had been allocated Hardtack 14, but, as has been mentioned, this was cancelled. According to Maurice Chauvet, who wrote an article about his Troop Commander after the war,[11] Trepel was so upset at having apparently missed his chance at striking back at the enemy he hated so much that he went to London and somehow inveigled the authorities into allowing him to lead a raid which was originally going to be led by Lieutenant Hulot. This was Hardtack 36 which had quite different objectives to the other Hardtack operations.

The Intelligence requirements for this raid were as follows: 1. To ascertain whether it is possible to penetrate inland clear of the immediate coast defences unobserved, and reach a position from which a clear run into the interior seems feasible. 2. To ascertain whether the obstacles encountered en route can be overcome or circumvented by an intelligent single individual of Dutch nationality. 3. A description of the obstacles encountered. 4. Any landmarks likely to be useful to the individual in question. 5. Estimated time it would take the individual in question to penetrate to or from the position referred to in para. 1 above. 6. Description and position of any cover available along the route referred to in para 1 above. Another document also makes it plain that they were to reconnoitre as far as the Aankver canal and to find a place where it could be crossed.[12]

The background to the requirement for such an operation is made clear in a memorandum issued by the Deputy Director Operations Division (Intelligence) in September, 1943. This stated that until the spring of 1942 DDOD(I) had executed numerous operations with coastal forces craft, landing and embarking agents and materials on the Dutch coast on behalf of SIS (Special Intelligence Service) and SOE. After that time the enemy had become too alert to allow agents to reach, or leave, the coast. Agents were thereafter picked up by Lysander, but the losses of these aircraft were now too high to continue this method of extracting them. It was therefore thought necessary to reopen a line of communication so that agents could be taken off from the Dutch coast, but it first had to be established that a feasible route existed. "The reasonable

---

* While COSSAC banned raids on the French and Belgian coasts they still allowed operations on the Dutch coast and on another area under consideration by COHQ, Ushant.

assumption that the enemy's defences cannot at the very best (in the face of his present predicament) be stronger than they were last year, combined with CCO's recent experiences on the French coast east of the Cherbourg Peninsula, leads DDOD(I) to the conviction that a line of sea communications with Holland can be re-opened."[13]

In fact DDOD(I) had been trying for some months to gain the information it required and, under the codename Madonna Able, had mounted four separate operations under the command of Captain Porteous VC, but on each occasion something had prevented the raiding party from landing. As Operation Premium, the raid was first mounted, after a training period at Great Yarmouth, on the night of 24/25 February, 1944, and from surviving documents it is clear that though it was mounted on behalf of Naval Intelligence it came under the aegis of Laycock as Commanding Officer of Layforce II.[14]

The party left Great Yarmouth aboard MTB 682 on schedule at 1600. The sea was moderate, but under the influence of the easterly wind became calm near the Dutch coast, so landing conditions were good and Trepel must have thought that at last he and his men were going into action. But it was not to be for at 2130 the CO of the MTB, Lieutenant William Beynon, informed him that the direction-finding transmitter was not working and that as he could not guarantee to find the exact landing point he was returning to base. Trepel asked him if one of the four escort vessels could lead the party to the right spot but was told that they, too, were not receiving the transmission correctly. Trepel then asked the Dutch navigating officer if he could navigate the MTB to some point on the stretch of coast that was within half a mile of the landing point but the navigator said he could not.

On the return voyage the four escorting MGBs were drawn away to attack some E-boats which had been operating in the Humber area, and two of them were damaged.

The raid was mounted again on 27 February, and at 1600 the same MTB left Great Yarmouth with Trepel and his five men, the dory coxswain, Quartermaster Rossi, two other French Commandos, Grinspin and a wireless operator called Bougrain, the MTB signaller and dory signaller, Lance-Corporal Farr and Private Sayers,* both X-Troopers, aboard. Conditions were again perfect; the sea was flat calm and there were intermittent flurries of snow; but they nevertheless arrived at the landing point two hours behind because the direction-finding transmission again misbehaved and because they had had to skirt an enemy convoy.

The MTB anchored about half a mile from the shore and at 0130 the dory,

---

* Documents in the possession of Dr Guy Vourc'h show that Sayers had already operated with the French during the earlier Hardtack operations and was later awarded the Croix de Guerre for his part in them.

with the intruder dinghy in tow, left for the shore which could dimly be seen. Ten minutes after leaving the MTB red rockets went up and fell on the beach between two fortified points which were about 3000 metres apart. At 0150, when about 30 yards from the beach, the raiding party transferred to the dinghy. As they did so a red over green over white flare went up from what was assumed to be a strongpoint north of the landing point. But Trepel did not hesitate and ten minutes later, after returning to the dory to collect a small mooring anchor, he and his men landed on the steeply sloping beach.

As they went ashore white flares began to be fired from the southern strongpoint which seemed to those on the MTB to be almost in front of the landing place. According to Rossi one lit up the dory as he and Sayers crouched in the bottom of it and those on the MTB could see some men silhouetted on the beach. Three minutes later another flare fell only ten feet from the dory, so Rossi took it out to about 100 yards from shore and then dropped anchor again, but then another flare dropped only 50 yards from the new position. It seemed to those in the dory that the strongpoint on the left was firing flares at the beach while the one on the right was firing them out to sea. They could see the dunes which were about 20 feet high as well as a group of three men moving. At any moment, Rossi reported afterwards, they expected the dory to be machine-gunned, but nothing happened.

What did happen was rather more extraordinary because both those in the dory and on the MTB now heard shouting. To those on the MTB, carried as it was by an offshore breeze, the shouting seemed amplified, as if a tripwire had set off some kind of recording. But in their report to Laycock both Sayers and Farr simply said it sounded "hysterical in character" and went on for about three-quarters of an hour, while Rossi described it as "cries of attack" which continued for about fifteen minutes.

The flares continued to light up the area and Rossi saw torches shining on the ground around the strongpoints. It was then 0330. Another flare landed near the dory and Rossi moved it another 50 yards out to sea, and re-anchored. The flares continued until 0445 and then ceased, but the torches continued to move around for another five minutes. At this time Sayers called the MTB as the dory should have returned at 0430. He was told to stay until 0500, and then return, which they did. The dory was lifted aboard on its davits, the light sisal rope holding the anchor, weighted so that it would sink, was cut with an axe, and the MTB headed for England at top speed. During the whole time both craft had lain at anchor no radio message had been received from shore and not a shot had been fired.

The normal routine under such circumstances was for an MTB to return to the landing place of an unsuccessful operation the following night in the hope of picking up any survivors. However, the Flotilla Officer in charge of MTB 682, Lt-Commander Donald Bradford, remembers receiving an order from

London that 682 was not to return. In his report Laycock wrote that the MTB was unable to go back because of unfavourable weather conditions. This may have been what he had been told, but, as it was only blowing force 5 from the north-east, it was certainly not true.

More mysterious was the eventual fate of the six French Commandos. Nothing more was heard of Trepel and his men until the area around Scheveningen was liberated. Soon after Germany surrendered Lieutenant Hulot of No 8 Troop was sent to the area to investigate the circumstances surrounding the disappearance of his comrades. Despite a thorough investigation, which included interrogating SS and Gestapo personnel in Rotterdam prison, he could find no trace of them. However, soon after he had returned to his unit stationed at Bergen-op-Zoom, he was again ordered to return as Captain Miles Bellville RM, a COHQ officer who had been given the task of investigating Trepel's disappearance, had tracked down where the men had been buried. The graves of the five described them as unknown Allied airmen, but the fact that the date of their deaths coincided with that of Premium aroused Bellville's suspicions. Their bodies, along with one who had been buried at a later date nearby as an unknown English soldier, were disinterred and identified. Though it seemed to Hulot when he saw their faces that they had died in terrible agony (*"tous portent l'expression d'avoir terriblement souffert"*) there were no marks on their bodies.[15] Bellville subsequently tried to trace some Germans who were in the area at the time and might have known how the Frenchmen met their fate. He later wrote a report, but this is no longer in the Public Record Office. In his history of the Commandos, Hilary St George Saunders wrote that "five had died of exposure, the sixth of drowning" which was presumably the conclusion Bellville officially arrived at – though such causes would be impossible to establish for certain with corpses dead over a year. But Saunders also added: "How they met their fate is not known", so it must be assumed Bellville was unable to trace the Germans concerned, or at least received no satisfactory answer from them.[16]

However, more recent investigations into Operation Premium have unearthed a German report on the death of the six Frenchmen from one of the strongpoints (Widerstandsnest 37).[17] This stated that at 0230 on the morning of 29 February, 1944, men in the strongpoint were alerted by cries coming from the sea. On investigation a rubber dinghy with three bodies in it was found. It seemed to the Germans that the men were so recently dead that an effort was made to revive them. A fourth body was found washed ashore immediately afterwards, that of Trepel's* the following week, and that of the last man not until over two months later when it was washed ashore some distance south of Wassenar. This fits with the facts in so far as the cemetery

---

* Trepel was posthumously made a Chevalier of the Legion of Honour and a battalion of the French Commandos is now named after him.

keeper confirmed that they were not all buried at the same time. But from what was found in the dinghy and on the dead men – including two identity discs and a list of the nine Frenchmen involved in the raid – the Germans concluded that the men were French Canadians who had been taking part in a Commando raid, so the fact that they buried them as unknown allied airmen has led some to wonder if the German report concealed more than it revealed. At least one of the French Commandos, who was on the MTB that night, is convinced that the report is a cover up and that his comrades were somehow captured by the Germans, then tortured and killed, though not necessarily by those who found the bodies. He could be right.[18]

4

In April, 1944, Bomber Command attacked a number of German coastal batteries at Houlgate. One plane dropped a bomb short. It exploded when it hit the water and caused a sympathetic explosion all along the foreshore, just beneath the water. Photographs were taken and the matter reported, and Professor J. D. Bernal, the Experimental Scientific Adviser to COHQ, suspected a new type of mine.[19]

The fact that the enemy might have produced some sophisticated device previously unknown to the Allies must have greatly worried the D-Day planners, and, despite the ban on any more small reconnaissance raids on the French coast, Admiral Ramsey and General Montgomery requested that investigations should be made as an urgent priority. Four raids were therefore planned for the next dark period, 14–19 May, these to take place simultaneously. The target areas had to be well away from the proposed landing beaches and Bray Dunes, Les Hemmes, Quend Plage, and Onival were chosen. The operation was codenamed Tarbrush and Hilton Jones, now promoted to major and 2 i/c of the Inter-Allied Commando, was named the Military Force Commander. The men Hilton Jones chose for the operation were the most experienced he could find from within SS Group. They were concentrated at Dover and codenamed Hiltforce, and before the raids took place they were briefed by Professor Bernal as to what they must look for. He warned that the new type of mine could be magnetic, acoustic, contact, electrically controlled, or voltaic – or it could be a new type altogether. "When he had finished talking," said Hilton Jones, "we didn't know if the mine would go off if we looked at it," and when someone asked what would happen when the dory's engine was started if the mine was acoustic, the not altogether reassuring answer was, "Wait and see".[20]

Tarbrush 3 (Bray Dunes) was commanded by Lieutenant I. D. C. Smith, who had accompanied Fynn on the St Pierre raid; Tarbrush 5 (Les Hemmes) was under the command of Captain McGonigal, who had recovered from his injuries sustained during the Hardtack raid on the Channel Islands; Tarbrush 8

(Quend Plage) was commanded by Lieutenant E. L. Smith; and Tarbrush 10 (Onival) was commanded by Lieutenant George Lane from X-Troop. Except for the Royal Engineers personnel, all Hiltforce members were either part of the Inter-Allied Commando or were temporarily attached to it. There is no record of who they were, but Lance-Corporal Howells, ex-12 Commando, and the Dane from X-Troop, Jack Davies, who was the dory coxswain for Tarbrush 10, were certainly among them as they were both Mentioned in Despatches for their work.

Each party consisted of the force commander, who usually acted as the coxswain of the rubber dinghy, two Commando other ranks as dory crew, with one Commando other rank as dinghy crew and signaller. One Royal Engineer officer and one NCO, both volunteers from 21 Army Group, were to carry out the beach and mine reconnaissance. The method of landing, perfected during the Hardtack raids, was by powered dory which took the raiding party from an MTB close to the shore before they transferred to a rubber dinghy. Only the two Royal Engineers personnel and the Commando signaller were to make the beach reconnaissance, and the fact that Lane decided on a further reconnaissance led to one of the most astonishing stories of the whole war.

In total eight raids were launched during the three nights, 15/16, 16/17 and 17/18 May. On the first night Tarbrush 3 and 5 did not land, either because the sea was too rough or because of lack of time due to enemy sea patrols. Tarbrush 8 landed and remained ashore for 1¾ hours. Whilst working to remove one of the mines off a stake, the Sapper officer slipped and hung onto the mine to save himself. "As nothing happened," the report noted phlegmatically to the Prime Minister, "it did not appear very sensitive." The device could not be removed, but was recognizable as an ordinary Tellermine 42.[21]

The landing party for Tarbrush 10 also got ashore that night, though briefly. The dory was launched at 0146, but the MTB had been having trouble with its navigational equipment and at 0316 the dory returned and Lane reported that the landing had taken place too far to the south.[22]

The following night all three of the raids which had been aborted the previous night were relaunched. Tarbrush 10 had to turn back because of the weather but the other two parties landed. Those with Tarbrush 3 remained undetected for their 45 minutes ashore despite seeing a German smoking a cigarette about 150 yards from them. They too only found Tellermines. Tarbrush 8 were only ashore about 20 minutes when they were challenged by a German patrol. Both sides opened fire before withdrawing, but those in the party were able to report that there was no indication of any mines between the four rows of posts they found and the water.

There was now pretty conclusive evidence that the sympathetic explosions spotted by the British bomber had been caused because the Tellermines tied to underwater posts had not been sufficiently waterproofed – or had not been waterproofed at all – and that the sea water had corroded the firing pins and made them extra-sensitive. Nevertheless, it was decided that Tarbrush 10 should try for a third time and was given the additional task of taking photographs with an infra-red camera of Element C in the area.

The party landed on schedule and the Sapper officer, Lieutenant Wooldridge, and his NCO, Sergeant Bluff, followed by Lane and his signaller, Corporal King RM, swept a path up to the beach defences but found no mines. The defences consisted of four rows of obstacles, details of which were carefully noted, but no mines were attached to them or had been laid amongst them, nor was there any sign of Element C. The party moved inland in search of this, but it was then decided that as they were getting some distance from the dinghy the two NCOs should return to it while the two officers went in search of some Element C they knew from aerial photographs to exist in the direction of Ault. If the officers had not come back by 0300 then the two NCOs were to return to the dory with the information they already had.

"The two officers then moved off south-westwards between the second and third rows of obstacles at about 0140 hours, where it was understood Element C would be found. Meanwhile Sgt Bluff jotted down some notes and remained with Corporal King near the dinghy. The two officers disappeared in the darkness and soon after Sgt Bluff and Corporal King saw a red flash which seemed to them to be the flash bulb used with the infra-red camera which the officers had taken with them; it was a very bright flash about 300 yards away. As the flash died away a challenging shout in German rang out and within about ten seconds it was followed by a scream which sounded as if somebody had been knifed. Three single shots followed."[23]

All hell now broke loose with starshells being fired which illuminated both the beach and the MTB. The two NCOs lay flat on the sand and looking along the beach spotted a German patrol. This passed between the grounded dinghy and the dory and proceeded to lay a row of canisters above the waterline which when lit burst into a reddish glow and exuded smoke. This effectively cut off the retreat of the two NCOs and as it was obvious to them that they had been spotted they moved inland. However, they were now seen by another patrol which fired Very lights and two single shots at them, but did not approach them.

By now it was nearly 0300 and as the flares on the waterline had gone out the two NCOs decided they had better try and return to the dory. However, this meant leaving their officers without any means of escape, something neither man was prepared to do. So instead of taking the dinghy they dragged it up the beach and then swam out to the dory which they could plainly see as it was illuminated by starshell. Bluff even tried to swim back with the mine detector, but found it too heavy and dropped it in about six feet of water. As the dory made out to sea it was fired at by one of the German patrols.

The rumpus ashore had, of course, alarmed those on the MTB and her anchor had been slipped so that a quick getaway could be made. As a consequence she had drifted southward, but the dory found her and came alongside at 0309. The two NCOs then reported to Hilton Jones, who was on board, that the two officers were missing and Hilton Jones immediately decided to try and find them. There was some delay as the MTB was manoeuvred back into the correct position but this was achieved by 0331 and two minutes later the dory left for the shore, Hilton Jones having been told by the MTB skipper that he would not be able to wait beyond 0415. The dory returned at 0358, not having found the two officers, and at 0408 the MTB withdrew at 35 knots and returned to base.[24]

It appeared to those who returned to England that Lane and Wooldridge had almost certainly been intercepted while taking photographs of Element C and had been captured, or even killed. This, however, was not the case.

As the two of them set off towards Ault it began raining hard, but they were able to keep up a brisk pace and only stopped to examine some Tellermines strapped to a number of wooden obstacles designed to prevent landing craft from opening their doors. After ¾ of an hour they were still some way from Ault, so they decided there was not time to go any further, and returned. It would appear that neither heard the scream or the three shots, or saw the red flash. When they returned to the vicinity of the landing place it seemed to them that they had gone beyond where they had left the two NCOs, so they turned back. But they now found themselves between two German patrols who spotted them, for both groups opened fire – though, in fact, they were probably firing at the dory. "As we flattened ourselves on the sand," Lane said later, "they fought quite a battle over our heads."

Eventually the patrols moved on and Lane started to flash a prearranged signal out to sea. When there was no answer, he flashed a continuous red light, but this did not bring any response either, so they continued along the beach still flashing with the torch. After about half an hour they found the dinghy and as it was only about an hour before dawn they decided to try and get out to sea in it. But as dawn broke they saw they were only about a mile offshore. They dumped all their equipment in the sea but kept their escape outfits and pistols. They then continued to paddle but soon heard the engines of a German patrol boat.[25]

"Shivering in our wet clothes, we were trying to cheer one another up by talking about the possibility of a Catalina flying-boat landing on the water to take us home. What a forlorn hope it was, and yet, talking about it helped to keep our spirits up. In fact, we were so confident by the time we saw a boat approaching us from the direction of Cayeux, full of German soldiers, that we decided to look destitute so when they came alongside, we could overpower them, pinch their boat and run for home. Unfortunately, they were not taken in. They circled us with five Schmeisser machine-guns pointing at us pretty menacingly. Fight was out of the question so we threw our pistols into the water with a somewhat theatrical gesture to show that we were ready to be rescued."[26]

They were taken back to Cayeux where they were interrogated separately, with Lane pretending, perfectly successfully, that he was Welsh which accounted for the different inflexion in his speech. They were both told they would be shot, and both were threatened with being handed over to the Gestapo who would certainly have disposed of them. Luckily for them, Rommel's Chief of Staff ordered that they should be kept by the Wehrmacht and he must have also told Rommel about them. That night they were locked up separately. Lane removed a piece of wire supporting the chimney pipe in his room and picked the door lock. It was pitch dark and as he moved into the corridor he fell over the German sentry stretched out on the floor. "I'd go back if I were you," the German advised, "there's another sentry round the corner."[27]

For several days they were moved around the countryside being questioned in different places by different German officers, some of whom masqueraded as members of the Gestapo. Eventually they were both blindfolded and bundled into a car.

"I sat in front, next to the driver, and to my great surprise I found that if I leaned back far enough I could peep between my nose and the bandage. In this way I was able to read the road signs . . . Shortly before we stopped I had been able to see a signpost that said 'La Petite Roche Guyon', and I tried to make a special mental note of this name although I still do not really know why.

"We got out of the car, my hands were untied and I took off the blindfold. I naturally blinked a bit at first, but then I looked up and saw a most extraordinary castle built against a rock. As I looked up I saw that all the chimney pots were in line with the trees which grew out of the rock. I turned to Roy Wooldridge and said: 'My God, what a strange place; just look at it!' – but our guards did not seem to like my remark and we were quickly pushed indoors."

Lane and Wooldridge were then taken to separate cells. Later an officer, accompanied by one of the guards who gave Lane some sandwiches, entered the room and told Lane that he was about to meet an extremely important person and that he had to promise to behave like an officer and a gentleman, to which Lane replied that he always did. He was then led into the next room where a very elegant, handsome-looking officer of much higher rank was sitting – probably the Chief-of-Staff of Army Group B, General Hans-Georg von Tempelhoff, who told him he was going to meet Field-Marshal Rommel.

"We rose, he led me to the door and we went into a very beautiful, large room. When we entered, I could recognize the Field-Marshal, who was sitting at a table right at the other end of the room, and I remembered the saying that some people like to make you cross an enormous room in order to intimidate you; but here the opposite happened. The Field-Marshal rose, came the whole length of the room towards me, and we gathered round a table – several people were present, but I cannot now remember their names. An interpreter was there – I think his name was Captain Lang."

After everyone had sat down Rommel said to Lane: "So you are one of those gangster commandos?", and Lane replied: "I do not know what the Field-Marshal means when he says that; there are no gangster Commandos! Of course I am a Commando, because Commandos are the best soldiers in the world." Rommel seemed to like this attitude for he smiled and said: "Perhaps you are not a gangster, but we have had some very bad experiences concerning Commandos. They have behaved very badly on several occasions", which Lane countered by saying he could not believe that. Rommel now switched conversation to Lane himself. "Do you realize that you have been taken prisoner under very strange circumstances?" he asked, to which Lane replied: "I hardly think they were strange, more unfortunate and unhappy." "Do you realize that you gave the impression of being a saboteur? And you know what we do with saboteurs here, don't you?" "If the Field-Marshal took me for a saboteur I would hardly have been invited here," Lane replied. Rommel smiled again and said: "So you look upon this as an invitation?" "Yes, of course," Lane said, "I feel very honoured." Once again Rommel smiled and everybody smiled with him – the atmosphere was really very friendly, and Rommel began asking Lane about the expected Allied invasion, which Lane parried by saying he had read in *The Times* that there might be one. Then, after Lane had been allowed to ask one or two questions the interview was terminated with Rommel giving Lane an assurance that he would be safe.[28]

Wooldridge was also interviewed by Rommel, but when Wooldridge refused to divulge that he was a Royal Engineer officer he was dismissed. Both officers were then taken to Fresnes gaol and put in separate cells, and the interrogations continued. Finally, however, the Germans must have decided that they would not get anything out of either of them, but Rommel kept his word, and instead of being shot they were sent to a prisoner-of-war camp. Lane ended up in Oflag 9/AH whose senior officer was Colonel Euan Miller. Lane knew that while he could fool the Germans by pretending to be Welsh there was no way he could bluff Miller and the other British officers. He therefore told Miller the truth. The camp had links with the outside world and Miller was able to check the veracity of Lane's story. When he knew Lane was who he said he was he then passed on all the information on the whereabouts of Rommel's HQ. A few days later two British aircraft opened fire on Rommel's staff car as it was returning to the Château and he was so seriously wounded that he took no further part in the war.*

* A recent historian of the Commandos, Charles Messenger, has been unable to confirm any connection between the information Lane gave and the attack on Rommel. Maybe it was just a coincidence, but maybe not.

For their parts in the Tarbrush operations both Hilton Jones and Lane were awarded the Military Cross. "The whole of the Tarbrush operation was only made possible by the outstanding leadership and organizing ability of Captain Hilton Jones," General Sturges wrote in his citation for Hilton Jones. "In spite of lack of sleep on seven consecutive nights, it was largely due to his untiring efforts that these urgent operations were brought to such a successful conclusion." He wrote of Lane that the raid was mounted on three consecutive nights but that "despite the physical fatigue resulting from this, Lane, with superior seamanship, navigated his dory to the selected landing point without error although there were definite indications of the presence of enemy patrols in the beach area", and that, "having landed, Lieutenant Lane accompanied and gave material assistance to his Sapper officer in obtaining a large part of the required intelligence. . . . Although strictly speaking it was not part of this officer's duty to go any further than the landing point, he insisted, with the greatest devotion to duty, in taking his share of the hazards of the operation, and by his tenacity of purpose assisted in obtaining vital information."

In all no less than six Military Crosses, two bars to the Military Cross, five Military Medals and four Mentions in Despatches were awarded to members of the Tarbrush Raids, and in writing of them to the Under-Secretary of State to the War Office, the Chief of Staff to the CCO, Major-General V. D. Thomas Royal Marines, said that he found it impossible to differentiate between the measure of gallantry displayed by all the officers and men who were mentioned in the citations.[29]

6

The Mediterranean

Before the start of the Forfar series of raids, on 26 May, 1943, four members of X-Troop were detached from the Inter-Allied Commando and attached to two Royal Marine Commandos, Nos 40 and 41, stationed in Scotland at Troon and Irvine where they were in training for the Sicily landings. This quartet, Lance-Sergeant Miles, Lance-Corporal Streeten and Privates Franklin and Anson, were the forerunners of a system – which was to work so brilliantly during the Italian and the Normandy campaigns – whereby members of X-Troop were attached to other Commando units as interrogators, interpreters, military intelligence experts, and, on occasion, for work behind the German lines. Miles and Anson went to No 40 Commando while Streeten and Franklin were attached to No 41 Commando. On the night of 9/10 July, 1943, they landed in Sicily.

"Just before midnight we went to Action Stations, put on equipment, took up our arms and waited silently. We shook hands with those who were staying on the ship. I thought, 'Can this be the last day of my life?' Everything suddenly seemed different, bigger and more important.

"But then I was too busy running to the assault craft to think any more. We jumped in, squatted down and soon we were lowered and touched water. The big iron hook suddenly swung out of control and nearly hit our captain on the head.

"And then we were off, a silent, dark flotilla of landing craft. The tossing was terrible, like a mad see-saw. It was very cold and water splashed over the sides and came running in streams from the door. We held our rifles and tommy guns up, but they got wet. Many were sick over the sides. I felt bad but could not be sick. The captain dozed silently in front of me. Only the naval ratings worked efficiently and unruffled. Soon I got cramp from squatting and tried to stand up and stretch. A wind howled and dark shapes moved near us. Searchlights shone in the distance. One felt too cold and wet and sick and cramped and sleepy and weary to feel fear. Even the thoughts, 'Are they expecting us?' or 'Is the beach mined?' were not exciting.

"I must have fallen asleep, for it was two hours later when a general stir began. Soon came the order, 'Prepare to land'. This was the moment for which we had trained for many months, the climax in the life of a commando. But I did not think of anything except of gripping my mortar bombs and rifle.

"The rattle of a machine gun was the first sound, then the crunching when we touched sand. The door opened and I jumped out. The water came up to my hips and my rifle got wet. I raced with all my might to the beach.

"A sharp, strange, sweet, spicy smell was the first thing I noticed, as of vines and southern leaves and fruits. I stepped on sand. Everywhere figures were moving, but a few yards in front of us there was barbed wire. The idea was to cross the beach as fast as possible, but all drill had been forgotten, and many stood and gazed as if we were on a half-hearted night manoeuvre at home.

"Somebody said, 'wirecutters', and that word electrified us. Soon there was a gap in the wire and we crept through.

"We were the first troops to land on Europe.

"Although on the ship we had spent many hours bent over the maps, air-photos and panoramas of our landing ground, the chances were very small that the Navy had beached us on the correct spot.

"As we were lying in the dark on the dunes beyond the beach with rifles loaded and bayonets fixed, machine guns spluttered in short busts and voices chattered in rather unmilitary fashion about where we might be. There was a narrow white path in front of us. Our captain rose, apparently for a reconnaissance, and fell down with a groan. Afterwards, we were all clever and thought he ought to have known that such paths might be fixed lines for defending machine guns.

"Bunched together, we pressed against the earth as if for protection, and some Oxford voices went on chattering, concerned about the captain, about our location, and we began to get 'sticky'. I could not get rid of the impression that we were on a miscarried night scheme in Wales.

"But then the big, dark mass of figures crossed the path, and the Troop leaders tried to sort out their men. My job was to be with P Troop until we had taken the first machine gun position, and then to join Commando HQ for interrogation of prisoners. I was a bit worried as to whether I would find them in the dark.

"Somehow I got hold of P Troop in the muddle and we found the machine-gun post. It turned out to be a derelict shed without inhabitants. I made my way back to HQ and was relieved when I saw the long beanstick aerials and bulky wireless sets of Commando HQ which squatted between the high exotic stalks. No one could have mistaken the Colonel's voice. 'Who are you?' he asked."[1]

All four members of X-Troop survived that first landing unscathed, but later, when No 40 Commando was being transported to Italy, its ship was bombed and Anson was severely wounded in the head by shrapnel; when No 41 Commando was landed to cut off the Germans' retreat Streeten was also severely wounded.

"We landed behind the lines on the road and railway line from Catania to Messina along which the Germans were withdrawing, in order to prevent them from evacuating too many of their weapons and men. We established a small bridgehead and were just about to enlarge it (I had by then been promoted to the dizzy rank of sergeant), when an 88mm gun shell hit the railway platform from which I was operating and knocked me out. I was later told that I had not been expected to survive. I still carry pieces of shrapnel in my neck, skull and arm as momentoes."[2]

By then, however, the members of X-Troop had more than proved their worth and at the end of the year several more were sent out to join 2 SS Brigade, under Brigadier Tom Churchill, in Italy.

While a handful of X-Troop men were being blooded in battle in Sicily and in the Forfar raids, the vast majority of the Inter-Allied Commando, apart from a handful of the Norwegians and one or two of the Frenchmen, had still not seen any action. Pressure now began to mount, both from the men themselves and from their governments, for the various Troops to be deployed on active service. The French, at first earmarked for the invasion of Corsica, were, as we've seen, then involved in the small-scale reconnaissance raids; the Norwegians were again about to be involved in operations from Lerwick; and the decision must have already been taken to use X-Troop individually and not as a sub-unit. This left the Belgians, the Dutch, the Poles and the newly-formed No 7 Troop, the Yugoslavs. The Mediterranean theatre was chosen and the Poles and the Dutch, along with a detachment of Yugoslavs who had just completed the course at Achnacarry, were picked to be sent to Italy to come under the command of No 2 SS Brigade. However, Mountbatten must have intimated just before he left for the Far East that he might need the Dutch, so they were replaced by the Belgians.

The Belgians (seven officers and seventy-seven ORs) and the Poles (nine officers and eighty-six ORs) embarked for Algiers on 13 September preceded by a note from Lister to Robert Laycock, who then still commanded 2 SS Brigade. "Herewith my best two Troops," he wrote, "with my blessings and personal regrets at losing them."[3] Towards the end of October they were followed by 2/Lieutenant Tripovic and fifteen men of the Yugoslav Troop, and by eleven men from X-Troop under the temporary command of Lieutenant

94

Emmet. The Belgians and Poles disembarked at Algiers on 23 September and they were still in the transit camp at Birtouta when Emmet and the second contingent joined them on 7 November. This detachment of the Inter-Allied Commando was under the overall command of Captain Lutyens, a British Liaison Officer who was attached to the Belgian Troop.

After the personal intervention of the new No 2 SS Brigade Commander, Tom Churchill, who considered that the Inter-Allied detachment would be useful to him in Italy in the roles he was then likely to be offered by Fifth and Eighth Armies, the Inter-Allied Commando detachment moved to Phillipeville (now Skikda) on 23 November and embarked for Taranto. After being inspected by Brigadier Churchill at the Brigade's HQ at Molfetta on 4 December, the detachment was broken up. The men from X-Troop and the Yugoslavian Troop were divided up amongst the units of 2 SS Brigade, which now also included Nos 4 and 6 Troops, and Churchill told the Belgians and Poles that he had arranged to give them battle experience in the mountains of Italy with the Eighth Army, news which delighted them, and they spent the next ten days preparing for battle.[4] "Tentative arrangements had been made with General M. C. Dempsey CB DSO MC Commanding 13 Corps for the employment of certain sub-units of Commandos on his front in order to give them experience in active patrolling and infiltration in the face of the enemy. It was my original intention to use certain sub-units of No 9 Commando in this way, but operational reasons made this impossible at the last moment. Instead, I visited General Dempsey and found that he would be glad to accept the Polish and Belgian Troops for this role, and he pointed out that his extremely mountainous front which was thinly held by both sides was ideal for the purpose which we had in view. He also agreed to take a personal interest in the activities and welfare of the two Troops. Accordingly, I arranged for them to move into the line on Monday 13 December 1943."[5]

In fact 13 Corps was moved away from the part of the front chosen by Dempsey and Churchill, and was replaced by 78 Division commanded by Major-General Charles Keightley, with the two Troops being put under the command of 56 Recce Regt, whose front extended from Villa Santa Maria to Castel di Sangro near the Sangro River. The Polish Troop, after a short stay at Capracotta, was stationed at Pescopennataro, on the 56 Recce Regt's northern (right) flank, and the Belgian Troop at San Pietro Avellano, on its southern (left) flank. Both villages were in ruins, having been systematically destroyed by the Germans before they retreated across the river – which, at that time of the year, was about four and a half feet deep with a 9-knot current – and there were no bridges standing in the area. Both Troops had to find shelter amongst the ruins as best they could. Merton* of X-Troop – who with Marshall, also

* Merton recalls that to the Poles the Germans had to be disposed of because they were in the way of getting at the Poles' real enemies, the Russians.

of X-Troop, and two of the Yugoslavian Troop, Corporal Anton Banko and Private Franz Trebizon, was attached to the Poles – remembers sleeping on the altar of the local church. The weather was bitterly cold and low cloud lay over the mountains most days, cutting visibility to about 30 yards in places. Few of the roads were open and supply to the Poles was by mule train.

The two Troops were active immediately, the Poles sending a patrol down to the river the night they arrived and the Belgians mounting their first patrol the following evening, and during the month they were in this part of the line rarely a night passed without some kind of encounter with the enemy.

A typical clash occurred during the Poles' first day patrol on the German-held side of the river – crossed by means of a rubber dinghy hauled by a rope which had to be taken across by a member of the Troop – when seventeen men under the Troop Commander, with Merton from X-Troop, went to search two buildings. While Smrokowski led some of his men towards the houses the rest, under one of the section officers, Lieutenant Czyński, set up a defensive perimeter. As the Poles approached the houses, fire was opened on them from the left-hand one and then a German patrol approached and, catching one of Czyński's men, Senior Rifleman Rogucki, too far forward, shot him in the thigh. Czyński, hearing the firing, went forward and was able to bring back the rifleman on his back, an act of great bravery for which, along with his part in the action across the Garigliano, he was later awarded the Silver Cross of the Virtuti Militari. Unable to attack the Germans across the open ground between himself and the house occupied by the Germans, Smrokowski ordered the patrol to withdraw. Rogucki, a Polish-American volunteer from Pittsburgh, was carried back across the river, but he died soon after Capracotta was reached at 2200 that night.[6]

The Belgians, too, lost a man almost immediately when, on 14 December, Captain Danloy sent out several patrols. Lieutenant Meny and two men crossed the Sangro during the morning to search some woods on the far side of a railway line as a reconnaissance for the larger patrol he was to take across later that day. While he was doing this Lieutenant Deton took some men to try and surprise a German sentry who had fired at him the previous day, and perhaps surprise, too, the advance post to which the German must be attached. The patrol found the spot where Deton had been fired on, but could find nothing. However, after they had proceeded about 400 yards they ran into a German patrol and opened fire on it. In the confusion the Germans were convinced they were being shot at by their own men. One of their number was killed and two others were probably wounded. However, the Belgians had losses too, for Lance-Corporal Mairesse was badly wounded in the leg. They carried him back across the river, while one man ran ahead to find the doctor, but by the time he arrived Mairesse was dead of shock and loss of blood.[7]

On another occasion the Belgian Troop only escaped having one of its members killed by a near-miracle. A small patrol crossed the river in front of San Pietro and reconnoitred the area of Carceri. A house full of Germans was encountered. The Germans were called upon to surrender but their answer was a fusillade of fire. Fire was returned and one German, standing in the doorway, was killed. In this exchange one burst of German fire hit one of the Belgian sergeants in the stomach. Five of the bullets hit his tommy gun magazine pouch, while one hit the magazine itself, but amazingly none penetrated and the sergeant did not receive as much as a bruise.[8]

The most severe test for the two Troops during this period came when, on the night of 20 December, an Italian civilian came into Capracotta with the story that the Germans were about to attack the Poles' positions at Pescopennataro. He said that he had been taken by the Germans three days previously on the far side of the river and had been closely questioned as to the British dispositions in the Capracotta-Pescopennataro areas. He had been told that a German attack by 200 mountain Jäger troops would be carried out on the night of 21/22 December, with the intention of cutting out the British field guns just east of Capracotta, and that the attack would cross the Sangro at San Angelo at 7pm, clearing Pescopennataro before proceeding to the main objective. He himself had been detailed to guide the attacking troops during the approach march.

There was no means of knowing whether the man was telling the truth, but it seemed clearly unwise to ignore his story. Accordingly, the artillery at Capracotta was ordered to fire concentrations on the San Angelo crossings at 7pm, and the Poles were warned of the impending attack.

At 8pm the Poles reported that they were being attacked from the east by two groups of Germans, each forty strong. Shortly afterwards they reported that another party of approximately the same strength was attacking from the west. Between 8pm and midnight the Poles were entirely surrounded, and had to beat off successive attacks launched in different places. During this time the artillery was firing concentrations close to the walls of Pescopennataro as directed by the FOO (Forward Observation Officer) in the village. At midnight the Poles announced that the fighting had died down but that the enemy were still in the area and were probably regrouping for a large final attack.

At 3am this attack was launched and for two hours, with the aid of an artillery barrage, the Poles fought off the Germans desperate to break through to Capracotta. By 5am they were beaten and in full retreat and though the Poles sent out five patrols in all directions no further contact was made, nor could the reserve squadron of the Recce Regt, which searched the area between Capracotta, Pescopennataro and the river, find any trace of them. For nine hours during the night the Poles had been in continuous battle with a force twice their strength and had fought them to a standstill, suffering only three slightly wounded in the process.[9] For his exemplary conduct during this encounter, Captain Smrokowski was awarded an immediate Military Cross. "His example," the citation stated, "his complete disregard for his personal safety and his absolute control of his Troop throughout the whole night undoubtedly contributed largely to its success in driving off the attack in spite of being outnumbered by two to one."

2

On 30 December the Belgians moved to the small mountain village of Montenero on the extreme left flank of the Eighth Army where they shared the line with three companies of the London Irish Regiment. Again they were extremely isolated and with the area covered in thick snow it was sometimes almost impossible to get food and ammunition through to them. It was here that "Nobby" Kendal, a member of X-Troop attached to the Belgians, "learned a practical lesson which I am anxious to pass on to future generations. If a mule, whether your own or adopted ad hoc, gets into a snowdrift, it is pointless to try jerking him free. The wall of the narrow hole made in the snow by each leg is too unyielding for this method to succeed. There is, as far as I know, no other way than to dig out each leg separately, and if there is no shovel handy, it has to be done by hand and if it happens during a snowstorm, it has to be done fast."

Many of the Poles were expert skiers – one, Officer Cadet Adam Bachleda, was a promising international competitor – and they noted with dissatisfaction that while the Germans were equipped with both skis and white clothing, these were unavailable to them, which restricted considerably their freedom of movement. Later four pairs of skis were found by the Poles in a house but nevertheless the honour of forming the first ever Eighth Army ski patrol probably fell to Kendal. "Through the village mayor I obtained narrow skis made of chestnutwood with frayed bindings and flimsy poles, and also white cowled cotton robes which normally were worn by the local *fraternita* in funeral processions. We used these robes over our gas capes – winter clothing arrived in the spring – and practised on our skis for two days. Almost none of the men had been on skis before. We then set out for a plateau in the Luperian mountains on our first – and last – ski patrol. The name of the mountains notwithstanding we did not meet with any wolves but approximately at the 3000-foot level came upon a stone hut in which an outpost of the opposing Austrian mountain troops was ensconced, with a light mortar in position nearby. We were greeted with some fairly accurate mortar fire. Due to the deep snow it proved to be as ineffective as the return fire from our personal arms. I had decided to proceed without a PIAT (which could have breached the walls of the hut) as my novices had difficulty enough to stay on their feet without this unwieldy load. Soon we beat a hasty retreat downhill during which some spectacular tumbles were observed."[10]

On 9 January the Belgian Troop was withdrawn from Montenero for a well-earned rest. Then on 17 January, now under command of 46 Division, they joined the Guards Brigade at Lusciano and that evening crossed the Garigliano with the loss of only one man who was wounded by a mine. However, they were not needed during this initial thrust across the river and returned across it and spent two nights in reserve in the village of Sorbello. They were then ordered up to the front once more and on the evening of 20 January arrived at the Tremensuoli feature, one of the most advanced positions in the British line. They based themselves in the ruined houses of the village of Minturno and that night sent out three separate patrols, all of which were involved in fire fights with the enemy. The next day they again recrossed the Garigliano and rested at Sorbello and Villa Literno until 30 January when they were attached to No 2 SS Brigade for the attack on Mount Ornito. They crossed the Garigliano yet again and after a two-day wait moved up to Mount Tuga where they were assigned the task of defending the Brigade Command Post positioned there. At 1630 they were badly mortared and lost four men wounded, but that evening drove off a German patrol that was approaching their lines.

While the Poles and Belgians were having their baptism of fire in the mountains, some of the members of X-Troop attached to units of No 2 SS Brigade were also initiated into the grim battle conditions of that Italian winter, and immediately suffered casualties. The sergeant in charge of the detachment, Groves, took part in Operation Partridge, when No 9 Commando, on a diversionary raid, landed behind the enemy's lines north of the River Garigliano on the night of 29/30 December. The operation was successful but when Groves was detailed to lead a party back the next night to retrieve the bodies of the British casualties he stepped on a mine and had a foot blown off. Then on 19 January, 1944, probably while operating with No 40 (RM) Commando during the crossing of the Garigliano, Private Wells was killed by a mine, the first member of X-Troop to be lost in action. The Anzio landings took place on the night of 21/22 January, 1944, but soon afterwards No 2 SS Brigade was withdrawn from the bridgehead and Brigadier Churchill was briefed by General McCreery on the latter's plan to extend his foothold in the hills west of the Garigliano by capturing the trio of peaks which made up Mount Ornito, an operation for which the Brigade was to come under the command of 46 Division.

Detailed to take rock-strewn hills which were devoid of any cover were Nos 9 and 43 Commandos, with the Belgian Troop in reserve. Again, X-Troop members were among the casualties with Barnes being severely wounded by a mortar bomb and Ross by a shell. "I was with No 9 Commando and we were up on the mountain without any cover when German artillery started firing a box barrage on our positions. I was knocked out and fell with my tommy gun under me. When I came to I heard German being spoken. It soon became clear to me that they wanted to surrender to me as soon as I recovered consciousness. They were Czechoslovakian conscripts. When I decided to come to, I did not let on I spoke German but let it be understood that I wanted them to carry me down the mountain to our lines. They knew the way better than I did as it turned out. The shrapnel had lodged in my dried rations in my rucksack and most of it had not penetrated, which was why I was still alive. I was taken to hospital in Pompeii. The day I arrived Vesuvius erupted. Penicillin had just arrived and this apparently saved my life. Before I was released from hospital my Colonel came along and said he needed me as the Commando was going back to the Anzio beachhead. So I went, but I was wounded again at Anzio, in a bayonet charge and was sent back to a forward general hospital. While I was there it was bombed and I was wounded for a third time and was in hospital for a month."[11]

When the Belgians left for Montenero their positions in the village of San Pietro Avellano were assigned to the Poles. This prospect did not please them for at least at Pescopennataro one or two buildings remained standing, and the church had given some shelter from the freezing weather, while at San Pietro hardly one brick or stone remained on top of each other, so complete had the Germans' devastation of it been. As it happened, a snowstorm trapped them in Pescopennataro and completely isolated them for five days, and it was not until 5 January that the Troop's expert skier, Bachleda, was able to get through on skis to Capracotta and ask for an air drop. Then on 10 January they received orders to dig themselves out and move back down the mountain where they would be picked up by lorries.[12]

The Polish Troop was now put under the command of the 56 (London) Division for the crossing of the Garigliano near its mouth, which was spearheaded by No 40 Commando. "At 18.00 hours on 17 January the Company moved to their base on the southern bank of the River Garigliano. After strong artillery barrages, lasting from 20.00 hours to 21.00 hours, the Company followed attacking units of the 56th Division and crossed the river on boats under intense enemy artillery and machine-gun fire."[13]

The task of the Polish Troop was to move through the forward troops once the river had been crossed and to penetrate through the German lines to cut communications and to act as a diversion in the area around Coreno and Ausonia. They crossed without loss and followed the white tape that had been laid to avoid minefields but this ceased after a while and, despite proceeding with the greatest car, four of the Troop were wounded when they entered an orange grove which was mined. They reached their rendezvous at 0330, but there was no sign of the leading battalion of the 56th Division which had been assigned the task of taking the village of Sujo, so this objective was now given to the Poles.

"The ridge above the village of Sujo had to be captured – a straightforward

100

task but one so far attempted without success. Before one was an almost vertical wall covered in places with bushes and precariously balanced rocks. To the right there was a less steep rockface but 100 metres high, then a precipice, then another rockface, running up to near the top of the hill. The enemy had now become vigilant though also nervous. We learnt later they were veterans from Stalingrad reinforced by fresh troops. In other words a determined and menacing enemy was sitting above our heads. We moved warily and slowly towards the summit. We had already begun to crawl on all fours when shouts of '*Hände hoch*' broke the silence. 'Fire!' I ordered."[14]

A sharp skirmish ensued, but by 0430 the Poles were in position on the ridge and after two hours they were relieved by men from No 40 Commando and the Queen's Royal Regiment.*

Later in the morning Section 1 of the Polish Troop, commanded by Lieutenant Czyński, was given the task of capturing the Monte Valle Martina hill to the north-east of Sujo, while the Troop's second-in-command, Captain Woloszowski, led another group down Valle Zintoni to one side of it.

"A sub-section, under my deputy, Zemanek, entered the ravine and there surprised a mortar team of six Germans and made them prisoner. Then my group overpowered an artillery observation post, and we cut their telephone wires. I rested for a moment and made contact with Zemanek, and when the Troop Commander came up I went on to join up with him. There were sounds of firing – rifle, Schmeisser and machine gun – and we hurried forward. As I came out onto the open ground I saw a group of prisoners and the sub-section withdrawing behind them. The Troop Commander now ordered me to hold the hill at all costs. I learnt that Captain Woloszowski had been wounded and saw others who had been wounded withdrawing on their own or with the help of others and we covered their retreat with machine-gun fire. I was under sniper fire and distant machine-gun fire throughout. On the hill to the right there was a sharp exchange at short range and the sound of hand grenades. They were fighting at very close quarters."[15]

At first Woloszowski's patrol had gone well, but then they had run into a small German patrol on the mountainside and though these were soon captured the brief fire fight alerted a larger group of Germans near a farm further down the hill. Czyński managed to get his men to the top before the Germans but in the confused hand-to-hand fighting that followed on the bare hillside both sides suffered casualties with at least one member of the Polish

---

* One of the Polish Troop, Lance-Corporal Rozen, who spoke good English, was attached to a company of this regiment for the crossing of the Garigliano. Immediately after the crossing the Company ran into a minefield and two of the leading platoon commanders were wounded. Rozen immediately went to the front and took charge, and encouraged the men forward. When the enemy wire was reached, he cut it himself, led the platoon through, and then took it to its objective. Throughout, Rozen showed a complete disregard for his own safety, and for this outstanding example of leadership he was subsequently awarded the Military Medal.

Troop having to use his Commando knife to defend himself. On the hill Captain Woloszowski went to the aid of a wounded rifleman, but as he was putting on a dressing he was shot dead by a sniper. The wounded man raised his head to see what had happened and he, too, was killed by the same sniper. At one point Senior Rifleman Brauliński's tommy gun jammed. Quite undeterred he continued to charge the German positions shouting as he went, causing several Germans to stand and raise their hands. Nevertheless, the Poles were outnumbered and it was not until Smrokowski sent up his second section under Lieutenant Zalewiski that the battle began to move in the Poles' favour, and by 1015 they had cleared Monte Valle Martina of Germans who left thirty dead behind them. But the Poles had suffered severely, too, their casualties amounting to four dead and twenty-two wounded in an action which confirmed the Troop as a fighting unit of exceptional courage and tenacity.

While the Polish and Belgian Troops were in the thick of battle, a battle of another kind was being fought over their futures, for in January, 1944, one of the Belgian liaison officers, Lieutenant Roger Taymans, returned to England with the specific request that both Troops be allowed to return to take part in the coming invasion of Europe. Both the Polish Commander-in-Chief, Major-General Kopanski, and Lt-General van Strydonck de Burkel, the Inspector General of the Belgian Army, agreed that this should be done and welcomed it as both Troops had suffered casualties and needed reorganization. On 17 February Sturges wrote to Major-General Robert Laycock, now Chief of Combined Operations that "The Belgian and Polish Troops of this Commando (10 [IA]) are now operating in Italy under the command of 2 SS Brigade. It is considered highly desirable in addition to being a possible political expedient that they should return to the UK in sufficient time to train for and take part in OVERLORD with the remainder of the Special Service group. In addition, these troops who have gained operational experience, especially in active patrolling, will be a valuable addition to the SS group, especially as is well known they are composed of first-class fighting material."

In his reply Laycock replied: "You will remember that the PM has ordered that no commandos or similar units be withdrawn from the Mediterranean or SE Asia without his permission. As I see it, this request for these troops to take part in OVERLORD has come from the troops concerned, and their governments. 21 Army Group have only asked if 10 Commando is available. General Montgomery's requirements for eight Commandos will be met without calling on the Inter-Allied Commando. I would suggest therefore that before the PM is approached 21 Army Group should be asked if 10 Commando is a firm requirement. It should be pointed out that the Dutch Troop is now in SE Asia."[16]

It was soon established that 21st Army Group did not have a firm requirement for the Inter-Allied Commando and the decision was taken to leave the two Troops, for the time being at least, in the Mediterranean. Therefore at the end of March the Belgian Troop joined No 2 SS Brigade on the island of Vis where, along with the Yugoslavian Troop of the Inter-Allied Commando, it had been sent to join Force 133 whose task it was to bolster Tito's Yugoslavian partisans in their fight to clear the Germans from their country.

When the Belgians first arrived on Vis there was a danger of the Germans invading it from the other Dalmatian islands which were in their hands. But as this threat receded the British and Yugoslavian forces went on to the offensive and in the succeeding months there were several hit-and-run raids on the German-occupied islands, while at sea marauding MTBs with small groups of Commandos on board attacked the Germans' supply routes. It was an ideal war for Commandos and one which the Belgians relished. They had some difficulty with the language for they could never pronounce the passwords the partisans, always quick on the trigger, used. Eventually, the Belgians used to just say "Belgski" when challenged with the partisans replying, "OK".

Many of the MTB patrols were abortive, though sometimes the booty obtained from German supply ships was very rewarding indeed. "For three hours I lay on deck jammed between a torpedo tube and a gun mounting. It rained continuously and waves kept sweeping across the deck. I was soaking wet and feeling rather sick, but the excitement of the trip made me forget all that. Because of the bad weather it was quite out of the question to disembark the British agent on the coast and we made straight for Cibenic instead. We saw the harbour lights, but after waiting for four hours without any sign of the convoy we returned to base. But not all the raids on enemy shipping were as fruitless as this one. On one occasion we were able to return with three small boatloads of Danish butter, flour and ersatz coffee, and this was divided between the crew and us 'pirates', and turned out to be a nice change from our usual rations of biscuits and corned beef."[17]

Sometimes the booty was rather unusual as when Lieutenant Roman and five of his men took part in the ambushing of a German supply ship on the night of 14/15 April, 1944, an operation he later described with great vividness. "Extra grenades had been issued, and when we arrive at the port a naval officer meets us and tells us to report to MTB 95. A Petty Officer takes us aboard and shows us around and introduces us to the crew. Some of them are evidently surprised to have Belgian Commandos aboard. Then we are given an excellent meal, typical of Royal Navy hospitality, and we leave harbour just before dusk, followed by MTB 99."

They headed south and near midnight approached the enemy coastline.

"Battle stations! We grab our weapons and climb a small metal ladder to get into the bows. Everything is quiet. The MTBs are entering a small rocky bay. Ahead, we can see the lights of a small port. Right in front of us are some high rocks which hide the northern part of the coastline. It is quite cold now and after waiting some time we start to shiver. Then, at half past three, we hear someone whisper: 'There it is. To starboard.' A shiver ran down my spine. Then behind the rocks ahead of us we see a plume of black smoke drifting towards the sky. We wait, the MTB's motors idling almost soundlessly.

"Suddenly the ship appears about 800 metres in front of us. 'Full speed ahead!' snaps the skipper, and the two MTBs leap forward and circle in front of the ship to cut him off. The ship sees us and starts shooting. Tracer bullets, white and red, pass over our heads. 'Fire!' orders our skipper, and the oerlikons, pom-poms and machine guns all open up, an incredible spectacle.

"Suddenly, the siren on the German ship, an armed tug, howls and the Germans cease firing. They have surrendered. We approach them cautiously, our searchlight trained on their decks. We can see now that some of the crew are struggling in the water. We come alongside and orders are given in German and Italian for the crew to get in the bows of their ship. Then we go aboard, search the prisoners and put them aboard MTB 95, which has picked up the men from the water. There are four Germans and twelve Italians. Four more lie dead on the deck of the sinking tug.

"Meanwhile, MTB 99 is dealing with the tug's three barges that it is towing. One of them is full of cement, another of petrol. Both these are sunk. The third is loaded with hay and this is taken in tow. Hay! What a present for our mules on Vis! They have helped us so much in the mountains. Now it is their turn for a special treat.

"It is time to go, for flares are going up on shore and searchlights are stabbing the darkness. We start our long journey back. I am exhausted and go up to the bridge to see the dawn breaking. Soon we can see Vis. As we pass some of the German-held islands they fire on us, but without any effect."[18]

By now the pressure being exerted to have the Belgian Troop returned in time for Overlord was having its effect and on 15 April Sturges wrote that the Belgian Troop "is known to be one officer and nineteen ORs under establishment. It may be more by now. It is doubtful whether the present moment is opportune to press for further reinforcements. Legionnaires are unacceptable. The Belgians are expecting their country to be reoccupied in the near future and naturally have no great desire to join their Commando comrades in Italy. There it is suggested that the unit return to UK when it might be possible to give it the reinforcements it needs . . . Monsieur Pierlot would welcome the return of the unit, though of course he is prepared to stand by the decision of the COS to employ it where it is most effective."[19]

The following week Laycock had lunch with the Belgian Ambassador "who is now very anxious that the Belgian Troop should return to the UK", and when the Chiefs of Staff committee were requested to allow their return they concurred.

The last operation the Belgians took part in was on 9 May when Lieutenant Meny and fifteen men from his A Section were detailed to protect the Signals section of No 2 SS Brigade which was to take part in a partisan raid on the island of Solta. "The partisans had a division of 1500 men and two batteries of 75mm guns for the raid," Meny wrote afterwards in the Troop War Diary. "The whole party was embarked on 6 LCI and 4 LCA protected by MTBs. We embarked at Komiza at 1700 and arrived at Solta at ten minutes past midnight on 10 May, 1944. We disembarked at Uvala Tatinja Bay and stayed on the beach until 0425 by which time the partisans were formed up in front of Grohote, the principal village due to be attacked before dawn. The guide led us 2km to the south-east of Grohote where the divisional HQ had been established and we prepared an all-round defensive position. The bombardment of Grohote started at 0530 and at 0700 the partisans attacked. The attack, with artillery and air support, went on all day and by 1800 the only German defences remaining were two pillboxes. They remained untaken when the order was given to withdraw at 2115 and we re-embarked at 2330."[20]

Three days later the Belgian Troop left for England, but was too late to take part in the Normandy landings. On 9 August the Troop was paraded before General van Strydonck de Burkel who presented the Belgian Croix de Guerre with palm to Captain Danloy and to three of his men, while two officers, seven NCOs and one other rank were Mentioned in Despatches for their work in Italy and on Vis. Then on 25 August five men under Lieutenant Dauppe took part in the one cross-Channel raid, codenamed Operation Rumford, in which the Belgians participated. The raiding party was taken to the objective, the Ile de Yeu in the Bay of Biscay, in a Hunt Class destroyer, HMS *Albrighton*, with Lt-Colonel Laycock also aboard. The dory coxswain, Lance-Corporal Legrand, landed the party safely. A short reconnaissance of the island was made and a Frenchman was brought back who could give information on harbour facilities and the whereabouts of the Germans. It was discovered that the Germans had withdrawn and had taken a battery of 75mm guns with them, and the raid might have concluded without any incident worth recording, but on the way back the destroyer was instructed to intercept two enemy trawlers which had been sighted making their way north from Brest. The trawlers were intercepted and surrendered immediately. The Belgians sent across one boarding party while the destroyer provided another. The vessels were searched and then sunk by gunfire after twenty-two Germans – who had apparently murdered their officers and were heading for neutral Spain – had been taken aboard the destroyer.[21]

3

By the time the Belgian Troop arrived back in England both the Polish and the Yugoslavian Troops had left the Inter-Allied Commando.

It appears that the attachment of Lieutenant Tripovic and his fifteen men to various units of No 2 SS Brigade worked smoothly at first for at the beginning of February the balance of the Troop, ten men under the command of Lieutenant Kerovin, was dispatched to the Mediterranean theatre to join them. However, soon after the arrival of Tripovic and his men on Vis, in the middle of February, it became evident that the Yugoslavian Troop were *persona non grata* with the partisans. The reason for this animosity was not hard to find. At first the Allies had backed both the Royalist sympathiser, Colonel Dragolyub Mihailovitch, and the leader of the banned Communist party, Tito, in their guerrilla war against the Germans. But as the war progressed Mihailovitch became increasingly pro-Axis. The two factions started fighting and then Mihailovitch and his Chetniks sided openly with the Italian occupation troops. At the end of 1943 it was decided at the Teheran Conference that the Allies would only continue to back the partisans, and the Yugoslavian National Liberation Committee banned King Peter from re-entering his country until his people had decided on the fate of the monarchy. The British, however, continued to try and save the monarchy and it was not until May, 1944, when Mihailovitch lost his post in the Yugoslavian government in exile, that they finally withdrew their support and threw in their lot with Tito who by then commanded a disciplined army of some 300,000 men.[22]

The Yugoslavian Troop of the Inter-Allied Commando, however, had been recruited from the Royal Yugoslavian Army, which had been stationed in Egypt, and they still wore the initials of King Peter on their berets and epaulettes. This did not suit the partisans at all and on one occasion there was a fight between the two factions in Komiza which the Belgians, with the help of the British, had to break up. As a result of this it was decided to dissolve the Troop. Some of the men returned to Italy, where the infighting became so bitter than one officer belonging to No 2 Commando remembers Tripovic being chased into Molfetta church by some of his Troop and having to be rescued by the priest. Others preferred to stay and fight with the partisans, and abandoned wearing the green beret. This did not go down well with the British Commandos who looked upon those who joined the partisans as nothing more than deserters. Kerovin and his men almost certainly never even reached Vis but were retained in North Africa where, Sturges reported on 15 April, the Yugoslavian Troop was "for political reasons in a state of disbandonment".[23]

While the Yugoslavian Troop, always something of an experiment, must be said to have ended as a failure, the Polish Troop, by the time it left the Inter-Allied Commando, had been one of the unit's most outstanding successes. In April, 1944, the Troop was transferred to the command of 2 Polish Corps and on the 24th of that month was reinforced with twenty battle-hardened volunteers from various Polish units. It was intended to be only a temporary attachment while No 2 SS Brigade was on Vis, but in fact the Poles never returned to it. Officially, however, they remained part of the Inter-Allied Commando until 3 August, 1944, and in the intervening months they experienced some extremely heavy fighting, fought with great gallantry and suffered severe casualties.

The Troop was by now used to operating independently and they viewed their move to 2 Polish Corps with some trepidation. It seems, however, that though they were by no means always used in the role in which they had been trained they settled down well enough with the Polish army units with which they worked.

The Poles' first fierce encounter with the enemy after coming under command of 2 Polish Corps was on 17 May,[24] when they were moved up to take part in the fighting to take Monte Cassino. Attempts to capture this German stronghold that dominated Highway 6 to Rome had been going on since January and 2 Polish Corps had been involved in trying to subdue it since 11 May. In the Polish Corps' second attempt to break through the German defences, codenamed Operation Diadem, Smrokowski, who now also had an assault squadron of the 15th Poznan Lancers under his command, was detailed to give cover on the right flank of the battalion designated to take one of the Germans' main positions on Colle San Angelo.

By climbing another feature, Monte Castellone, it was possible to cross over the northern part of a ridge known as Phantom Ridge and thence to the north-west slope of the main objective. However, before they had begun to climb the steep, rocky side of Monte Castellone the northern part of the ridge was almost entirely conquered by the Poles, although Germans still lurked in many well concealed bunkers with the expectation that their side would counterattack – which, at 0530, they did, though they were eventually driven off. When the Commandos mounted their attack towards Colle San Angelo later that morning they came under heavy fire and one officer, 2/Lieutenant Bachleda, and another man were killed and several wounded; they were forced to withdraw to tend to their casualties and to reorganize. At 1115 a fresh attack was ordered and at 1300 after crossing Phantom Ridge the Commandos and the Poznan Lancers were on the northern side of Colle San Angelo where other Poles were fighting fiercely to retain their positions.

The Polish Troop now came under heavy mortar fire once more as they lay on the hillside. In Section 2 both Lieutenant Zemanek and his 2 i/c, Senior Sergeant Gradowski were wounded, along with two others, and Cadet Officer Henryk Jedwab took over command. The Germans pressed home their counterattacks and by early afternoon were once again masters of the whole of Colle San Angelo. Then later in the afternoon the Poles regrouped and launched their own counterattack, managing to clear the Germans off most of the mountainside but were unable to dislodge them from the summit. By the close of that day the Polish Troop's casualties amounted to one officer killed and three officers, three sergeants, eight corporals and six men wounded.

Early the next morning men of the 3rd Carpathian Rifles finally captured

Monte Cassino Hill and by 1000 the red and white flag of Poland was flying over the ruins of the monastery. Despite this victory the Germans refused to give up their second key position, Colle San Angelo, without further fighting, and as the Polish flag was being raised over Monte Cassino itself the Poles launched yet another attack on the summit of Colle San Angelo, but yet again they were stopped below it.

In the afternoon the Commandos and the Poznan Lancer Squadron, plus what remained of the other Polish infantry units in the area, moved yet again to conquer the peak of Colle San Angelo and at 1745, after a severe struggle, they drove the Germans from it, and then drove off a German counterattack, though Captain Zalewski, in charge of the Polish Troop, was wounded, and the command of the Troop passed to Captain Czyński. Czyński's Section 1 was now taken over by 2/Lieutenant Rzemieniecki while Cadet Officer Jedwab remained in charge of Section 2. During this final phase of the attack on Colle San Angelo the Troop lost one NCO killed, with three officers, four NCOs and four ORs wounded.

By now the ranks of the Polish Troop were thinning in an alarming fashion, and by the evening of 18 May only seven officers and forty-five ORs remained to carry on the fight, but by 1730 they had managed to capture nearly the whole of Colle San Angelo ridge. Then at 2000 Cadet Officer Bartosiewicz reported that the enemy had withdrawn and at 0415 the next morning two white rockets were fired over Colle San Angelo tracing a V for victory sign in the sky. At midday the Polish Troop was relieved and went into reserve. Their part in the battle for Monte Cassino had cost them two killed and thirty-four wounded.

After a period of well-deserved rest the depleted Troop was transferred to the Adriatic side of Italy and was quartered in the little town of Oratino. There they had attached to them what was called 111th Company for the protection of bridges, a unit composed entirely of Italian volunteers anxious to fight against the Germans. It was an unusual unit which certainly saw more active service than guarding bridges and the Commandos took it under their wing. The unit was given Polish uniforms, Polish insignia, and was commanded by a Polish officer and NCOs, and in one of its first actions against the Germans with the Commandos was involved in clearing Monto Freddo when the enemy was being driven north to Anacona, an operation that cost the Polish Troop one officer killed.

After Section 1 of the Troop raided behind enemy lines in the area of La Montagnola to obtain information and take a prisoner – which was successful though they lost one man in a fight with a German patrol – the Polish Troop, on 15 July, were sent to operate under 2 Polish Armoured Brigade on the left flank of 2 Polish Corps. On the night of 15/16 July, acting as infantry support for the tanks, they attacked across the River Musone to take the village of Case Nuove that lay beyond. From their position on Monte Polesco they could see the church tower and roofs of the village that lay beyond the maize fields that concealed a series of German defences, and to their left was a deep ravine that ran down to the river and divided the village from some brickworks with a tall chimney, an ideal observation post for the Germans.

In the severe fighting which followed five of the Polish Troop were killed and three wounded before they even reached the edge of the village. Section 2 now worked its way round to the left flank to attack the brickworks, while Section 1 entered the village. The latter cleared its objective without casualties, but Section 2 soon found that the brickworks had been turned into a small fortress and four more Poles were killed before Smrokowski ordered the section's withdrawal. By 1000 the area, except for the brickworks – which was reduced to rubble by tanks that afternoon – was in the Commandos' hands, and they were then transported to the next objective, Castelferretti, on the tanks. This proved to be an uncomfortable journey as they were continuously mortared and shelled, and one man was killed before the order was given for the Troop to be taken inside the tanks. Just in front of the town the Commandos' left the tanks and advanced, but found that the Germans had left that morning. During the preceding 48 hours they had lost eight men, including one officer and four NCOs killed, while nine, including one officer and three NCOs, had been wounded, though they had killed many Germans and had taken fifty-six prisoners.

The battle for Case Nuove was the fiercest the Poles fought, and it was also the last they were to fight as members of the Inter-Allied Commando, for on 3 August they ceased to be No 6 Troop – or the 1st Independent Commando Company, as they called themselves – and became the nucleus of a much larger Commando Motorized Battalion which took part in the battle for Bologna.

During the Italian campaign the Polish Troop lost in total eighteen men killed and seventy wounded, an 80% casualty rate. For their courage in battle they won one Cross of Virtuti Militari IV Class (the Polish equivalent of the Victoria Cross), nineteen Crosses of Virtuti Militari V Class, two Crosses of Bravery with two bars, nine Crosses of Bravery with one bar and thirty-six Crosses of Bravery without bar, plus a Military Cross and a Military Medal. "For one single company," the author of *Poles in the Italian Campaign* wrote, "this was an amazing achievement."

By August, 1944, the only Inter-Allied troops remaining in the Mediterranean theatre were members of X-Troop who were proving invaluable as interrogators and interpreters. But they too had suffered losses and at the beginning of 1945 Bartlett, Stewart and Shelley, who had all received field commissions for their services during the Normandy campaign, arrived in Italy and began to recruit new members for an enlarged detachment of X-Troop with Bartlett as its commanding officer. Sixteen were recruited altogether and with Anson, now a sergeant, as their senior non-commissioned

109

officer, the three officers gave them the kind of training they themselves had been put through by Hilton Jones and the instructors at Achnacarry. Then in April they were transported to where No 2 SS Brigade was operating at Lake Comacchio, but were engaged in only one or two minor skirmishes before the war ended on 8 May.

7

The French
go Home

While the Belgian, Norwegian and Dutch Troops were lobbying to become part of the vast invasion force, the two French Troops and those members of X-Troop not in Italy were training hard for D-Day, for all three had been allotted specific tasks which they were to undertake while attached to other Commando forces.

In February, 1944, Lt-Colonel Robert Dawson, then Commanding Officer of No 4 Commando, was called to Scotland by Brigadier "Shimi" Lovat, commanding the 1st Special Service Brigade of which No 4 was a part, for a preliminary briefing on No 4's role in the forthcoming landings. Lovat, in fact, had picked out Dawson and his men for the special task of destroying a German battery on the extreme eastern flank of the invasion beaches, at Ouistreham, and of then securing the town and port while ensuring that the sluice gates of the Orne canal remained intact.

Lovat's choice was a good one, for No 4 Commando was an extremely experienced unit. It had taken part in several raids and, under Lovat's command, had stormed the battery at Varengeville during the Dieppe operation. If any unit could succeed in the vital task of taking out the Ouistreham batteries, No 4 was it. Even so, it seemed to Lovat that Dawson would need to be reinforced if he was to succeed quickly. He had heard that the two French Troops from 10 (IA) Commando might be available. Would Dawson like to have them?

Dawson was enthusiastic. He spoke French perfectly (he had been brought up in Switzerland and France) and already knew the French from a recent exercise, and from the Forfar and Hardtack operations in which both units had been involved the previous year, and he had liked what he had seen.

111

Lovat promised he would do what he could do, and on 16 April, 1944, the two French Troops joined No 4 Commando where they were stationed at Bexhill, and, although they were still officially part of 10 (IA) Commando, they were allowed to replace their 10 (IA) flashes with those of No 4 Commando.

Initially the two nationalities eyed each other warily, but both soon became accustomed to one another. Eventually they became such close allies that when the French became involved in a Belgian dance hall fracas with a British unit members of No 4 Commando waded in too – on the side of the French. On the parade ground, however, the French did at first cause some problems for their drill movements were different to the British ones. Dawson was too wise a man to try and alter the Frenchmen's way of drilling, and he and the regimental sergeant-major devised a method whereby the British were able to co-ordinate their fewer drill movements with the more complicated French ones. It worked so well that when on 10 May the head of the Free French Naval Forces in Britain, Admiral d'Argenlieu, came to decorate some of those who had taken part in the small-scale raids the previous winter, Dawson was congratulated on his men's parade-ground drill.

With de Gaulle's intransigence during the war now a legend, it might be thought that Dawson had bitten off more than he could chew, but in fact he found that the chain of command worked as well with Kieffer and his officers as it did with Dawson's own. Dawson later remarked: "If I wanted both French Troops to do something then I'd ask Kieffer to get it done, but if it was just a matter of one of the Troops then I would give the order to the Troop Commander concerned but always with Kieffer present. Kieffer was there to command the French Troops and as my second-in-command of them. He turned out to be a very able operations officer indeed."[1]

Soon after No 4 Commando amalgamated with the French – the French called the new unit the Franco-Britannique Commando – Dawson was offered a version of the Vickers K-gun* to help the Commando in its assault on the Ouistreham battery and its outlying defences. Originally this weapon had been designed to be mounted in the open cockpit of an aircraft. It had a drum mounted on top as a magazine and had a very high rate of fire. Dawson decided that such a weapon could be extremely useful for low-angle fire support and one Troop of No 4 Commando was equipped with eight of them, for the more he looked at the plan for taking the battery the more essential it seemed to have the heaviest possible weight of fire available during the assault period.

* These were normally mounted in Catalina amphibious planes and had a very high rate of fire – 1000 rounds per minute from a drum magazine. They were fitted with bipods for use on land and proved their worth, but at the end of the Normandy campaign had to be abandoned through lack of spares.

The plan was to land 2000 metres west of Riva-Ouistreham on the beach at La Brèche, codenamed "Queen Red", which was itself the eastern flank of the British landing area known as "Sword Beach". Once ashore and off the beach – which it was hoped would at least have been partly cleared by men of the 8th Infantry Brigade which were to land at H-Hour – Troop 8, commanded by Alex Lofi, had been given the task of overrunning the nearest German strongpoint, while the rest of the Commando went on along the road that took them into the back part of the town.

As the French entered Ouistreham it was planned that Lieutenant Guy Vourc'h and Troop 1 would turn left and move towards the beach and take a German strongpoint, centred on the demolished Casino, from the rear, while the British Commandos moved on to the eastern end of the town before turning and attacking the batteries in the same manner. When Count Guy de Montlaur,* a sergeant in Troop 1, heard what his objective was to be he is alleged to have told Kieffer, "It will be a pleasure. I have lost several fortunes in that place."[2]

It was part of Dawson's plan to give the French their own independent objectives. "It gave them the opportunity of getting to grips with something within their own competence and under their own steam, whereas the battery No 4 Commando had to attack was so complicated in its layout that it could have been difficult to integrate the French into an attack on it when they spoke a different language and so on. You see, we'd never all been together in action before, and although subsequently we never had any problems, on this first operation I thought it better to give the French their own targets."[3]

Once No 4 Commando had cleared Ouistreham it was to join the rest of the Brigade and race inland to reinforce the bridgehead which it was planned would be made beyond the Orne River by the 6th Airborne Division.

Because the French were to operate independently, it was decided that they too should have K-guns, and so a K-gun section, with four of these lethal weapons, was formed by Lieutenant Amaury, with Lieutenant Hubert as his second-in-command.

On 25 May the whole of 1st Special Service Brigade were sent to Titchfield Camp, near the mouth of the Hamble, and from then until D-Day they were, as were all the invasion forces, isolated from the outside world. In the camp they rehearsed again and again their exact roles in the landings. Kieffer had been shown maps of the No 4 Commando plan before they had moved to Titchfield and though the names on it had been replaced by codenames it did not take him long to fathom out where he and his men were going to land. Now it was his men's turn to try and guess.[4]

---

* Like many of the stories of the French Troop this amusing aside has no foundation in fact. When the makers of "The Longest Day" wanted to put it in the script, de Montlaur, who was an adviser on the film, said he would sue them if they did.

Before the Frenchmen left Titchfield on 5 June Lord Lovat addressed them in their own language. "You are returning home. You will be the first uniformed troops to fight the Germans on your own soil. You are going to show us what you know and what you can do. Tomorrow morning, we're going to get them."

The two French Troops were then taken by truck to Warsash where they embarked on the two LCI(S)s which were to take them right on to the beach, Troop 1 in LCI 527 and Troop 8 in LCI 523. The rest of No 4 Commando were taken to Spithead where they embarked on the *Princess Astrid* and *Maid of Orleans*, both of which had been converted to Infantry Landing Ships equipped with LCAs which would take the Commandos the last mile or so onto the beach. They went aboard "in a grotesque gala", as one witness described it, "more like a regatta than a page of history . . . At 2100 the Commando 'set out to war' in the first of nineteen ships in line ahead with Lord Lovat's piper playing in the bows . . . it was exhilarating, glorious and heartbreaking."[5]

It was a rough crossing for the French, but it did not stop Kieffer, for one, from going to sleep. As he rolled himself up in his blankets, the prayer of Sir Jacob Astley at the Battle of Edgehill in 1642 came into his mind. "O Lord, thou knowest how busy I must be this day. If I forget Thee, do not Thou forget me." He repeated it to himself, and then drew up his blankets and fell asleep.[6]

Some of his men, however, remained awake and reflective. Among them was young Maurice Chauvet who had been given command of what must have been one of the most unportable pieces of equipment devised during the whole war – a folding bicycle. He wrote of those tense hours vividly and simply:

"5 June 1944. 10.30pm. We know now where we are going. We shall land tomorrow, 6 June, at H-Hour + 20 = 7.30am,* west of Ouistreham. When I saw this for the first time, the real names of the places we used to know instead of under exotic Anglo-Saxon codenames, I felt that this time it was for real.

"Forgotten details are rushing back to our minds. Up till now, this part of France has been for us nothing more than maps and snaps. For twelve days we have been learning by heart the minutest details about the roads in the area we are going to invade, but all this had been too abstract. It had not sunk in that we were actually landing in France. I needed to see those proper names on the map, then the operation meant something: liberation. I think that we all felt the same way. With the maps we had been given Montgomery's message: very English but very friendly.

"All we can do it wait. I feel very tranquil, have no special desires at all. The sea is rather rough, and the LCI is rocking rather more than when we were training, but I'm not bothered. I am thinking of the cigarettes I have in the pocket of my battledress, and I hope that they will not be soaked when I disembark. I am in the bows of the LCI in a small cabin five or six metres

* The French were actually scheduled to land at 0755, which they did.

square. It has two large ladders leading to the deck. When the hatch is closed, the only light is an electric one. On either side are wooden benches, rather like the ones you see in a railway station. The fact that 25 men with all their equipment can squeeze into such a small space is amazing. The radio sets take up a lot of space. The light is dim and though the walls are painted white it is hard to distinguish the faces of my comrades sitting opposite. Their faces are familiar, of course, but I do not know their real identities. In the Free French Forces you seldom know who you have in front of you, most have changed their names especially those in the Commandos. We live without any past or any future, like children do. . . . Often during these last years we felt we were just mercenaries, but since we have joined No 4 Commando we have felt at home. The Colonel speaks to us in French and the last months have been pleasant . . .

"There is what sounds like thunder in the sky above us and I go on deck. It is hundreds of planes flying above us, most of them towing gliders. This is the 6th Airborne Division which will be dropped inland from where we're going to land in about an hour. If we do not succeed in joining them in the morning, they won't survive. Dr Lion is on deck with all his medical orderlies and says that the news on the radio is good, Rome has been taken and now everyone's eyes have turned to Paris . . .

"It is cold outside and I go back below. The room is dim but warm. In a corner I can see X, a young boy who found out a few days ago that his English girl friend was pregnant. He applied to get married, but was told it was impossible. So he went to the Colonel and explained that he knew he was going to die on the first day and that he wanted to give his son his name. Somehow the Colonel arranged it and he got married just before he went to Titchfield Camp. He is certainly going to die, and he knows it. I am wondering whether soldiers in earlier wars had the same premonition that they were going to die but carried on just the same. Beside him sits the Luxembourger, Reiffers, as still as a statue. He is smiling to himself, lost in his thoughts. Before the war he was a professional hunter in Africa. Maybe he is thinking that it is ironical that he is now the prey instead of being the hunter.

"The cabin is full again, no one can sleep, no one is hungry. Silently, we wait with our equipment around us. In our group there are graduates, workers, all mixed together, brought together because they were disgusted with France in 1940, or just because of personal matters. They have chosen to live among commandos and to die if necessary and be buried with the words 'Unknown Allied Soldier' on their graves . . .

"It is almost 6am. We are not nervous, there is too much to do. H-Hour is coming up. We have to get our equipment ready. Within 90 minutes 177 French Commandos are going to land: all equal even if they have different ideas about life and death."[7]

The task of landing the French was given to Sub-Lieutenant J. W. Berry RNVR who commanded LCI 523 and to Lieutenant Charles Craven RNVR who commanded LCI 527. 523 carried Lofi and his men, plus a sub-section of K-guns, 527 Vourc'h and No 1 Troop, plus Kieffer and his HQ, and the other K-gun sub-section.

Kieffer had requested that he and his men be landed as far to the left as possible without running on to the rocks which hedged Sword Beach, and Berry, with LCI 527 close behind, kept as much to the left as he dared as he made his run in to the beach. He'd been told that the plan was to clear a way through the obstacles and minefields the previous night, but, as he drew nearer, he could see that this had not been done. He saw about six rows of stakes and tripods in the water which had some converted captured shells on top of them acting as mines. Bits of wire and chain hung between them. Fortunately, as it was just after low water, Berry had a good view of the obstacles and could guess where the beach minefield would be. Just then LCI 527 must have also seen the jungle of lethal metal for it hailed Berry and suggested they try further along the beach. Berry refused and told LCI 527 that they were going straight in. He then went full ahead and, with everyone crouching low, the LCI smashed straight through the obstacles, and hit the beach so hard that it was ashore as far as the bridge. The idea of doing this was that, as Berry thought he had not the slightest chance of ever getting his ship off again, he might as well use her as a bridge for the French across the beach minefield. He then let down both ramps and watched the French charge on to the churned-up sand.[8]

The two LCIs hit Queen Red Beach on time, but what the French saw there must have appalled them. Bodies lay everywhere, littering the sand and floating at the water's edge. Some of the H-Hour assault troops were still in the water and some of those on the beach were actually trying to dig themselves in.*

LCI 523 was able to haul up its ramps and, despite Berry's worst fears, refloated herself. LCI 527, however, was not so lucky. She fouled her propellers on a beach obstruction, some of her crew were wounded during the landing, and a direct hit smashed her ramps. Scaling nets were lowered over the side and the Commandos swarmed ashore. Others were too impatient to wait and simply dropped into the water and waded to the beach. Some transferred to 523 which had managed to manoeuvre herself alongside and she then rebeached.[9]

---

* There is conflict about exactly what happened on that section of Sword Beach during those first hours. The official history of the 2nd East Yorkshire Regiment who landed on Queen Red Beach at H-Hour said it was "just like a training show, only easier", a statement vehemently denied by some of the men who were there. Brigadier Cass, in command of the 8th Brigade, asserted that the 2nd East Yorks were off the beach by the time the Commandos landed, but it is now generally thought that most of the 200 casualties they suffered on D-Day were hit on the beaches.

Despite these delays, Guy Vourc'h was one of the first ashore and, caught up in the fever of the moment, yelled with the rest of his Troop as he staggered inland towards the dark lines of dunes. He had only taken a few steps, however, when there was an ear-splitting explosion immediately behind him. He felt a numbing blow in his back and right arm as he was hurled forward on to the sand. For a moment he lay dazed, scrabbling weakly at the sand. He saw his men moving on ahead and he felt bitter that for him the battle was over. Then the numbness gave way to pain, and he saw the mortar bombs dropping all round him, and knew that if he didn't do something he would not only miss this battle but would never survive at all. He struggled clear of his rucksack and managed to get off the beach. Later in the morning he was evacuated with other wounded.

Vourc'h at least was still alive and recovered sufficiently quickly to bully the hospital authorities into letting him return to his beloved Troop in the middle of August. But several others were already dead, and a number were wounded. Reiffers, Dumanoir, Laventure, Lahouze, Casalonga, Leostic, Cabellan, Piauge, Flesch, Beux, Rousseau, Bucher and Lieutenant Pinelli were all out of the battle before the Commando even got off the beach, and, while they were in the dunes, Kieffer was another early casualty when he was hit in the left thigh by a mortar fragment. Out of the 177 men of the two French Troops (including six English wireless operators and medics) who had landed, 114 reached the forming-up point, an old holiday camp in the dunes which was now half in ruins.[10]

On learning that both Vourc'h and Pinelli had been wounded, Kieffer now put No 1 Troop under the command of the Administration Officer, Lieutenant Mazeas. Mazeas went forward to reconnoitre and was wounded in his turn, and Kieffer took personal command of the Troop with Warrant Officer Faure as his second-in-command.[11]

The French had requested the honour of advancing first. This had been granted and they now began to form up at the head of the Commando ready to advance on the town just as soon as Dawson returned from reconnoitring ahead. However, when he came back his face was a mask of blood and he was not in a good mood.* "What the hell are you doing," he yelled at his adjutant, Donald Gilchrist. "Get them moving." Gilchrist opened his mouth to protest that Dawson had not given any orders to push on. "Move," shouted Dawson, and Gilchrist did. He ran to the Frenchmen in a fury. *"Allez! Allez!"* he screamed at them. *"Vite, vite! Sacrebleu!"* The French looked at him in utter amazement but obediently began to move off to their objectives, and it wasn't until after the war that Gilchrist was told by the French that they thought he

* He'd been wounded in the head and temporarily had to hand over to his second-in-command, Major R. P. Menday. After his wound had been dressed he returned to the fray and refused to be evacuated until ordered to hospital by the Assistant Director of Medical Services.

had been shouting "Allah! Allah!"[12] As they moved off they passed the wounded Dawson who said, "Go ahead – we're counting on you."[13]

After dumping their rucksacks as planned, the first to leave the column progressing cautiously towards Ouistreham was Troop 8 led by Alex Lofi. So far his luck had held, for his Troop had managed to clear the beach without losing a man. But his task, to take out a small but well-defended blockhouse about 800 yards from the landing beach, which marked the western edge of the German strongpoint centred around the demolished Casino, was a tough one. To help him Kieffer allotted him half the K-gun section under Lieutenant Hubert and it was Sergeant Saerens* from the section who first made contact with the blockhouse.

"I gave the order to move off with Hulot's section at the head," Lofi wrote later. "We had already been bracketed by some mortar bombs and we had to cross another minefield before we reached the grounds of a large house. Hulot arrived and went in, but Bagot, with his 2 i/c Chausse, was given the task of clearing it. Just then we were caught in a heavy artillery barrage and the house was hit by shells.

"Progress was now rapid. We found several machine-gun posts empty. We skirted round the obstacles set up by the Germans at the entrance to Riva Bella. Notices saying 'Achtung Minen' were fixed on the walls of villas. As we closed in on the strongpoint a mortar, which must have been biding its time, dropped a bomb on Hulot's section and there were a number of wounded including Hulot himself. I helped get the wounded under cover and then ordered Bagot's section to take over the advance. As we approached our objective we came under heavy machine-gun fire and four scouts were wounded, though only lightly. We took up our positions in surrounding houses from which we could command the complex of very well-hidden trenches in the middle of which a large blockhouse stood still absolutely intact.

"Bagot placed his section carefully for the assault. Hulot, with exemplary courage, rejoined the Troop despite his wound. I put him in reserve with Chausse's sub-section on the left flank of the blockhouse, but with enormous determination he managed to reach within grenade-throwing distance of the trenches. Chausse, well installed on the left flank, opened fire with everything he had, but though it was effective – as were Hulot's grenades – the blockhouse remained intact and the Germans increased their fire. The anti-tank gun which was part of the German defences demolished one of the houses but I kept up the attack so the Germans wouldn't guess how few of us there were. Our PIAT was also ineffective on the blockhouse but we registered some lucky shots with it on the trenches full of enemy.

"We then saw that the Germans were leaving their trenches and were trying

---

* Sergeant Saerens was awarded the Military Medal during the Normandy campaign, but his citation cannot be traced.

to surround us by outflanking the K-gun section on the right flank. I gave Bagot the order to reinforce the K-gun section and when he did so the section was able to disengage, but during this fighting Bagot was caught in some automatic fire and he fell, and one of the bren gunners, Lechapponnier, was also wounded."[14]

The two K-guns had been set up in a bomb crater and had given covering fire to Hubert and Lance-Sergeant Coste who had led the first attack. At first everything had gone well, but then Hubert, in trying to signal Saerens to join him, exposed himself and was shot through the head. Matters were made worse when first one and then the other K-gun jammed, and Saerens had to order his men into a nearby house where the K-guns were stripped, cleaned and reassembled, before being repositioned in the house so that fire could once more be brought down on the blockhouse. It must have been this lapse in firing that the Germans took advantage of to try and outflank the sub-section, and moments after the sub-section left the house in which they were sheltering it was hit by the anti-tank gun and collapsed in a cloud of dust.[15]

While Lofi and his men were having problems in reducing the first German blockhouse* the rest of the Commando continued on into the town. On the outskirts Kieffer and Troop 1 turned down a side street and made their way to the rear of the Casino strongpoint while the rest of the Commando carried on to the eastern end of Ouistreham to take the battery from behind.† "Troop 1 crossed Riva Bella in 40 minutes. The street in which they found themselves had one feature which had not been noted in the aerial photographs. 50 metres from the blockhouse it was closed by a concrete anti-tank wall, two metres high. In the middle of the wall there was a gap just wide enough to let a man through. The advance on the pavements to left and right took place in the shelter of this wall, and the Germans who were to be eliminated were unable to see their enemy. Once the wall was reached it was enough to make a quick movement through the gap and to disperse down each side as had been planned. Though the strength of Troop 1 had by now been reduced by a third, its fire power had not been, as the automatic weapons of the wounded and dead were now being used by those who previously had only been armed with rifles.

"The Troop was spread evenly on both sides of the street, with two bren guns, four tommy guns and one flame thrower on each side. Everyone had orders to fire on the embrasures of the strongpoint which was now only 40 metres away.

"On the left-hand side of the street the Petty Officer in charge of Troop 1 [Faure] and Petty Officer Lardennois set up the two PIATs, with their crews

---

* It in fact surrendered soon afterwards to British infantry which took over Ouistreham when the Commandos left the town.
† It was found later that the Germans had removed the guns inland, but the British Commandos still had to overcome a complex network of fortifications that surrounded the empty batteries, which they did with grenade and bayonet.

on the first floor of a small villa. They had only four projectiles which were very heavy to carry. The first two, fired simultaneously, destroyed the 20mm anti-aircraft guns on top of the blockhouse and disabled the men manning it. The second two widened the embrasures; it was only later that we were told that the blast produced inside had had the most devastating effect on the defenders. The Frenchmen hastily left the villa just as it was about to collapse as it was being hit by an 88mm gun 800 metres away which had pinpointed the fire from the PIATs."[16]

An old man with a long white moustache now appeared and introduced himself as Marcel Lefevre, a 1914–18 veteran and a member of the local Resistance. Lefevre said he wanted to fight alongside the French Commandos so he was given a rifle. He then told Faure that he knew where some telephone cables – which linked a strongpoint in a water tower overlooking the Casino position with the fortifications at Riva Bella and with St Aubin d'Arquenay and Caen – were buried. He led Faure and Nicot to the place and a hole was dug down to them. Two 4kg of plastic explosives were then laid in the hole and the cables severed.[17]

This vital piece of information interrupted the enemy's lines of communications but it did not solve the problem of how to capture the Casino position. Kieffer, who had been worried about the progress of Lofi and his men, now returned to Troop 1 to find them unable to move forward. Kieffer saw that he now had virtually no choice but to launch a direct attack, though he must have known that it would probably fail and that his men would be decimated. It was then that he heard a message over the radio that perhaps saved many of the Troop from certain death: several DD tanks* had managed to land and make their way off the beach. This set Kieffer off down the street with his batman, Devager, to try and get one of them to help his men. After some difficulty, he managed to do this and returned riding on top of it. It was now 0925.

"I decided to keep the wall as a protection and went with the tank through an adjacent courtyard where we set up in front of the Casino and commenced firing under my directions. The first two shells went straight into the Casino which stopped two of its guns from firing. At that moment I was once more lightly wounded in the right arm by a rifle bullet, and I came down from the tank and went forward five metres behind a wall to continue directing the tank's fire by hand signals. I ordered the tank to pump fire into all the German positions, and the fire from the machine guns stopped. I now ordered Faure to send Montlaur's section on the left to clear up while Lardennois' section was ordered to clear up on the right. It was then 0955.

"Resistance seemed to be most intense on the right side in the direction

* Amphibious tanks. They should have turned to the right after landing, but a few turned left and found themselves in Ouistreham.

120

taken by Lardennois and his section. It came from the water tower which was firing on our right flank. After bandaging my arm we got back on the tank and got it to turn and face the water tower, so that we were no more than 100 metres from it. With four shells it was silenced. The section on the right now moved forward and cleared up the area, and Lanternier brought back the first eleven prisoners of whom three or four were Poles. While they were being brought back one of them threw a grenade which slightly wounded two of my men. At once we fired and killed three of them."[18]

Kieffer was later awarded the Military Cross for successfully leading the attack on the Casino position. "The dash and resolute action of this officer," the citation stated, "led to the final liquidation of a series of enemy strongpoints in the coastal built-up area, and of an enemy company in the town itself."

The Frenchmen were now in control of the western end of Ouistreham, but the cost had been high, as Bolloré, more than anyone, was in a position to know. Only eighteen at the time, he was the sole medical orderly to be able to help Dr Lion, for the other orderly, Bouarfa, had been wounded. But worse was to come for the medical team: as Lion and Bolloré were attending a wounded man two snipers fired at them simultaneously. Moments before, another Frenchman hiding in the rubble had called out, "You're mad, you'll be killed." Bolloré turned to see who had shouted and the sniper's bullet hit the wall where his head had been split seconds before, but Lion, giving the wounded man a morphine injection, was shot through the heart and died instantly.

Bolloré now started dragging the wounded man back to the bomb crater and seconds later Sergeant de Montlaur was at his side to help. Between them they got the man into the crater. He had been shot through the head, but he was still alive. No sooner had he finished doing what he could for the dying solider than Bolloré was called away to deal with another member of the Troop, Renault, who had been hit by a mortar fragment, but he too was beyond medical help and died minutes later.[19]

During those first hours of fighting Troop 1 alone had lost all five of its officers and twenty-three other ranks, but in the days to come the casualty rate was to rise even higher.

2

With the capture of their objectives completed, No 4 Commando returned to where they had landed, and, following the route opened by other units of 1 SS Brigade, began to make their way to the two bridges, across the Orne and across the canal, which had been taken during the night by men of 6 Airborne Division. As they marched inland the long column was sniped at and several men were lost. Lieutenant Amaury had his arm broken by a sniper's bullet, and, with Hubert dead, the K-gun section had no officers left so Kieffer attached them to his HQ section, with Sergeant Saerens leading one sub-section and Sergeant Coste the other.

The French, along with the rest of No 4 Commando, crossed the bridges under cover of a smokescreen. The fresh wind made it less than perfect and three more Frenchmen were made casualties, but by 1915 they had reached Ecarde on the road to Cabourg. It was then decided to move eastwards and for the Commando to take Amfréville south of Le Plein and to dig in for the night ready for the inevitable counterattack. They occupied Amfréville without any problems and prepared their defensive positions. The bulk of the Commando moved up to Le Plein, leaving the two French Troops holding the gap in the Brigade positions between Amfréville and Le Plein.

The attack when it came was launched from Franceville Plage and it drove a hole in the bridgehead set up by No 1 SS Brigade and 6 Airborne Division under whose command the SS Brigade had now come. Snipers infiltrated the British positions making contact with the rear increasingly difficult and six tanks approached the Brigade's positions, though these were driven off by Allied planes which destroyed two of them.

Major Menday decided to take a blockhouse near Sallenelles and move towards Franceville to try and plug this gap, which meant he needed to know if Sallenelles was still occupied by the enemy. Three men from No 1 Troop were chosen for this task. "Sgt-Major Lardennois, who on 6 June had succeeded in leading an equally hazardous patrol in the direction of the locks at the mouth of the Orne at Ouistreham, was put in charge with orders to enter Sallenelles without being noticed and without any fighting, to contact the inhabitants, if any were still there, and to gather information about the Germans' dispositions and strength. Lardennois made up a small patrol with two tried men: Corbin and Guyader. He succeeded perfectly in reaching and entering the village without being seen. The majority of the inhabitants had fled the fighting; only a few farmers remained and a baker gave Lardennois especially invaluable information. A well-placed look-out observed the German blockhouse for over two hours, after which Lardennois and his team came back to our positions. I accompanied Lardennois to the Major's HQ for debriefing. Lardennois revealed that the blockhouse* at Sallenelles was in a marsh, at some distance from the village with minefields all around. The garrison was composed of fifteen or so men under the command of a fanatical sergeant-major. Their weapons included an 88mm gun in a gun turret which was able to fire only towards the shore to the east of the Orne. No direct view over the disembarkation beaches was possible. Several machine guns completed the available fire power."[20]

* This blockhouse indirectly caused the death of a member of X-Troop, Fuller, as will be seen in the next chapter.

By early afternoon, however, the pressure on the British Commandos' positions increased to such an extent that Menday was obliged to postpone his move. German snipers were so active that the French were pinned down in their trenches and mortar fire rained down on them with increasing ferocity. Then at 0200 the next morning Kieffer received the message that German tanks were only 2 km to the south of his positions. He sent a patrol towards Bréville but it returned without having found anything. The Frenchmen's PIATs were strategically placed, and Kieffer waited. At dawn a tank appeared, but then disappeared behind a small hill by Bréville and was not seen again. The French were still relatively unscathed, though they lost their Commanding Officer that day. After attending the Brigade O Group in the morning and organizing supplies for his men, he went to a first aid post to have his wounds dressed. The doctor there ordered him to be evacuated immediately, as his leg had become infected. Kieffer* implored Lovat and Dawson to allow him to stay, but Lovat ordered him to the rear. He then handed over command of his men to Lofi. Lieutenant Francis Vourch now took over No 8 Troop, No 1 Troop remained under the command of Warrant Officer Faure, and Sergeant Coste was given command of the K-gun section.[21]

The next day passed without incident, but then at dawn on 10 June after a fierce dawn bombardment which left the French in no doubt that they intended taking Le Plein, the Germans threw two battalions of infantry, supported by tanks of the 21st Panzer Division, at the Commandos' lines. A desperate struggle ensued, and in that one morning the French lost twenty-nine men, including seven killed.[22]

"Soon the woods of Bréville were reduced to a cloud of dust by their shells with, here and there, the burning hulks of tanks. But some Tiger tanks filtered through towards our lines, and some even penetrated our rear positions where our anti-tank guns destroyed them. One of the Tiger tanks positioned itself some 300 metres from our position, out of the range of our anti-tank guns dug in behind us. One could see with binoculars the accompanying infantry squatting in the wheat fields. The K-gun section machine guns were doing splendidly, nailing the infantry to the ground, helped by our bren guns and those of No 8 Troop which we could see to our right firing without pause. The tank was firing with everything it had on our positions. I saw the courageous Gersel of the near-by K-gun section fall, killed instantly by a bullet in the forehead, and there were others too. A shell from the tank's 88mm gun tore off the lower half of the face of our poor comrade Bégot. The upper and lower jaws and the nose were torn off and smashed; he was losing blood in abundance, and it ran into his lungs producing an unbearable gurgling. His friends around him

---

* Kieffer's leg was saved from amputation by penicillin. He returned to his command on 13 July and received the Military Cross which he had won on D-Day from General Montgomery three days later.

had their morale sapped by the sight. It was obvious that any delay in evacuating Bégot would reduce his chances of surviving. On the other hand, the problem was that there was about 40 metres of open ground to cross before reaching shelter and then the First Aid Post, and this was covered by the tank. We were able to do this in the 60 seconds following Bégot becoming a casualty. It seems that the gunner in the enemy tanks saw a man running with Bégot* on his back, understood what was happening and ceased fire."[23]

The fighting continued throughout the day with some of the British Commandos being forced back but then counterattacking with such ferocity that they retook all the ground they had lost. The French showed their valour that day. They stood their ground and French accounts of the fighting recount individual actions of great bravery. Sergeant de Montlaur, for instance, raced forward to take over a bren gun when both of its team became casualties, calmly shooting the German that had hit them both as he rose to kill de Montlaur. Then, as the two sides became locked in hand-to-hand fighting, Laot, attacked by three Germans, killed two of them before himself being bayoneted by the third. "That day of 10 June," wrote one of the Frenchmen many years later, "was lived by all with such intensity that we lost all sense of time."[24] By the end of that day only seventy men of the two French Troops remained out of the 177 that had landed four days earlier.

10 June was a critical day for those holding the vital eastern flank, for though there was hard fighting ahead the Germans never again attacked with such determination and weight, and before long became purely defensive in their operations. Slowly the initiative swung to the Commandos and the parachutists defending the Orne bridgehead, and they began mounting an increasing number of patrols into no-man's-land so that in the end they came to dominate it. The French especially revelled in the night probes among the Germans' positions and were delighted when prisoners told them it was what the Germans dreaded most. In fact, so popular did these nightly excursions become that a strict rota had to be set up to make sure that everyone had a chance to take part in them.

The weeks of static warfare, with its incessant mortaring and shelling, began to take its toll on morale, however, and Lofi more than once – to the annoyance of more senior British officers – arranged for some counter-action to be taken against the Germans. "You will reveal our positions," he was chided on one occasion after starting some counter-mortar fire.

"They know our positions all too well, mon Colonel," Lofi retorted with a shrug. "Hardly a day passes without someone having to be evacuated." By the time the breakout from the bridgehead came and the French had helped take Bavent, which they did on 16 August, No 8 Troop had been reduced to twenty-seven officers and men.

* Miraculously, Bégot survived and his face was reformed by British and then French surgeons.

124

The breakout came as a godsend to the French and they pursued the Germans with such verve that they often caught up with them and forced them to fight. On one occasion they did so with particularly good effect when, on 20 August, after crossing the Dives River they came upon some Germans at La Ferme de l'Epine.

Lofi wrote later: "I was about to halt 8 Troop and wait for dawn when I heard a voice about 10 metres in front of me call out what sounded like, '*Halt. Wer da?*' On the other hand we were expecting Guy Vourc'h and his Troop to join us, so I decided it was probably a Frenchman shouting '*Halt, la!*'. So I shouted back, 'Don't make fools of yourselves, this is 8 Troop. Who is there?' The answer was a burst of machine-gun fire that hit the ground around my feet. I took a grenade and threw it at where I thought the fire had come from, but another grenade thrown by Senée landed there before mine. I felt a very slight pain in the corner of my eye and found that a splinter had got in there. The enemy marksman had aimed badly. Messanot who was behind also received a few splinters. Apart from these two no one was wounded."[25]

Lofi now withdrew his Troop and planned a counterattack for dawn. Chausse urged that they make a bayonet attack. Lofi agreed and arranged for Chausse and his men to be covered by the K-guns, Hulot's bren guns and the Troop's 2-inch mortars. The attack went in and though eight of the French were wounded several of the Germans were killed, including one officer shot dead by Chausse with his revolver, and they were eventually routed.

Five days later St Maclou was swiftly overrun and the French were also involved in liberating Deauville, Honfleur and several other towns before reaching the Seine. Then, on 5 September, along with the rest of No 4 Commando, they returned to England for rest and reorganization. Out of the original 177 men who had landed on D-Day only forty had survived the campaign unscathed.

8

X-Troop in
Normandy

The only other Troop of the Inter-Allied Commando to be in action during and after the Normandy landings was X-Troop, by now officially renamed No 3 (Misc) Troop. Unlike the French, however, they did not fight as a unit, but were divided into small detachments of between two and five which were then attached to each of the Commandos, and to the two Brigade Headquarters, which took part in the D-Day landings and the fighting afterwards.

Those members of No 3 Troop who had been on active service already, in Sicily and Italy, had been regarded basically as interpreters, but neither they nor Hilton Jones – nor the men who were about to see action in Normandy – regarded this as their principal role. They were by now a highly trained group of individuals with an unrivalled knowledge of the German army, and for some time Hilton Jones had been campaigning to give the Troop more recognition. He lobbied the relevant authorities to allow the most promising to apply for OCTU, and to acknowledge that the role of the Troop in the imminent invasion of Europe would be a far more active one than acting as interpreters. His views were well summed up in a memorandum sent by one of the Troop to Lt-Colonel Broad at COHQ at the behest of Hilton Jones in March, 1944. It was based on the writer's experience with No 9 Commando in Italy and, besides recommending that a proportion of the Troop be allowed to attend OCTU, and that the skill of those not commissioned should be recognized by the appropriate non-commissioned rank, he summed up how the Troop could best be used in battlefield conditions:

a) Interrogation and Identification
Experience shows that because 3 Troop personnel speak the German

language perfectly (i.e. both colloquially and in dialect) prisoners enjoy talking to them. Consequently much information is forthcoming which is unlikely to be disclosed through ordinary interrogation methods.

b) Treatment and Exploitation of Prisoners
If tactical information required urgently is to be received in time it is essential that the interrogating personnel should be right forward. This is necessary not only to obtain the information but also to ensure proper treatment and search of prisoners from the moment of capture. In this connection, with 3 Troop personnel right forward, it was found possible in Italy to use prisoners as guides walking ahead, thus avoiding minefields, to make them assist in the evacuation of wounded, and to help in carrying equipment.

c) Interpretation of Captured Documents
The following examples indicate some of the uses that can be made of a trained interpretation of captured documents.

In Italy, on one occasion, a sketch of minefields and defensive positions, expressed in tactical signs, was found in the tunic of a captured NCO. The sketch was immediately interpreted by a 3 Troop man and life undoubtedly saved.

Similarly, in raids on HQs 3 Troop personnel know what to look for.

d) Patrols
An important offensive function for which 3 Troop is specially trained is to operate with fighting patrols, as specialized recce troops with particular reference to: roadsigns, vehicle markings, military abbreviations on sign-posts, and enemy weapons.

In conclusion it is submitted that acceptance of the proposal to raise the status of No 3 Troop as well as their employment as indicated above will contribute considerably to the success of future Commando raids.[1]

In due course this submission – and doubtless others like it – had its effect and at the end of April eleven members of the Troop were interviewed for OCTU and seven were accepted, six for the shortened course and one for the normal one. Then early the following month two men were promoted to sergeant, three to lance-sergeant, three to corporal and seven to lance-corporal.

The War Diary for the Inter-Allied Commando records that altogether one officer and forty-three other ranks of No 3 Troop were deployed on D-Day – the balance of the entire Troop then stationed at Littlehampton, less those in Italy and those at OCTU – though there is no record of which Commando each man was attached to. Hilton Jones, now 2 i/c under the new Commanding

Officer, Lt-Colonel Peter Laycock, was the one officer and he was attached to the HQ of No 1 SS Brigade. With the exception of the No 6 Commando detachment, each Commando detachment consisted of four or five men commanded by a sergeant or lance-sergeant, with corporals as their seconds-in-command. In the case of No 6 Commando the detachment was commanded by Nichols, who was a corporal, with Masters, a lance-corporal, as his second-in-command. When the detachment complained that this wasn't fair, they were told that No 6 Commando was a bullshit unit and that they'd get "busted" anyway, though in fact rather the opposite occurred. Some detachments were divided amongst the Troops of a Commando, while others were kept as a pool with Commando HQ and then assigned special tasks.

Altogether seven Commandos landed on 6 June, with 46 (RM) Commando landing the following day. These were organized into two Special Service Brigades: No 1 commanded by Brigadier the Lord Lovat and No 4 commanded by Brigadier Leicester, Royal Marines, and the Headquarters of both these Brigades had members of No 3 Troop attached to them.

The task for No 1 SS Brigade, which consisted of Nos 3, 4, and 6 Army Commandos and 45 (RM) Commando, was to land at Ouistreham, the extreme left flank of the invasion forces, and for Nos 3, 6, and 45 Commandos to push inland to link up with the 6th Airborne Division, whose task was to seize the bridges over the Orne canal and river, while No 4 Commando cleared the town before joining the rest of the Brigade. The Brigade was then to hold the high ground in the area of Hauger, Le Plein and Amfréville, and so help hold the vital bridges over the Orne canal and river and at the same time safeguard the invasion force's left flank. It was also given the task of capturing Franceville Plage and to "infest" the coastal area eastwards towards Cabourg.[2]

No 4 SS brigade was to land farther to the east with Nos 41 (RM) and 48 (RM) Commandos being given the task of destroying the coastal defences situated around Lion-sur-Mer and St Aubin while No 47 (RM) Commando, operating by itself, captured Port-en-Bessin. No 46 (RM) Commando was scheduled to storm a coastal battery situated to the east of the Orne, but when this was put out of action by the RAF they landed the following day behind No 48 (RM) Commando to take a strongpoint at Petit Enfer.

The task assigned to those in No 3 Troop was a formidable one, for though they had now been given far wider briefs than being interpreters they still had to persuade the officers they were to work with that they indeed possessed the wide range of talents claimed for them. The advice Hilton Jones gave them was brisk and to the point. "Make yourselves useful. If a CO won't use you, keep nagging until he does."

As interrogators and decoys, and experts on German units and the arms they used, 3-Troopers were to become invaluable members of the Commando units, but no one was to know that before D-Day. It seems that the Royal

Marine Commandos, being new units, regarded the newcomers as seasoned soldiers and welcomed them for this reason. The army Commandos, on the other hand, had already done a lot of fighting and as veterans they sometimes viewed the strangers in their midst with some scepticism. If this is true, then their scepticism was soon dispelled, but equally every member of No 3 Troop had a lot to learn in action. Most, happily, learnt fast and survived, but some had little or no chance to do so. Franklin, Webster, and Laddy – one of the Troop's medical orderlies – died on the beaches or before they even reached them, while others were soon killed or wounded in the fierce fighting to keep the Orne bridgehead intact. The detachment with No 4 Commando, for instance, was wiped out, with Howarth, its sergeant, being wounded on the beach, Graham killed on 13 June, Sayers – a Hungarian who had served with the French army before the war – wounded in the arm and chest on 14 June while attached to Kieffer's two French Troops, and Thompson captured on the night of 19/20 June.

On the extreme left flank, after crossing the Orne, No 45 Commando had the unenviable assignment of capturing the powerful Merville battery and clearing the village of Franceville Plage. It had a brush with the enemy on D-Day as it made towards its objective but it was not until the following afternoon, when the Commando launched its attack on Franceville Plage, that the determination with which the Germans were fighting became really apparent. The attack was checked, so Arlen, one of No 3 Troop detachment with the Commando, walked out of the unit's positions with a white flag and told the Germans to surrender as the Commando had three divisions behind it and it was useless to fight on. "The only answer to this was a heavy burst of machine-gun fire followed by even heavier mortar fire."[3] Arlen, a prizefighter in civilian life, who had vowed to win the VC, was infuriated that he should be shot at while carrying a white flag. He went back to his position, collected his tommy gun, and rushed forward to assault the machine-gun position that had fired at him and was immediately killed.[4]

Another member of No 3 Troop with the Commando was Hepworth. He, too, was used to try and get the Germans at Merville to surrender, but without success, and Lieutenant J. E. Day remembers taking him on patrols whenever it was likely that they would come across wounded Germans, or had been detailed to take prisoners.[5]

Lance-Corporal Saunders was another early casualty of No 45 Commando's 3 Troop detachment; on 7 June he was hit in the leg by a piece of shrapnel from a grenade. By now the wounded on both sides were beginning to mount and when at 1015 two German ambulances accidentally drove into the Commando's lines at Merville it seemed an ideal opportunity to evacuate the more seriously injured. Eight Commandos and one badly wounded German were loaded into the ambulances which were put in Saunders' charge in an effort to get them back to the Brigade's lines at Le Plein. Unfortunately, they were captured by the Germans soon after leaving Merville, though Saunders himself managed to escape back to his unit the following day. It must have been a highly dangerous situation for him but he had foreseen that he might be captured and had told the German driver to do and say exactly as he was told because the British were winning the war and he would die if he didn't. Luckily this bluff worked and the driver did not reveal that Saunders spoke German, but his luck did not hold for two days later he was again captured while leading a patrol behind the German lines and, after a fruitless attempt to try and escape from the train which was taking him to Paris, spent the rest of the war in a prisoner-of-war camp near Zagan not far from the River Oder.*[6]

The same day as Saunders was captured with the ambulances his Commando was cut off from the main British positions and several German attacks were mounted on Merville. One small group worked their way into the village from the east but these "were effectively dispersed by Sergeant Stewart and Corporal Shelley, both of 3 Troop, 10 (Inter-Allied) Commando, who put in some rather skilful grenade work in doing so."[7] According to another member of 3 Troop what they did was rather more than that. Some of the Commando were trapped in the farmyard into which the Germans were lobbing hand grenades. Shelley and Stewart reckoned that if the Germans could lob them in then they could lob them out, but no one seemed very keen to try this. So Shelley and Stewart went round gathering everyone's grenades in a large camouflage scarf. Then, whenever they saw a grenade coming in they threw one out in the same direction. This seemed to have the desired effect so they then took a bren gun to one of the entrances, stuck it out, and without exposing themselves sprayed the surrounding area to keep the Germans at bay, and under this covering fire the others managed to extricate themselves. That evening the Commando withdrew from the village through the German positions and safely reached the Brigade lines near Hauger later that night. Soon after this action both Shelley and Stewart were given immediate field commissions in the Royal Marines.

No 6 Commando landed with Brigade HQ at 0840 and immediately struck inland towards the bridges that had been seized at dawn by the Airborne Division. The Commanding Officer of No 6, Lt-Colonel Mills-Roberts, had

---

* Near the end of the war, when the Russians were drawing close to the Oder, the prisoners in the camp were moved and Saunders took his opportunity to escape. He rolled down an embankment with another soldier and made his way to the Oder. He managed to swim across but his companion was drowned. After shooting at him and missing, the Russians took him in and employed him to drive some Russian officers around in a horse-drawn cart. He was then put in a Russian camp on the Oder where the occupants were persuaded to help the Russian army build a bridge over the river. Saunders decided he would have no part in this slave labour and escaped yet again, and walked and hitchhiked and jumped trains eastwards with another companion until he eventually reached Odessa. In the harbour he found a British ship and persuaded the captain to take him back to England.

split up the No 3 Troop detachment among the various Troops, though he kept Nichols with him. Masters was attached to the bicycle Troop commanded by Captain Robinson. "The most irritating thing about the D-Day accounts, to me, was the fact that we were meant to have stormed up the beach. That was the last thing we did. Nobody stormed. I went down after the first man, holding my bicycle, and waded in knee-deep. There were a couple of tanks which had been knocked out and were smouldering, and there were also two soldiers digging in in the water. I have never been able to fathom what they were doing. I can only imagine they were trying to dig something up – unlikely – or they had started digging in in the sand and the water had come in. There were also a few bodies around but it was nowhere near as bad as Lovat had led us to expect. Lovat was landing on our right and with him was the Skipper. I caught his eye and for some reason I saluted him! He just nodded. There were meant to be flags showing where there were gaps through the mines but there were no signs of these, though someone said later that he saw some floating in the water. We had what was called a very good beach. The people before us got cut up and those behind us had an artillery barrage put down on them, but we were OK. Mind you, if you were hit it was a bad beach whatever else it might seem to anyone else."[8]

As the Commando moved inland the first bewildered and shell-shocked prisoners began to appear, and Lovat told Masters to try and find out from one of them the position of the German artillery. The interrogation was not a success as the German Masters chose turned out to be a Pole who knew no German at all. Masters then remembered that French was taught in Polish schools and launched into that language, but with equal lack of success, firstly because the Pole obviously knew nothing and secondly because "his Lordship, it turned out, spoke much better French than I. I caught a phrase here and there of their animated conversation before pushing on towards Colleville sur Mer."[9]

Drew, working alongside Masters, did not have much better luck with his first interrogation either. "I had to interrogate two German prisoners we'd taken soon after landing. I thought I'd show what a liar Goebbels was in distorting the news of the war and not telling them what was really going on. 'Do you realize,' I said to them, 'that the Allies are just ten miles from Rome?' They looked at me in surprise, and then one of them said that I was out of date for they had just heard on the radio that Rome had fallen!"[10]

Robinson's bicycle Troop now started its dash inland to link up with the Airborne Division. As it approached the high ground before the bridge someone was shot by a machine gun and fell off. Robinson told his men to dismount and leave the bikes by the road, and to climb the knoll that overlooked Bénouville. Robinson looked around him and then told Masters to go down to the village and see what was happening.

"Well, it was rather obvious what was happening. They were shooting at us. But Robinson obviously hadn't seen from what angle the machine gun had been firing and he needed to know this. I asked him how many men I should take with me, and he said none. That was fine by me, we'd been trained in just this kind of work. I told him I'd go round the left flank, reconnoitre the village and come back from the right flank, which is what we had been taught to do. 'No, no,' said Robinson. 'I just want you to walk down that road and see what's going on.'

"It was now quite clear to me that what he wanted was for me to be shot at by the machine gun so he could see where it was positioned. It was a bad moment for me, and I began to think feverishly. I knew he had to know, but that didn't help me. We'd been trained to try and figure an angle, to improve the odds. I remembered an old Cary Grant film, set in the Khyber Pass or somewhere. He had walked straight into a rebel stronghold alone because he'd had no alternative and had said, 'You're all under arrest', which I'd always thought a very funny line indeed. So I decided to do the same, so I walked down the centre of the road where everyone in the village could see me and began shouting in German, 'All right, everybody out with your hands on heads. It's no use fighting, you're totally surrounded. For you the war is over. Come on, give yourselves up.'

"No one came out, of course. On the other hand no one shot me either. Below me was a parapet wall. On the left was a 10-foot hedge, quite impenetrable. There was no ditch but a grass border a few feet wide, no place to hide at all. I guess they didn't shoot because they were curious to see what else would show. They knew they could always shoot me when they wanted to, and this is eventually what they decided to do. A man popped up from behind the parapet and shot at me with a Schmeisser. He missed, because he fired too quickly and perhaps because he was a bad shot anyway. I didn't see where the bullets went but assumed they went right high because that's how a Schmeisser fires. Then he ducked back and as he ducked I went down on one knee and fired. My tommy gun fired one round and then jammed, because the 30-round magazine had caused a double feed,* though I didn't know it at the time of course.

"I couldn't look because my eyes were glued to where the man had been. I cleared the gun quickly, but when he popped up again and missed me again, it jammed without firing. By this time I was lying down in the grass by the verge, and I forced myself to look and see what had gone wrong and saw that two rounds were crumpled in the breech. I cleared them and thought that this time

* The tommy gun magazine normally held 20 rounds, but a 30-round magazine had been brought in for D-Day to give the weapon extra fire power. The idea didn't work as the spring became too compressed and caused double-feeding. Worse, the magazine became too heavy for the catch so that it often fell off. Harry Drew, another 3 Troop member with No 6 Commando, remembers landing and running up the beach only to find that he had no magazine on his tommy gun.

I had to get him otherwise he was bound to get me. But then I heard a noise behind me and saw the rest of the Troop charging down the road with fixed bayonets. One of them was firing a bren from the shoulder – most unusual – and it was he who shot the machine gunners who had retreated a little way down the Ouistreham road. Then some of our tanks turned up and put some shells into the village and we were able to move across the bridge."[11]

Farther to the west the No 3 Troop detachments with the Commandos of No 4 SS Brigade were also early into action and some suffered severely. Those with No 41 (RM) Commando, for example, were all wounded or killed within days of landing. Both O'Neill and Swinton had to be evacuated, and did not return. Latimer had a minor injury but it went septic and he, too, had to be evacuated, though he returned later, while Gray was hit five times on D-Day, but not sufficiently seriously for him to be evacuated.

"For D-Day I was attached to No 41 Commando. I was disgusted with their level of training. The others from No 3 Troop in the same camp often met to compare notes. Moody, for example, came to chat quite often. He was with No 4 Brigade HQ. He was a very brilliant, amusing sort of guy, but he was very depressed at the level of training. I was with the CO during the landings. The troops were allowed to drink much too much on the boats going over. They were much too slow, and they were what Montgomery had warned us about, 'beach happy'. We couldn't get the buggers off the beaches. We lost a lot of people that day. Yet by Walcheren it was one of the best – if not the best – unit in the British army.

"When we landed I found a group of German prisoners and I got them to show me the path through the minefield, so I was able to get to the forming-up point. Only a few others appeared, it seemed, though Latimer was there, but eventually one officer managed to get his Troop through and we went towards Lion-sur-Mer. I remember we heard a gun – it sounded like an anti-tank gun – go off in the same house we were in. We didn't have any anti-tank guns so we thought it must have been a German. But the gun seemed to be firing at the strongpoint. So after it had fired several times we went very quietly – I was wearing gym shoes, I refused to wear army boots – to investigate. On the second floor we found an Arab firing an old muzzle-loader at the Germans. He spoke no English and hardly any French. He became a mascot and stayed with us until the winter when he was wounded.

"After we'd taken our objectives we were sent to contain the radar station at Douvres, a strongly fortified position surrounded by a minefield. We tried to penetrate it with patrols at night. I was sure if I could get a 15-man patrol into the strongpoint I could take it, or at least half of it because it was split into two. So I took in the patrol but I came across two *Schuhminen* which had not been there the night before. I marked one with a handkerchief and held my hand over the other, but someone stepped on the one I had marked with the handkerchief and that exploded another. That was the end of trying to penetrate the defences, so next we tried sending a petard tank in. I marked out the route for it and put a big white T with tape in front of an anti-tank ditch so that it wouldn't fall in it. But after firing a few times the tank moved position and fell straight into the ditch. This was when Latimer was injured. He was in a diversionary attack on the other side of the strongpoint when he came on this German. He didn't want to make any noise so he hit him over the head with his pistol and injured his finger. After some days it was decided to make a full-scale attack on the strongpoint. Flail tanks made a passage through the minefields and we went in in broad daylight, but there was no sign of any Germans. They were all underground. Latimer found a periscope so he kicked it in and threw a phosphorus grenade down it. In no time at all the doors opened and out they came."[12]

The War Diary for 41 Commando noted the bravery of both O'Neill and Gray during these early days. "Patrols were out nightly to the radar station," it noted on 11 June. "CSM O'Neill was particularly valuable in this work", and when on the night of 13 June the radar station was attacked, it recorded that "CSM O'Neill and party commence blowing gap: this was successfully completed and at 0200 the AVREs had moved up." And on 1 July, by which time the Commando was at Sallenelles, the War Diary records what was to become a normal No 3 Troop method of working: "On afternoon of July 1st as a result of exchange of fire between a patrol and the enemy FDLs Cpl. F. Gray (10 IA Cdo) became detached from patrol. As he had not returned at dusk a search party was sent out to locate him, without success. Cpl. Gray returned early in the morning of 2 July, uninjured, having lain up close to the enemy and having gained much useful information."

Further still to the east No 47 (RM) Commando had an equally tough time in fulfilling its task of taking Port-en-Bessin, the small town on the border between the British and American beaches. The Commando was heavily shelled as it approached the beaches and several of the landing craft were hit. By the time many of the men struggled ashore, in the wrong place, they were without either their arms or vital supplies.

Again, the No 3 Troop detachment was to suffer heavy casualties: Corporal Webster was drowned after his LCA had been hit; Fuller, the Viennese-born sergeant in charge of the detachment, was killed on 16 June; and Lance-Corporal Terry and Private Andrews were both wounded during the first hours after landing. They were evacuated but both returned to their unit at the end of June. Terry was again wounded, this time seriously, on 23 July, and Andrews was killed on 17 August. Only the Danish-born Davies, Mentioned in Despatches for his work during the Tarbrush raids, remained unscathed.

Going ashore Terry was in the same landing craft as his sergeant. "Fuller was quite extraordinary. He was the closest to the John Wayne-type hero I ever met. He and I were good friends, partly because he, too, was Viennese and we often were amused by the accents and expressions used by the Germans in No 3 Troop, who were in the majority. He looked not unlike John Wayne and was oblivious of fear. Once, near Eastbourne, we saw a parachute wash ashore on the beach. There was barbed wire and notices saying the beach was mined. Fuller (we called him Didi for some reason) decided to get it in order to sell it as fabric in London. He just ran across the beach, grabbed the 'chute and dragged it back.

"During the landing he sat at the stern facing the rest of us. When, after about ten minutes all hell broke loose, with enemy mortar and rocket fire as well as the heavy stuff from the battery at Le Hamel, most of us just sat there, crammed tight, being seasick and scared out of our wits. But Fuller stood up, grinning as usual, exhorting us with cries of 'This is fantastic, just how it should be. Enjoy it boys', and cracking jokes, and generally trying to keep our spirits up."[13]

Soon after landing it seems that Fuller, realizing the Commando was desperately short of weapons, persuaded the Germans in one strongpoint to surrender so that their guns could be used against their own side. He was, as another member of 3 Troop said with affection, a second-hand car dealer who would sell you anything, and on this occasion used his powers of persuasion to great effect.[14]

What remained of the Commando was now gathered together and the move westwards began. Terry took a small party into La Rosière and there accepted the surrender of about twenty of the enemy who were awaiting him with their hands in the air. They turned out to be Poles, and were only too eager to help, and two ended up carrying some of the Troop's bangalore torpedoes.

In the afternoon someone spotted a German riding a bicycle along a road and Terry and Fuller were called to investigate. "I waited hidden in a ditch beside the road. He was riding quite slowly with his heels on the pedals so that his toes pointed outwards. He appeared to be an officer and evidently felt quite safe: he was after all several miles from the beachhead and the road seemed quiet. Just as he passed me, I jumped from my cover, pointed my tommy gun at him and called, 'Halt! Hände hoch!'

"For an instant I felt very silly. The man calmly dismounted, carefully placed his bike on the ground, then raised his hands and said, '*Ich bin Regimentsstabsfeldwebel. Ich habe nach den Gesetzen der Genfer Convention behandelt zu werden.*'*

"My first reaction was one of pride: I had been told at the German Army Intelligence Course in England that this was a very rarely used rank in the Wehrmacht and that we were unlikely to come across it. It appeared that this

---

* I am a Regimental Sergeant Major. I have to be treated according to the rules of the Geneva Convention.

man had been on the Russian Front, where he had suffered from frostbite and had obtained a medical discharge. Earlier that year, when things began to go really badly for the Germans, he was called up again for light occupation duties in France. He was put in charge of a camp for Spanish Republican refugees who had entered France across the Pyrenees after Franco's victory. That morning he had been woken early by one of the guards who had seen the Allied invasion fleet on the horizon. Seeing literally thousands of ships from the edge of the camp, he decided that he had had enough of war and had told the guards either to surrender or to make their way inland. He himself was now on the way to his favourite brothel in Ouistreham, after which he intended to give himself up to the first Allied troops in order to spend the rest of the war in the safety of a prisoner-of-war camp. He had heard that German prisoners were sent to Canada, where he wanted to settle after the war.

"He was indeed some character, and we took him along as he knew the local terrain. Fuller, of course, asked him for the address of the brothel, which he noted in the back of his paybook."[15]

In the evening the Commando occupied a small feature behind Port-en-Bessin, known as Point 72, where the following morning they were joined by the stragglers which included the Commanding Officer, Lt-Colonel Phillips.

"Several Poles from the German garrison appeared and asked to surrender. We sent a German Medical Captain, whom we had captured on Point 72, into the town with a note which I had composed in German, telling the Garrison Commander that he was surrounded on all sides and ordered all Germans to march along the road towards our hill before 3pm, carrying white flags."

In the meantime the mayor of Commes appeared and said that an injured British Spitfire pilot was hidden in the village, so Terry set out with a small party to pick him up. "Under the guidance of the mayor of the village he and his party reached the village taking several prisoners on the way. Being the first troops to enter Commes, they were given a hearty welcome by the inhabitants, and in the midst of the celebrations shots were fired from the windows of La Bauquèrie. Under small arms fire Corporal Terry ran up the street and entered the house, shouting in German, and after some minutes he emerged from the house with four prisoners."[16]

In the event the pilot requested that he stay where he was and on the way back the small party came under heavy sniper fire and one of the party was killed.

"We left him there while we tried to evade the constant sniper fire and made our way back to Point 72. The place had changed since we had left it earlier: a German parachute unit was attacking the position from the rear and we were under heavy fire. I was told that Fuller had been taken prisoner and Colonel Phillips had given the order to evacuate the position. It was every man for himself and Corporal Thornton and I decided to return to La Rosière. After a while we were overtaken by several men from our Commando who had been forced to abandon their position at the foot of Point 72. We were again being sniped at, but were unable to determine where the shots came from. I got shot in the left thigh, luckily only a graze. It was professionally bandaged by Thornton and we continued on our way.

"Meanwhile, our Commando had regrouped and, although it had been forced to abandon Point 72, had begun its attack on Port-en-Bessin, aided by a heavy naval bombardment. We were now alone, about ten of us. One of the Marines who had taken a Lewis gun from a wrecked naval vessel on the beaches set it up and fired at one of the strongpoints above the town."

Soon afterwards the small party ran into a German ambush and attempted to make their way separately back to the port to rejoin the rest of the Commando. By now Terry was beginning to feel the effect of his wound and took refuge for the night with a French family who next morning took him in a horse-drawn cart into the town which had now been captured by the Commando. On the way they encountered some German naval personnel who wished to surrender and they followed them on foot. "As we entered the town, I was greeted with some hilarity by the battleworn Commandos. Among them was Fuller, who had been able to escape from a Troop of German parachutists."[17]

Fuller, in fact, had spent the previous 24 hours in and out of the enemy's hands, for he had escaped after his first capture down the road to Port-en-Bessin. However, he had then run into a Troop of German bicyclists who had taken him prisoner. They took him to a château, where they had found his cosh* tucked into his gaiters and had proceeded to hit him on the arms with it, though not too hard, saying that coshes were forbidden under the Geneva Convention. Fuller was then put into a cellar alone and was left to worry about being tried as a Commando with an illegal weapon. Somehow, during the confusion that followed, he escaped and rejoined the Commando. When he saw Terry he told him to dispose of his cosh at once, which Terry did.[18]

At first Terry refused to be evacuated but the next day, while with his Troop Commander, Captain Walton, he collapsed and was taken by jeep to the beachhead. There he remembers seeing the Regimental Sergeant Major he had captured on D-Day, who was full of complaints about the lack of food and sanitary facilities. On his arrival back in England he took the train to where his parents lived.

"When I stepped off the train, I had a week's growth of beard and was filthy, having not having taken off my clothes for six days. My left trouser leg had been cut off by Corporal Thornton when I had been hit by the sniper and the thigh was bandaged. I was carrying a pair of German Zeiss binoculars with the German eagle engraved on them, and I also had various other morbid souvenirs

---

* The coshes used by some members of 3 Troop were in fact the straps that hung from the roofs of the London underground trains.

of the past few days. When I realized that I had been on the beachhead the day before, I could not help reflecting on how close the war was to home. I saw my parents run towards me and strangers at the station came to pat me on my shoulder and ask questions. I had difficulty in holding back my tears and suddenly felt not like the returning hero, but like a small child running into the arms of Mummy and Daddy. It was two weeks before my twentieth birthday."[19]

2

As will already have been gathered from the fierce fighting in which Kieffer's men were involved, the first weeks following the landings were critical for the Allied armies, with the positions of 6th Airborne Division, which had No 1 SS Brigade under its command on the left flank, being constantly under attack. On 12 June No 4 SS Brigade, less No 47 Commando which had temporarily returned to England for re-equipment and reorganization, came under command of 6th Airborne Division as well and moved into the vital Orne bridgehead. It took up positions around Sallenelles, and from then until the breakout from the bridgehead by the red and green berets on 18 August the war was a static one in which both sides probed with patrols and sorties into no-man's-land. It was just the kind of fighting for which the men from 3 Troop had been trained. Though they were allotted to different Commandos they would often go out on patrols together and would also meet at the church in Amfréville,* to exchange notes and ideas.

After five days of heavy fighting the German attacks began to falter, and on the night of 11/12 June Hilton Jones, on orders from 6th Airborne Division, took a reconnaissance patrol of No 3 Troop personnel to Bréville to investigate the strength and dispositions of the enemy prior to an attack on the village the following day.[20] On this occasion Hilton Jones returned safely to report that Bréville was still occupied by the enemy in at least company strength, but three nights later he was not so lucky. With him on this second patrol were Nichols, Stewart, Shelley, Drew and Masters, as well as three civilians from the French underground who were to be passed through the German lines to Varaville – though at that time Bréville had not even been taken.

Masters was rather shocked by the appearance and behaviour of the Frenchmen. "They had absolutely no experience of patrolling at night. One wore a light blue smock you could see for miles, while another wore a white shirt. We just took them as they were. As soon as we were beyond our forward

---

* It was here that one of the residents of the church, Masters, light-heartedly now claims to have invented the wine and cheese party. The wine had been taken from a captured German half-track and the cheese came from the hoard of camembert Masters had acquired as presents for his friends and family when rumours circulated that the Commandos were to be withdrawn to England. The rumours kept proving to be unfounded and the cheeses became riper and riper until in the end Masters invited some of his friends to eat it while it was still edible.

138

positions, the Skipper leading, they wanted to crawl which showed us they knew nothing about it. I said that we only crawled when it was necessary and they asked how we knew when it was necessary. I was rather taken aback by that question. It was a hard one to answer. It just came from experience and if you were wrong then you didn't live long. We listened like crazy, we moved so that we could hear while we moved, we didn't bunch, and so on. When we told the Frenchmen to go down, they went down all right, but then they wouldn't get up again.

"Three times that night we heard the Germans. They were digging. That made sense to us as up to that time they'd been strung out very loosely with gaps in their lines. We had been hoping to pass through one of those gaps. We tried to skirt them but each time we heard them again. They were obviously making a solid line which would make it virtually impossible to get through, especially with a large number of men. So the Skipper decided to split us. He, Stewart, Shelley and the older Frenchman went to the right, and the rest of us went to the left. After we'd moved off to the left we heard a lot of shooting where the others had gone. We moved on through a fence which took forever as the Frenchmen kept falling asleep on us. Finally, when we heard the Germans ahead of us one more time, the Frenchmen indicated they wanted to talk. This wasn't easy but by lying down and cupping our mouths and ears together we managed it. Via me, because I speak French, they said they couldn't go on. We said that was OK, we'd go back and try again the following night, but they said they couldn't go back either, and that their plan was to lie up until broad daylight and then walk into the German lines and tell the Germans that they wanted to be with them because they felt safer and the Allies had no food. They had done this before, they said, and it had worked.

"So we left them there and returned to our own lines.* This could be hazardous, especially with the French who sometimes muddled the password, so we sang songs loudly and made sure they knew who we were. We'd only gone about a mile or a mile and a half before we turned back. We learnt later what had happened to the other group. The Skipper approached a hedgerow shaped like a T. Then the Germans must have heard something or someone – the Frenchman probably. Anyway, they let the patrol come close and then opened up with a machine gun. The Skipper was hit and fell, and the others dispersed to the right and left as we'd been taught to. Then the Skipper shouted out in German that he was a British officer and that he was seriously wounded and would the Germans come out and get him.

"Each person on that patrol thought he was the only survivor. They all tried to converge to the rear as we'd also been trained to do, but it didn't work. So they each got back on their own. Shelley and Stewart made it, but the

---

* According to the narrative of the part taken by No 1 SS Brigade in Operation Overlord the two men did get through the lines.

Frenchman came back through the French lines. He was challenged but he couldn't remember the password so they shot him.

"The Germans left the Skipper until morning, and then fetched him, not an unreasonable thing to do under the circumstances. Apparently, he was very nearly dead when they found him and a British POW was told to dig a grave for him. However, he pulled through and they transferred him to a hospital at Pont-L'Évêque where, by sheer chance, there was a German surgeon who specialized in the stomach which is where the Skipper had been hit. He saved the Skipper's life and became quite friendly. When the 6th Airborne Division was advancing towards the town he told the Skipper that we were bound to take the place, and that if he cared to risk the bombardment he'd say the Skipper was too ill to be moved. Naturally, the Skipper opted to do this and in due course he was found by us."[21]

When Hilton Jones was captured Stewart took command of the Troop until the arrival of James Griffith at the beginning of July. Griffith, a quietly spoken, highly intelligent man, was, by common consensus, one of the most outstanding members of No 3 Troop. Born the son of a German doctor called Glaser who had fought on the side of the Republicans in the Spanish Civil War, Griffith had been a medical student pre-war and had picked up sufficient medical knowledge to become one of the Troop's medical orderlies. When, belatedly, it had been acknowledged that a proportion of 3-Troopers should be commissioned he was one of six to be accepted for a shortened OCTU course.

From No 1 SS Brigade's point of view an even bigger disaster had occurred two day's previously when the Brigadier, Lord Lovat, had been severely wounded and had had to be evacuated.

"No 6 Commando was to take Bréville, but word come down that an airborne unit, I think the First Canadian Parachute Battalion, were better rested and would do it instead. My friend Gerald Nichols had done a reconnaissance patrol up to the crossroads outside the village the night before, and had seen no sign of enemy armour. So Gerald said to me, 'Let's go out and watch the attack get under way.' I replied that I was not sure that that was a smart thing to do. 'That fellow Dunlop was killed yesterday, when a gun fired short during the preliminary artillery bombardment. How do we know something like that won't happen again?' 'Look,' Nichols said, as we came out of Monsieur Saulnier's farm to the little triangular green. 'Who is standing over there? The Brigadier. Now don't you suppose he knows all about that gun firing short? He wouldn't be standing around if he hadn't taken care of it.' 'You have a point,' I conceded. 'Let's watch.'

"The airborne soldiers were moving up the road past the farm and the cemetery. We stood on the patch of grass a few feet from Lord Lovat. It was then that the artillery opened up. Shells exploded all around us, and the brigadier was hit – killed, I thought. It was not immediately clear whether it was the Germans firing at the most likely forming-up area, or yesterday's deliquent 25-pounder. We rushed towards cover in the sturdy Saulnier farm, but in the archway entrance the adjutant, Captain Powell, called out, 'We need wire-cutters, quick!' 'I'll get mine from the barn, sir,' I said, and at that moment two shells hit the barn, one on the reverse slope of the roof, and the other high up on the thick stone wall, collapsing it, surprisingly, precisely on to my kit. It took hours to dig out later, removing Norman boulder stones.

"The barn did not look attractive as a shelter then, and I ran across the courtyard to dive into a shed opposite. As I opened the door a gaggle of noisy geese, panicked by the shelling, emerged, like white bats out of hell. Hell seemed to be let loose all around. All this had taken only a few seconds, and suddenly Nichols made a wild dash out through the archway to where the brigadier was lying, motionless, and bleeding from abdominal wounds. He picked him up and, staggering under the weight of the big man slung over his shoulder, re-entered the yard. Shells were still bursting all around, and it seemed a foolhardy sortie, at best, to bring in a dead officer. Two of us ran to help him, for he looked as if he were about to fall. He put Lord Lovat down and shouted, 'Where's the MO?' The Medical Officer was taking prudent shelter diagonally across the long yard, under the huge cider barrels, I believe. Nichols ran across, darting past the captured Sdkfz 251* [half-track] and the people taking cover under it. Cover was hard to come by; every available space was crowded. Someone said, 'Don't get the MO out, we'll need him later!' But Nichols found him, and I saw him pull him by the hand back across the yard.

"We kidded Nichols† about it later. 'What some people won't do for promotion! I suppose you realized somehow that he was still alive, and saw your opportunity!' But it was a fine thing that he did."[22]

The No 3 Troop detachment was hard hit during these early days, for, on 13 June, the day before it lost its Troop Commander, it lost three of its best men. Two, Moody and Norton, were killed by a shell while on patrol with Envers and Broadman, the latter being wounded by the same round. The third man, Fuller, was, like Lovat, not hit by the enemy but by Allied fire.

There is no written documentation of this incident, but many surviving members of the Troop remember more or less what happened. "There was an 88mm well dug in on the eastern flank which was continuing to fire on the beaches. It caused a lot of trouble and in the end 47 (RM) Commando decided to call in American Mitchell bombers to destroy it. Fuller volunteered to go into a farm which was in the swamp and stay there during the day and direct the

---

* This large vehicle had been ambushed by Shelley and Stewart a few days previously when Shelley had put a phosphorus grenade down its air intake. When the crew had opened the turret to exit quickly he had lobbed in a 36 grenade with devastating effect.
† Not long afterwards Nichols was wounded in the face while on patrol. As he was carried back, he was told by the new brigadier, Mills-Roberts, that he intended making sure he got an immediate field commission, and he did.

bombers by radio onto the target. One of the bombs fell short and killed him."[23]

Two other totally fearless members of the Troop were Lawrence and Spencer who had both been placed with No 3 Commando, commanded by Lt-Colonel Peter Young. Spencer, a butcher by trade, survived his frequent incursions into enemy lines in search of a prisoner – Turner, also with No 3 Commando, went on one or two of these raids with Spencer and recalls his bravery with astonishment – but Lawrence did not.

Ernest Lawrence came from Darmstadt of a middle-class Jewish family. He was, like most of his comrades in No 3 Troop, very well educated and he soon came to mistrust – as did his friend Sergeant Ken Bartlett, who commanded the No 3 Commando detachment – the training standards and patrolling abilities of many of the Commando officers with whom they were working. In his book *Storm from the Sea* Young describes one of the raids Lawrence took part in with one of Young's officers, but Lawrence preferred going out without an officer if he could. As they had no idea which Germans were facing them, several attempts were made to take a prisoner, but without success. On the night of 22/23 June Lawrence went out to try and find a dead German and take his paybook. He said if he couldn't find a dead one he would kill one. About 30 minutes after he had left No 3 Commando lines, Bartlett heard some shooting and voices from the direction in which he had gone, and Lawrence was never seen again. To prevent further needless casualties among his detachment, Bartlett tried a different approach.

"Since we still had made no headway with identifying the Germans opposite us and had not made any prisoners for quite a while, I got permission to mount a couple of loudspeakers in the trees by our lines. I then started broadcasting to the Germans, giving them the latest news on the war, and, of course, told them to give up fighting and to quit, assuring them of good treatment if they decided to desert. By doing this we saved lives and soon had all the information we needed. The Germans shot madly in the direction of the loudspeakers, but the first batch of deserters arrived the following night. One of them told us that at the time of Lawrence's disappearance a British soldier had been captured and led away, and we assumed it was Lawrence."[24]

Lawrence, however, was never seen alive again. It could have been that his true identity was discovered, for he would then have been shot out of hand. But this seems unlikely as all members of No 3 Troop had been extensively briefed on how to behave if captured. It seems more likely that he was killed by Allied bombing or shelling as he was being transported to a prison camp.[25]

Another member of the Troop to be captured was Sergeant Thompson, in charge of the detachment attached to No 4 Commando. On the night of 19/20 June he accompanied Lieutenant Littlejohn on what must have been a typical patrol for those in No 3 Troop to undertake. It was suspected that the enemy were having supply difficulties so it was decided to try and pass the two men through the German's Gonneville-Longuemare line in the hope that they could observe a main crossroads at Varaville. They went out at about 1430 and crawled up and down in front of the enemy lines observing their positions along the Gonneville-Longuemare road in order to try and find the best place to penetrate the German defences. An attempt was made after dark to cross the road, but, finding it impossible, the two men lay up in a ditch all the next day, observed the enemy at a distance of about 50 yards, and then tried again that evening. However, as the two men tried to infiltrate between two enemy posts Littlejohn found himself facing the muzzle of a German rifle at point blank range. It had been agreed that if surprise was lost grenades would be thrown and the two men would make a separate dash for it, which is what Littlejohn did. But while running back to take cover he was shot in the leg, though Thompson managed to reach the shelter of a bomb crater in the open field. About an hour later a search party came out to look for them. Littlejohn pretended to be dead. A German shot at him from two yards' range but missed him, and then prodded him in the face with a bayonet. Miraculously, Littlejohn did not flinch so the Germans left in search of Thompson. Littlejohn knew they had found him because when they came back to strip him of his belongings he heard one of them say, "*Der eine ist gefangen; der andere ist tot.*"*[26] Thompson's true identity could never have been discovered by the Germans for at the end of the war he was released and returned to England.

By D+18, 24 June, the Germans attacking the bridgehead no longer held the initiative and the control of no-man's-land between the two sides was indisputably in the hands of the Commandos. In no-man's-land were three farm buildings called La Grande Ferme du Buisson where a cat-and-mouse game was played with the Germans. During the day it was held by the Commandos who used it as an observation post, but at night they moved out and it became occupied by the Germans who would leave messages in bad English for the Commandos scribbled on the walls. It was, according to Kieffer, a mysterious place which provided continual surprises – a half-eaten meal; a haversack with the owner's kit inside it; a map spread out on a table; and for six days a dead German stood sentinel in a doorway until the smell became so bad the Commandos buried him.[27] It was the jumping-off place for many of the Commandos' patrols and it was from here that it was decided that a fighting patrol of fourteen men from No 47 Commando should raid the enemy lines beyond Sallenelles on the night of 23 July, in preparation for the breakout from the bridgehead which was to come the following month. The orders for this raid came from General Dempsey who drove to Amfréville to brief those who had volunteered for it. The patrol was under the command of two officers but it was for Terry, who had returned to the unit at the beginning of the

* "The one is captured; the other is dead."

month, to lead it into the enemy's lines. The plan, when it was explained to Terry, seemed to him quite wrong. A few hours before the patrol was due to start, three Polish deserters walked into the Commandos' lines. They told Terry that mines had been freshly laid right by the route to be taken by the patrol, which increased Terry's sense of foreboding. However, the CO, Lt-Colonel Phillips, insisted that the patrol must go out.

"Because we would be up all night, the Colonel suggested we return to our respective slit trenches for a few hours' sleep. He told me to get a special non-censored letter form from the post corporal, on which I could write a note to my next of kin to be mailed in case I did not return safely.

"It was already dark when a marine called to me in the trench: a glass of rum, with the Colonel's compliments. I was now thoroughly depressed. At the command post we blackened our faces with camouflage cream, I handed my letter to my parents to the post corporal, and we set off down the hill to the Grande Ferme du Buisson. At midnight we moved off in single file, with me leading the way up to the T-junction in the hedges across the field where I had often been on patrol. We moved silently. At the T-junction, which we reached after about 15 minutes without incident, we had a short conference, as a result of which we split into two groups, with Lieutenant Collett leading six men along one side of the hedge leading to the German lines and myself with the rest moving parallel along the other. After some minutes there was a gap in the hedge and Collett's group came over to my side. He moved several paces ahead of me. Suddenly there was a flash in the darkness and an explosion. Collett had stepped on a mine. The rest of us threw ourselves down and for about a minute there was absolute quiet. Then Collett started screaming and seconds later all hell was let loose; tracer bullets seemed to be converging in our direction from all sides. I called to the men behind me to run for cover in the hedges and just then everything seemed alight: the Germans had sent up a flare. It was like bright daylight. Less than 30 yards in front of me was a concrete pillbox, with German soldiers running around shooting. I started running left towards the hedge, when I fell forward. All I felt was something wet trickling down my back. I remember calling out, 'I'm hit', and then began fighting for breath."[28]

When he came to after being hit by grenade splinters Terry tried to crawl back towards the Grande Ferme du Buisson, but was fired on by Canadian infantry on the left flank and was hit in the arm when about 200 yards from it. He fell into the hedge and then into the ditch that ran along it. He called for help and was eventually found by the Brigade Major and another No 3 Troop member, Harris.*

---

* Five out of fourteen of that patrol never returned, and Terry had to be evacuated again. When he arrived at a hospital in England the nurse asked how long it had been since his wounds had been dressed. It was not until they searched his belongings that they found it wasn't his wounds that smelt but the overripe Camembert cheese he'd brought back as a present to his father.

The casualties among the No 3 Troop detachments continued to mount during these weeks of patrolling and reconnaissance. On 19 August Andrews was killed by a mine when out beyond the Grande Ferme du Buisson; Gilbert was shot in the leg when he clashed with a German patrol among the farm buildings; and other casualties included Villiers – a brilliant soldier and an expert at picking locks – Drew, and Envers. One of the last to be wounded before the Normandy campaign ended was Harris who was still with No 46 Commando when the breakout towards Troarn started.

"During one night attack on a hill I was wounded by a grenade. After our second wave had passed through I began to stagger back down the hill and fell into a German slit trench – right on top of a German who was hiding there. I immediately grabbed him by the throat, and he said to me in German, 'Hans, is that you?' I told him it wasn't and he said he wasn't German and wanted to surrender. I could tell he meant it, because he practically carried me to our lines. I took him up to our HQ and handed him over. Before I left he said to me in German, 'You gave me my life, I want to give you my watch', and he insisted that I should have it, so I took it. The next day I was on my way back to the rear when I saw him in the road. He was dead."[29]

Out of the original detachment of forty-four men from No 3 Troop who fought in the Normandy campaign, twenty-seven were either killed, wounded or made prisoners of war.

9

The Dutch

Like the Yugoslavian and No 3 Troops, the Dutch never went into action as a unit. Yet the contribution of its members, in the Far East, at Arnhem, at Walcheren (described in the next chapter), and, lastly, behind the German lines in occupied Holland, was just as valuable as that of other members of the Inter-Allied Commando.

The fact that the Dutch fought as individuals, or in small sub-units, was caused, unlike the Hilton Jones' plans for No 3 Troop, entirely by the vagaries of war. Initially, as has been seen, they were earmarked for the Mediterranean, but Mountbatten must have intimated that he might require them in the Far East and they were therefore replaced by the Belgian Troop. Then followed months of frustration, for it was not until mid-December, 1943, that they eventually embarked for India. Captain Jan Linzel now replaced Mulders as Troop Commander, and, as several of the Troop did not wish to serve in the Far East, only three officers, ten senior NCOs, and 45 junior NCOs and other ranks sailed. They arrived a month later and were encamped, with units of the recently arrived No 3 SS Brigade, under Brigadier Nonweiler, Royal Marines, at Kedgaon, some 40 miles from Poona, and it was there the following month that Mountbatten visited them.

Mountbatten's original idea had been to invade Sumatra, and for this he wanted the Dutch Troop, but the Tehran Conference in November, 1943, gave the highest priority of men and material to the European theatre, and the invasion was cancelled. Mountbatten therefore had to tell the Dutch that the original reason for their presence in India was no longer valid, but went on to say that he expected them to be in action soon.

146

It may be that Mountbatten thought that Linzel's men could be employed with the other Dutch force in the area, the Corps Insulinde, for he suggested that Linzel visit Admiral Helfrich, the Dutch Naval Commander-in-Chief, in Colombo to discuss this possibility.

Although four men from the Dutch Troop were later seconded to the Corps Insulinde, nothing came of Linzel's visit and the Troop was sent on a jungle training course near Goa. However, some men from the Troop did see immediate action for Lieutenent Knottenbelt – on hearing, while Linzel was in Colombo, that two Commandos from the Brigade, Nos 5 and 44 (RM), were leaving for an operation in Burma – requested that the Dutch be allowed to go too. Permission for this was not granted, but Knottenbelt and four men, chosen by lottery, were allowed to be attached to the two Commandos to gain battle experience. One of the men became seriously ill before the two Commandos arrived at Cox's Bazaar, but Knottenbelt and Sergeant van der Veer were attached to HQ of 44 Commando while the two privates, Blatt and de Koning, were attached to HQ of 5 Commando, and all four saw action during the raids that both Commandos launched behind the Japanese lines, as did the fifth, Corporal Ubels, when he returned from hospital.

One interesting use of the four men was to employ them to pass messages to one another over the radio, for it was quickly found that the Japanese were adept at breaking into the Brigade wireless net, but though many obviously understood English none, it seemed, knew Dutch. While, however, this made the wireless link secure it infuriated the Japanese who, frustrated by not knowing what was being passed over the air, would start mortaring the British positions with great ferocity whenever the Dutchmen started to pass messages.

During one action near Maungdaw, Blatt was seriously wounded and had a miraculous escape from being captured: "All of a sudden, after we had walked for about an hour, a silent sign went through that long line of commandos – as if every man had been connected by a rope – and every man dropped flat on his stomach. There we were, lying in the muddy soil of the Arakan. There was nothing we could see or hear, and we did not have the slightest idea why we had to take cover.

"Then they were there. I could see them clearly. They walked one behind the other, somewhat bent, and they came straight towards us. Clearly we could hear their heavy steps in the wet soil. A few more minutes and they were almost on top of us.

"There was still no sound from us. With all our iron discipline, our trigger fingers itched. But we had to wait for the command. Then just a few yards from us, they also fell down.

"There were a few rifle shots from our line. Someone must have lost his nerve. That was the sign for the Japs. All hell broke loose. They jumped and yelled, shouting English orders – their old trick to confuse us. Then, crying

'Banzai', they came at us. There were shots everywhere and the rattle of machine guns, with hand grenades bursting. In between the bursts of firing I heard the anguished cries of the wounded.

"I just could not believe it. I was not scared, nervous, or afraid. There was just no time for it. I aimed my rifle – shot – another one down. There were so many. I did not even have to look for a target. They were everywhere. Our fire kept those few yards between us. They could not get close enough for a bayonet attack.

"Then there was a terrific fireball in front of me and a tremendous explosion. I felt a terrible shock against my right shoulder. I felt as if I'd been hit in a fight but that my adversary had not taken his hand away and the pressure of it remained. I could hardly breathe. My mouth was full of liquid. I tried to call Nick (de Koning), but there was no answer. I wanted to feel my chest, but I could not move my right arm. Where was my rifle? Everything was confused. There were bright lights, then darkness, and lights again. There was terrific noise, and then it was quiet. How long did it go on? Minutes? Hours? Who knows?

"Then I slowly returned to my senses. I was hit. How badly I did not know. I looked around then. Where were all our boys? Where was Nick? I was alone. But there was still all that noise, all that shooting. I had to get out of there. I saw a low bush behind me, a few yards away. I tried to get there. It would be some kind of cover. I made it and just fell down behind the bush. If I could only have breathed. All that blood and that pain in my chest. I was lying on my back. I thought, why not close my eyes and perhaps soon it will all be over.

"But I could not relax. I coughed all the time. I had to clear my throat. Then something happened. I looked up and I saw stars and the yellow light of the moon – the same moon we had in Holland. That was the essence of it – Holland, all Europe, lay occupied and tortured by the Germans, and it had been my goal to help to liberate my country. I did not want to die there in the mud of the Arakan. I had to get out and finish the job.

"But how? The pain grew worse. It felt like a burning iron in my chest. The morphine – it shot through my mind like lightning. The little box I had on my back. With my left hand I got hold of it. I fumbled around. There was the little tube. Unscrew the top. Push the needle in your arm, and squeeze and squeeze. Why not take the tablets, too. One, two. Let's keep two in reserve for later. After I was finished I was completely exhausted. Keep quiet now, and let the morphine work.

"It did not take long. My pain diminished. I had the feeling I was drunk. I realized fully that I could not stay there. There was still a lot of shooting going on. Somehow I had to get to the coast. Perhaps I could reach our defensive box. I got up. I could hardly walk. I saw a group of trees. That was my next goal. I just made it.

"After a little while I felt I had enough strength to get further. Getting up was the worst part. But there was some power that just pushed me further. I saw a low wall ahead of me. There I could have something to lean against, and it was cover. I had no idea how long I had been sitting there when all of a sudden I saw little figures coming over the wall. There was no end of them – more and more. I thought I must have been dreaming. I thought it was the morphine. But I saw those figures so clearly – and only a few yards away. I heard noises then, too. I pinched my leg. Yes, I could feel it. I was wide awake. It was not a dream. There were Japs all around me.

"There was no way out. They would discover me any minute. I was not scared. I only hoped the end would come fast. But I was not desperate. I was all attention. I pulled my green beret from my head and tried to control my breathing, which still gave me a lot of trouble. There they were. Three of them came right towards me. The one in the middle was helped by the two others. They were right in front of me. I could smell their breath. What next? Out of the corner of my eye I watched them. Now they took the one in the middle and put him right next to me. After that they left to join the others.

"It had been close. I could hardly believe it. I looked at the Jap at my side. He was half-lying, half-sitting. His breath came very irregularly. I started to understand what was going on. The Japs had taken me for one of their own wounded. They had put the wounded man next to me, and I was sure it was their intention to pick both of us up later and bring us to safety – their safety.

"I had to get away from there. The moment they came back I was lost. With all the strength I had left I crawled over the wall. But what was that? The wall ran like a circle, and in the middle of it was a pile of crates, metal crates like our ammunition boxes. The Japs had stored their ammunition there before going to attack us. What a chance to sabotage their efforts. But with what? I had one hand grenade left. I was not even sure it could do anything against those boxes; and I was sure it would kill me. At that moment my own survival was more important to me than all the ammunition in the world.

"I crawled to the other side of the wall and over again. I had to get away from there, but to where? In the far distance I thought I heard the faint noise of the surf breaking against the beach. Yes, I had.

"I walked and I walked. It was rough going. The ground was muddy, and the pain started to come back. I did not want to give in. I fell, but got up. I was sure that if I lay down to relax I would never get up again. I came to a river. I had to get through. I fell in the water, but a voice inside just shouted that I had to go on. Then I was out of the water. I walked, perhaps for hours, perhaps for minutes.

"What was that? I saw something moving ahead of me on the ground. It was not more than 50 feet away. I stopped. I could see it now. There were two men, their weapons pointed at me. Oh God, they were wearing berets! They were Commandos. I shouted: 'Don't shoot!' "[1]

Despite having a large hole in his chest and several smaller ones, Blatt survived and was later joined in hospital by Sergeant van der Veer who had malaria. Then the message came for them both to rejoin the rest of the Troop in India, as it was being returned to England.

The truth was that there was no way of using the Dutch Troop in the Far East, and as the realization of this sunk into the men their morale slumped. Their situation was made worse by the persistent rumours that the invasion of mainland Europe was about to take place, and eventually Linzel requested an interview with Mountbatten. As a consequence of this meeting Mountbatten sent the Chief of Combined Operations, Major-General Laycock, the following signal on 16 May, 1944: "I've just interviewed Captain Linzel O/C No: 2 Troop 10 (IA). Two years of training and no opportunity to carry out an operation despite various promises has made the men disappointed and disillusioned. They have a guarantee from the Dutch government that they can obtain their discharge six months after the liberation of Holland. If the liberation occurs without them having seen any action they will undoubtably claim discharge. I would like to avoid this if possible as there are tasks for them to perform later in this theatre for which I am particularly anxious to have them. As there is no immediate prospect of giving them an operation here I have asked the Dutch Minister for the Colonies to obtain their Government's approval for their return to the UK, with a view to them taking part in operations on the Continent. Therefore, in order to save them from disintegration through inactivity, I urge you to try and get agreement for their immediate return to the UK, to take part in the fighting in Europe. A failure to do so will lead to their loss. The numbers involved are only three officers and 48 OR. If they fight in Europe Linzel guarantees he can hold them together and many will volunteer for further service in SE Asia. Further, he considers he would have no difficulty in finding sufficient reserves to bring the unit up to full strength."[2]

The Troop sailed from Bombay and arrived in Liverpool in 15 August, and two days later the Inspector General of the Dutch Troops, Lt-Colonel P.O. Doorman, requested that the Troop be sent to the Princess Irene Brigade, then attached to 1 Corps in Normandy, as the Brigade urgently needed reinforcements. This obviously did not appeal to Laycock and his Chief of Staff replied to Doorman's request by saying that the Troop had gone on leave, that on their return they were to be inspected by Prince Bernhardt, and that after that a decision would be made. Doorman, however, was not to be fobbed off, and replied that his Government required an answer immediately. Permission was then granted for the Troop to join the Princess Irene Brigade after the Prince had inspected it on 5 September.[3]

The last thing the Dutch wanted to do was to become ordinary infantrymen and quite possibly it was Prince Bernhardt who intervened to ensure that they did not. On the day he inspected the Troop he decorated de Koning and Lieutenant Knottenbelt with the Dutch Bronze Cross for their bravery during the Arakan campaign, and announced that he needed volunteers for several special assignments. The Troop was now divided up into three different groups. One of the Section Commanders, a South African called Ruysch van Dugteren, and four other ranks, were assigned to Prince Bernhardt's staff as his personal bodyguards; Lieutenant Knottenbelt and seven other ranks volunteered for the special mission of being parachuted into Holland behind the German lines to liaise with the Dutch underground; and the rest of the Troop were divided amongst the British and American Airborne divisions for Operation Market Garden.

Captain Linzel, 2/Lieutenant de Ruiter and three other ranks were attached to the 52 Lowland Division, which was to be airlifted in once the airborne landings had been successfully completed; eleven other ranks were attached to 1st British Airborne Division whose target was the bridge at Arnhem; eleven other ranks were attached to 82nd American Airborne Division whose target was the bridge at Nijmegen; three other ranks were attached to the HQ of First Allied Airborne Army; and five other ranks were attached to the 101st American Airborne Division.[4]

When it became obvious that 52nd Lowland Division could not be airlifted Linzel's group joined First Allied Airborne Army HQ established at Nijmegen. The failure to hold the bridge at Arnhem also caused an alteration in the mission of Knottenbelt and his men. Instead of being dropped deep into occupied Holland Knottenbelt parachuted with 1st Airborne Division, while the other members of his party waited for the outcome of the battle. Despite the heavy and confused fighting Knottenbelt managed to make contact with the local Resistance. "I was put in a glider and we had a good landing at Wolfheze. There was a mental hospital nearby and I remember the nurses were out to greet us before we pushed on to Oosterbeek where the fighting was. My job was to organize the Dutch Resistance who were supposed to make contact with us. They did, and I became busy feeding information to Divisional HQ. I had to be very careful to make sure I was dealing with reliable people. Because of the Resistance workers on the telephone exchange I was able to contact several people who gave us vital information about the strength and whereabouts of local German units."[5]

On 20 September Knottenbelt joined a Canadian lieutenant, Leo Heaps, in an attempt to contact the Polish airborne troops who had been dropped near the bridge. Heaps asked for two jeeps filled with supplies, a Dutch guide and an interpreter. "The Dutchman, who was to come with us, spoke English with a heavy Oxford accent. He was Oxford educated and had been loaned from the

Dutch Commandos to the Airborne Division for this operation. His name was Martin Knottenbelt.

"Martin demands well-planned schemes under almost any circumstances. Before I could speak he went outside the house and reappeared with a sleepy-eyed local who carried a tommy-gun and had on an old British uniform and wore a pair of German jackboots.

"Then for one hour I gave Martin different plans, and after conferring in Dutch with the local, Martin would discard most of them. Finally I offered a plan which he accepted . . .

"We were to travel in two jeeps, with a tommy-gunner in the back of each, down to the ferry, which we presumed was still held by our Engineers. The jeeps were to cross on the ferry, and we were to head south until we contacted the tanks from the Guards Armoured Division. We were then to take a tank and clear out the Germans on the south side of the Arnhem Bridge and then take supplies across in the tank."[6]

The ferry, however, had been abandoned and its mechanism smashed by the Germans, and the party was forced to return. Knottenbelt survived the following day of battle unscathed, but during the final withdrawal he became "both bored and frightened waiting for a boat on that exposed bank"[7] and decided to swim the river, but was wounded in the thigh by a piece of shrapnel.*

The night following his attempt to cross by the ferry, Heaps tried once more to cross the river, this time taking with him as interpreter another member of the Dutch Troop called Gobitz. Just as Heaps was about to swim across the Rhine he heard men crossing in rubber boats lower down and, leaving Gobitz where he was, moved down the bank to find out what was happening. The men crossing the river turned out to be the Polish paratroops Heaps was trying to contact. He told the Polish officer where Gobitz was and told him to tell the Dutchman that Heaps was going to cross and that Gobitz was to show the Poles the way to Divisional HQ. The Polish officer said he understood but he never contacted Gobitz and the Dutchman remained waiting by the river. He was shot in the foot and captured by the Germans, who treated him as a partisan and kept him in solitary confinement[8], but, as will be seen, he escaped the firing squad and survived the war.

Several other members of the Dutch Troop were also captured during the fighting, one of them Private Beekmeijer, whose account of his part in the

* Knottenbelt was operated on in a field hospital where they found in his pockets the collar badges of a German general. This led to the long-standing rumour that it was he who had killed Major-General Kussin, the Arnhem "Feldkommandant", who was ambushed in his car during the afternoon of 17 September. However, in 1982 Knottenbelt told W. Boersma of the Arnhem Museum that he had passed Kussin's car just after he had been killed and had taken his collar badges. The General was, in fact, killed either by men from 8 Coy 3 Bn The Parachute Regiment or by those from 9 Field Coy Royal Engineers.

battle can be taken as typical of the Dutch Troop's involvement in the operation. "On Sunday 17 September, at about 1.30pm, the unit to which I had been attached [1st Bn King's Own Scottish Borderers] to serve in its Intelligence section, landed by glider to the west and north of Wolfheze within a hundred yards of the landing zone. The landing was perfect: only one accident occurred, in which a glider pilot was killed when his glider collided with a tree. The glider in which I landed was severely cracked and I had to use the butt of my rifle to break open the exit. The enemy was nowhere to be seen. We set off immediately in the direction of the heath, of which the north-east corner was formed by a farm called 'Het Planken Wambuis', and which was bordered to the north by the main Arnhem-Ede road. On our way I frequently questioned Dutchmen about the position and strength of German troops in the vicinity, but it became clear that our original information had been pretty accurate. We had soon captured our first twenty prisoners, but these consisted for the most part of Germans who were only too happy to surrender, which was a considerable boost to our morale. Towards evening we took up positions in a sort of triangle round the heath, but on the following day – when the parachutists were landing – this proved too large to be effectively defended, and the north-western corner in the direction of Ede was thus largely unprotected. By evening the first shots were heard, and firing continued throughout the night. A member of the Resistance from Wageningen (or Bennekom), a forestry expert, joined us, as did some other Dutchmen who probably came from the Delen airfield, where they had been forced to work for the Germans. As the only Dutchman in our battalion I was employed almost exclusively as an interpreter, and I well remember that I was none too pleased about that.

"The next day, 18 September, at about 10am, the battle started in earnest, becoming even fiercer when the parachutists landed, a few hours later than expected. In order to give as much protection as possible to both the parachutists themselves and to the aircraft, which could not defend themselves from the air and were under heavy fire, the Headquarters Company, myself among them, went out with fixed bayonets over open ground to divert the attention of the Germans who had settled in one particular part of the woods which surrounded the heath, and to drive them out. Reinforced by some parachutists we disposed of a number of them and I later had to interrogate quite a number of prisoners. To my shame I found many Dutchmen among them, they having come from Amersfoort where they were apparently stationed . . .

"During the night of 18/19 September we, together with the parachutists, advanced rapidly towards Arnhem but encountered opposition just past the 'Johanna Hoeve', which was burnt down during the fighting. Our CO decided to wait for daylight (which in my opinion Commandos would never have done) in order to oust the Germans from their fortified positions. Their defences

153

consisted of possibly a hundred Germans strongly entrenched on a wooded hill to the west of the 'Johanna Hoeve'. The occupants of 'Johanna Hoeve' behaved in an exemplary fashion and were very helpful. We were involved in skirmishes throughout the day [19 September]. The parachutists went off in various directions with the aim of storming the hill. We meanwhile kept the top of the hill under mortar fire until the moment when it might be expected that the attackers had reached their objective. What went wrong I cannot explain, but I do know that the 'Johanna Hoeve' came under very heavy mortar fire from the Germans, as a result of which the farm went up in flames and the occupants very calmly evacuated their home. In the meantime we had come under fire from about a dozen German fighter planes. I may add here that a police officer from Arnhem, whose name I unfortunately cannot recall, kept company with us the whole day long and assumed responsibility for escorting the occupants of the 'Johanna Hoeve' to a safer place. This man behaved extremely well, as did many other Dutchmen who reported to us in the hope of receiving equipment and firearms.

"Towards the afternoon of 19 September we came under further fire from snipers and from 88mm self-propelled guns which attacked us from the north. One particular sniper made it very difficult for us, and when a couple of volunteers were asked for to track him down I went forward, and thus parted company with my unit, which I was subsequently unable to rejoin. Under increasingly heavy fire the parachutists, after one or two unsuccessful attempts to dislodge the Germans from their fortified position on the hill, returned dejected. As a result of this retreat the Germans came closer and closer, and the moment came when we dispersed in the wood to decrease the likelihood of being hit. After some time I spotted an English column moving south, and I joined them as they crossed the Arnhem-Ede railway line. I was with a group of parachutists and I could not get permission from their CO to rejoin my unit because we were surrounded on all sides. We were about a hundred strong and we dug trenches for the night. On the first night I had not slept from excitement, on the second and third I had no chance to. Though the Germans kept their distance, we were under fire all night long.

"On the following morning, 20 September, we succeeded in shifting our positions a little further to the south, but were very soon more or less pinned down. After we tried a second time, I, with twenty others, found ourselves completely surrounded in a hollow in the ground on the left flank. Two tanks opened fire on us from a distance of about 20 metres, severely injuring two of us who – presumably out of fear – stood up and walked towards the enemy. We succeeded in putting one of the tanks out of action with a PIAT, and the other then withdrew. However, we remained surrounded, and when some snipers began to fire on us we had no alternative but to surrender."[9]

Beekmeijer, however, continued to give the Germans trouble. In his POW camp he met Gobitz and another Inter-Allied Dutch Commando, Gubbels, and all three were sent to Dresden. In the confusion that followed the bombing of the city in mid-February, 1945, they managed to escape and very nearly reached the Czech border before being recaptured. Towards the end of April they escaped again and, after nine days, managed to reach the American front at Wittgensdorf, near Chemnitz.

Sergeant de Waard, who was with 1st Airborne Division, was another member of the Dutch Troop who was wounded and then captured. "We got in a glider together with Major-General Urquhart, his batman, a wireless operator and a driver. We also had aboard the General's jeep and a few small motorbikes. We landed in a potato field near Wolfheze. The pilot only just escaped hitting a great heap of potatoes. Soon after landing I met a number of Dutchmen who had just returned from church. They were nervous and afraid. I explained to them what was happening, and that calmed them. They took me to a house where more Dutchmen were gathered. When they heard that we were here to liberate them from the Germans they started sing the National Anthem. I had a lump in my throat, I did not expect such a reception after an absence of three and a half years.

"On the way from Wolfheze to Oosterbeek we passed at a crossroads a German car with four dead in it. The Divisional HQ was set up in the Hotel Hartenstein. When we arrived there we found a complete meal for the Germans still on the table. In the meantime we had taken several prisoners and it was my job to interrogate them. There were also quite a few people who had been released from the jail at Arnhem, and these were allowed to continue to the Allied lines once they had been vetted.

"In the first days in Oosterbeek I was the liaison between the HQ and a dentist in Oosterbeek who could phone to a friend in Arnhem who lived near the bridge there. He could give us valuable information about the situation there as communication between HQ and the bridge was very bad. News about what was happening was so scarce that in the end we had to read about it in a British newspaper! While we were reading it we were mortared and I was wounded, and I still have a piece of shrapnel in my head.

"The situation slowly got worse, and there was hardly any ammunition or food. The streets of Oosterbeek were deserted, and we dug ourselves in in front of the Hartenstein. On the night of 25 September I went to HQ to ask what was hapening, but there was nothing they could tell me. The next morning it was extremely quiet around us, no gunfire or anything. I was with a glider pilot and two parachutists in a trench, and we decided to go to HQ. When we arrived there, we did not find anybody except a very tired doctor with many dead and wounded who told us that HQ had pulled out the evening before. Without giving us any warning they had left us behind! We cursed. For a moment I thought of taking off my uniform and trying to hide with the civilians in Oosterbeek, but decided not to. We'll stick together, I told the others, we'll try and cross the Rhine, it's not that far.

"I led the way, when all of a sudden there was a rifle shot and one of the paratroopers fell, wounded in the back. The glider pilot and I dived behind a big oak tree. Looking around I saw some metres away a British soldier squatting by a small wall. I called out to him but suddenly realized he was dead; for me, that was one of the most remarkable memories I have of Arnhem. Then high up in one of the trees I saw a German who was aiming at me. I brought up my rifle, but he fired first and shot me in the foot. We then discovered that we were surrounded and that our escape route to the river was cut off. The only thing to do was to give up. As soon as we put up our hands the Germans came towards us, and the first thing they asked was if we had any cigarettes. In the afternoon we were taken by truck to Apeldoorn where a long train of cattle waggons was waiting to take us to Germany."[10]

Although most of the Dutch Troop who took part in Operation Market Garden landed safely, two at least did not reach the target. One glider of 1st Airborne Division, with Sergeant Luitwieler of the Dutch Troop in it, was forced to make an emergency landing on open ground near Biezenmortel. The glider contained two jeeps and Luitwieler and his companions decided to try and drive through the German-held country to Arnhem. They encountered some Germans at Helvoirt, but managed to fight their way through, but near St Michielsgestel they were warned that a much stronger force was awaiting them so they hid the jeeps in a wood and a Dutch Resistance worker brought them a tent and some food stolen from the Germans. They hid there for some days before they were led by a local Resistance leader to where about a hundred Allied paratroopers were hiding near Campina Heath. This group was eventually reached by American paratroopers on the night of 24 October and Luitwieler was able to rejoin his Troop early in November.

The glider containing Private de Leeuw also had to make an emergency landing on the island of Schouwen and he and the two pilots were hidden by the local Resistance. Early in December they, and some Resistance members who had to get out of Holland, tried to escape by boat, but were betrayed by some locals. In the ensuing fighting de Leeuw and the two pilots escaped, but the Resistance workers were caught and hanged. De Leeuw managed to get to Amsterdam, but was captured there, though he survived the war.[11]

Though the Dutch Troop suffered heavy casualties with several of its members being wounded or taken prisoner of war, their losses in killed, compared to the British forces at Arnhem, were light, with only two dying in action. One, Private Hagelaars, was shot by the Germans after Arnhem when,

156

on 5 October, he tried to visit his parents near Den Bosch when the area was still occupied by the enemy. The other, Private Bakhuys Roozeboom, was killed in action at Arnhem while attached to 1st Airborne Division. Like Knottenbelt and de Waard, he was with the Divisional Commander and worked from the Divisional HQ at the Hotel Hartenstein in Oosterbeck. On 19 September two volunteer guides were called for to help try and get a patrol through to the bridge at Arnhem. Two Dutch Resistance fighters, Jan Diepenbroek and Hendrik Beekhuisen, immediately stepped foward. "We had to put on British uniforms. We got hand grenades and ammunition for our rifles. There was also an interpreter with us as we could hardly speak any English. This was a young soldier with a green beret. His name was Bakhuys and he took us outside to the jeep with a British major and four soldiers. With eight men on the jeep, legs hanging outside, the major at the steering wheel, we drove towards the bridge. Near it we were shot at from both sides, but were not hit. After 400 metres we saw a high-sided vehicle coming towards us. We stopped and took cover on both sides of the road. We forced the driver to stop. It was a German Red Cross ambulance with two soldiers. The major did not like the situation as, of course, Red Cross vehicles were protected by the Geneva Convention. Then one of us opened the back of the ambulance and found it was full of ammunition and weapons, so we took the Germans prisoner. Bakhuys told us that the major had decided to go back as we were surrounded by Germans, but we would try and get the ambulance back to Oosterbeek. On the way back the ambulance was stopped by a German patrol, but the major drove his jeep at them. Then about ten Germans started shooting at us from the bridge with automatic weapons. Bakhuys was throwing hand grenades while the major was driving. Suddenly, I realized that Bakhuys was sinking in between the major and I without a sound. It was a miracle to me that we were still alive. We stopped in Oosterbeek near a church which had been turned into a hospital, and the major and I looked to see where Bakhuys had been wounded. We soon saw that he had been hit in the head and must have died immediately."*[12]

Altogether, the bravery of the Dutch at Arnhem was quite extraordinary. Two of them dropped with the 82nd American Airborne Division without ever having had any parachute training, while Sergeant Visser served as the second pilot of a glider when he was attached to the HQ of 501st Parachute Infantry Regiment, and was recommended for the American Bronze Star. "From the moment of his landing until he left us he proved to be of invaluable assistance to the regiment," wrote one American officer. "When he was called upon to prove his quality as a soldier he acquitted himself of his tasks with skill and coolness."[13]

In the middle of October Linzel received orders to gather together the

* The Dutch Commando training camp at Roosendaal was named after Bakhuys Roozeboom in 1980.

remnants of his Troop at Eindhoven, and on 20 October they moved to Bruges where they were attached to No 4 SS Brigade for the forthcoming operation against Walcheren.

2

Of the eight men who had volunteered to parachute into occupied Holland only five eventually went, as it was found that three of them could not speak Dutch sufficiently well for the mission. These were employed instead as instructors for Dutch volunteers from the liberated part of Holland.

Four of the men now came under the orders of the BBO, while the fifth, Lieutenant Knottenbelt, joined the BBO later, jumping into Holland near Barneveld on 3 April, 1945. At the request of Prince Bernhardt, who had been made Commander-in-Chief of all the Resistance forces in the Netherlands,* Michels, de Koning and Blatt were made sergeants while van der Veer, already a sergeant, was promoted to sergeant-major.

Van der Veer, Michels and de Koning were dropped together on the night of 11 October, near Veenhuizen in northern Holland, while Blatt was dropped on 25 September 200 miles north of Arnhem, near Westerborg, with a group of Belgian SAS. Their contact man in Holland was an old colleague from the Dutch Troop, Peter Tazelaar, who had returned clandestinely to his country for a second time, this time by parachute and with a radio operator.

The task of all five was to make contact with the local Resistance and to organize its arming and training in readiness to attack the Germans when the Allies resumed their drive into Holland. Knottenbelt, de Koning and Michels all led groups of Dutch Resistance fighters in seizing bridges across various canals when the Canadians advanced into Holland in April, 1945, and after the war all five were decorated, Knottenbelt with Holland's highest award, the Military Wilhelms Order.

Rudy Blatt was the first to be dropped. On the night of 25 September he parachuted into occupied Holland 200 miles north of Arnhem with a group of

* In common with France, there were various Resistance organizations in Holland, with different functions, and not always acting in harmony. Prince Bernhardt had ordered that all these movements should be combined to form the NBS (Nederlandsche Binnenlandsche Strijdkrachten – Netherlands Forces of the Interior) in the hope that the Gemans would recognize that if it was one force with one Commander, Prince Bernhardt, its members would be accorded the Geneva Convention if captured. The five main organizations were the LO (Landelijke Organizatie – National Organization), which looked after those in hiding, the *onderduikers* as they were called; the LKP (Landelijke Knockploegen – National Fighting Teams), which did all the dangerous tasks like jailbreaks, stealing ration cards, bank robberies, organizing weapon drops and so on; the OD (Orde Dienst – Service for Order), which was concerned with building up an organization which would take over the liberation of Holland until the functions of Government and police could be resumed; and the RVV (Raad van Verzet – Council of Resistance), which was suspected by the other organizations of having Communist sympathies, and maintaining secret weapon dumps without doing any real Resistance work. I am indebted to Rudy Blatt for the above information which came from his book, *Rudy, Een Strijdbare Jood.*

158

Belgian SAS. Their orders were to report back on the strength and dispositions of the Germans, and they had been briefed that they could be expected to be joined by Allied troops within a week of being dropped. They soon heard, however, that the attempt to capture the bridge at Arnhem had failed, and that their mission was now aborted. Blatt now pushed for working more closely with the Resistance, and, though the officer in charge of the group was opposed to this, Blatt forced his hand by saying that unless they did the Resistance would stop supplying them with intelligence. Blatt then asked London for weapons and for instructors, and these were dropped to them.

The party had a narrow escape when the farm they were hiding in was searched by the Germans, and it was agreed that the only hope they had of avoiding capture was to head south for the Allied lines. They decided the best way of doing this was to strip themselves of their insignia and pretend to be a German parachute patrol on special duty. Blatt could speak perfect German and he felt he could bluff his way out of any problems. In any case it was the only hope they had. They stopped at isolated farms to rest and eat. After some days they came to the riverside town of Balkbrug, which had the only bridge to the south. With astounding panache Blatt marched the small group right through the town and up to the bridge. A sentry stepped out and saluted, and Blatt replied with *"Heil Hitler!"* and marched on.

In the end it was not the Germans that defeated the group but the cold and hunger and exhaustion which they suffered, and after six days of moving through enemy-occupied territory Blatt was forced to risk seeking contact with local Resistance leaders through a farmer. This they managed to do without being betrayed and eventually the group, with the help of the Resistance, found its way to the Allied lines, but Blatt stayed behind to work with the underground in the province of Twente in order to organize the NBS on proper lines by convincing the various Resistance organizations that it was vital to work. In this he was successful, as by the end of the year there were 2000 NBS men in the Twente province under military discipline.

One of the hardest things Blatt found working with the underground was denying his background. "For the first and only time in my life I had to deny that I was Jewish. This had been one of the few points of instruction I had received before leaving England. Not only might the fact that I was Jewish have endangered my own work, but also, if I was captured, it would have made things worse for those who worked with me. I knew it was necessary; but it weighed on my conscience."[14]

When the Allies crossed the Rhine and the signal came from England to start sabotaging the Germans' lines of communications, Blatt and the men he was working with went on to the offensive. And when the Canadians arrived the Dutch worked with them. "A report came through of a pocket of German resistance near Almelo. We took this report to the CO of the Canadians in

Almelo. However, he refused to go as he had only tanks and no infantry. We offered our boys. After some hesitation, he accepted. Our men jumped on the tanks and were off. They stayed in the field three days – till the last German was cleared out. The Canadian Commander could not get over the magnificent job these 'untrained' men had done . . . not one important bridge in our district was destroyed, thanks to the preparatory work of our men."[15]

It was as a result of Blatt asking for instructors that de Koning, van der Veer and Michels were dropped together on the night of 11 October near Veenhuizen in Northern Holland. They were met by members of the Dutch Resistance and given Dutch police uniforms to wear. Michels then went to Groningen, van der Veer to Drente and de Koning to Friesland.

De Koning worked from a small town called Swichum. Officially, he was a farmer called Harry Prinz but in February, 1945, the Germans got to know about this alibi when they arrested a Resistance worker with a letter from de Koning on him. So de Koning became a vet, the kind that specialized in delivering calves, so he was allowed to travel far more freely than would normally have been the case. Then, in April, when the Resistance was alerted that the Canadians were about to attack he organized the capture intact of three bridges across a canal. It was during this time that he had his narrowest escape from capture when the Germans began a thorough search of the town he was in, for by now his second identity had become known to them. "He wore false spectacles and grew a moustache when his identity became known to the Germans," his citation for his decoration, the Bronze Lion, read. "For the photograph he put on a charcoal moustache as he had not then had time to grow one. In early April, 1945, the Germans began a thorough search of the town. The only way to extract him was to send in a Dutch Resistance man dressed as a Dutch policeman with papers to arrest him as a black marketeer."[16]

De Koning, at least, was able to carry on with his work, but van der Veer found that the Germans were so hot on his trail that at first it proved impossible to carry out his orders. "I was taken to a very isolated farm at Garminge near Westerborg but I was betrayed by a courier who was engaged to a Gestapo man. The Germans searched the farm but could not find me. I hid under the hay in the stable and then for two nights in a potato pit. But it was obvious I could not stay there much longer as the farm was being closely watched. So on the third night a Resistance worker came along and took me away. This man was a policeman and by coincidence I had known him at the police college I went to. He said he was going to take me to the German HQ – the very people who were trying to find me! – as he lived under the same roof as they did. It sounded dangerous to me, but in fact it was safer than anywhere else as they never suspected I was not a policeman. I spent three months with him.

"Eventually it was safe enough for me to go in Dutch police uniform by bicycle to instruct members of the Dutch underground hidden in farms in the area. Then in the Spring of 1945 I went to a hideout in the woods which the local underground had created. There were thirty of us altogether, and it was there that I started giving instruction in weapon-handling and map-reading, and so on."

In April this group accidentally came across a party of French paratroopers who had been dropped to attack the HQ in which van der Veer had been sheltering for the preceding months.

"We were at Appelsha about 40 kilometres away from the HQ at Westerborg but I was determined to save my friend, who had a wife and a baby, as I was sure he would be killed in the attack. Somehow I got there in time and took my friend to the woods at Wiiteveen where the paratroopers were hiding, and then we both led them back to the HQ. By that time I knew every inch of the ground, and the Germans were taken completely by surprise. The battle lasted almost two hours and about forty Germans were killed or wounded. We lost three men.

"After this attack the Germans left the town and at 0400 the next morning the farmer where I was hiding woke me and said he could hear a strange sound. I got up and knew it was tanks coming our way, Allied tanks. So I decided that Westerborg should be free before they came. I went to the town hall and demanded to see the burgomaster. Although it was only 6am he agreed to see me and when I entered his office I took out my pistol and made him my prisoner. I then told the caretaker to change the flag on the roof so that the proper Dutch flag would be flying when the tanks arrived.

"As I was drinking some coffee the telephone rang. The burgomaster asked if he should answer it but I answered it myself. A voice in German asked about the situation in Westerborg, saying he was the Commandant of the local concentration camp. I told him they couldn't be better. By now the tanks were coming up the street and I put the telephone out of the window so that he could hear them. 'Who are you?' he shrieked down the telephone. 'Why not speak English,' I said in English. 'If you can't speak English, it's time you learnt'."[17]

10

The Dunes of
Walcheren

By striking towards Arnhem instead of first clearing the approaches to Antwerp, which had been captured on 4 September, 1944, with its docks intact, Montgomery had created a critical situation not only for his own army group but for the whole invasion force. As the British and the Americans pushed towards Germany, their numbers building all the time, so they moved further away from the source of their supplies. Organizations like the "Red Ball" convoys made supreme efforts to keep the advancing troops supplied, but it soon became obvious that only a major port like Antwerp could solve the acute problem of keeping the armies rolling. Not only was the advance slowed by this logistical problem, but actually halted.

To be fair, Montgomery thought that while he struck for the vital bridges across the Rhine the Canadians would be able to clear the banks of the Scheldt. But once Antwerp had been taken German resistance stiffened and the British drive into Holland petered out. The island of Walcheren, which dominates the mouth of the Scheldt, then became, and was so named by Hitler, a fortress, its powerful array of gun batteries and other defensive positions being manned by a mixture of tough Kriegsmarine gunners and medically below par members of the Wehrmacht.

It needed a series of major operations to drive out the Germans from the area but by the end of October the Canadians had, with great bravery and loss of life, taken almost all of what was known as the Breskens pocket on the south bank of the Scheldt as well as South Beveland on its north bank. British army units under 2 Canadian Corps were then poised to strike from South Beveland on to Walcheren Island to help clear the one remaining centre of resistance that was preventing Antwerp from being used.

The hub of the attack on Walcheren was the two amphibious landings that took place on 1 November by No 4 Special Service Brigade commanded by Brigadier Leicester, Royal Marines. The dawn attack on Flushing from across the Scheldt by No 4 Commando was codenamed Infatuate I, while the landing on the north-west part of the island, at Westkapelle, undertaken by Nos 41, 47, and 48 Royal Marine Commandos, and by two Troops of the Inter-Allied Commando, was codenamed Infatuate II. American amphibious LVTs – called Buffaloes by the British – and the smaller amphibious Weasels were employed in the landings. These were an essential part of the operation, for the island had been partially flooded when RAF bombers had blown a large hole in the dyke at Westkapelle and smaller ones in several other places. The inundations caused by this bombing had isolated the German positions from possible reinforcements. They had also flooded some of the defences situated inland away from the higher ground of the dunes that were an integral part of the island's dyke system against the North Sea.

This amphibious attack on Walcheren saw by far the largest contingent of the Inter-Allied Commando to go into battle at the same time, for not only were the two French Troops still attached to No 4 Commando but No 41 Commando was reinforced for its drive to the north-eastern part of the island by the Norwegian and Belgian Troops of the Inter-Allied Commando under the command of their own HQ.* In addition, eleven members of the Dutch Troop who had managed to escape from Arnhem were attached, under the command of Captain Linzel, to No 47 Commando and twelve, under 2/Lieutenant de Ruiter, were attached to No 4 Commando, while a number of No 3 Troop continued in their inimitable role of interrogators, interpreters, and in helping patrols snatch prisoners. Among those attached to the three Commandos or to Brigade HQ for this purpose were Sergeants Farr and Gray, Corporals Douglas, Hamilton and Latimer, and Private Watson.[1]

On 30 September the two Troops and their HQ sailed from Southend and disembarked at Arromanches, and from there were taken by truck to De Haan on the Belgian coast near Bruges where the captured German defences were very similar to the ones that were to be stormed at Walcheren. Intensive training then began, but there was time for the Belgian Troop to snatch a few days' leave to return to their homes. It was, as their historian wrote, a brief but joyous reunion, and for some it was also a time of additional anxiety. One man found that his father was in prison for collaborating with the Germans and that the rest of his family had fled to Germany. Another discovered that his wife had left him for a Luftwaffe pilot.[2]

On 28 October 4 SS Brigade was moved to its concentration area where

* 10 (IA) Cdo HQ included its commanding officer, Lt-Colonel Peter Laycock, the 2 i/c, Major Godfrey Franks, the Intelligence Officer, Lieutenant Dwelly from No 3 Troop, and Captain Emmet, now the Commando's Adjutant.

behind barbed wire the men were briefed on the role they were to play. They were not, of course, told their destination but it was an open secret that the landing was to take place on one of the islands in the area of the Scheldt and when they embarked at Ostend on the evening of the 31 October Segers of the Belgian Troop recalled a meeting with a French fortune teller in London. "I was told, 'Don't go swimming in November as this could be fatal to you.' I had laughed at the time but now I remembered and felt a cold shiver run down my spine."[3]

Those taking part in Infatuate I were moved to Breskens and spent the night of the 31 October in the ruined houses of the town. That evening the two French Troops gathered in the ruins of the local Catholic church where the French Chaplain, René de Naurois, held mass.*

For the attack on Flushing the Dutch section under de Ruiter was divided up amongst the two French Troops, now numbered 5 and 6, though de Ruiter himself was with Dawson, van Woerden was with the 2 i/c, and van Gelderen – who had won the Dutch Bronze Cross at Arnhem for organizing two supply air strips – and Persoon were with Kieffer. Their brief was to act as guides and interpreters, and to liaise with the local Dutch underground. They proved to be invaluable in this last role, for the Resistance rose against the Germans immediately the Commando landed and the British, the French and the local townsmen fought alongside one another to drive the enemy from Flushing.

"I worked as Liaison Officer for Colonel Dawson and after we landed one of my roles was to keep the Colonel in touch with Kieffer. I would also take back any German officers to the prison compound on the beach in case I could extract any information from them as I could speak German. One of these officers was mortified that he was in charge of someone so junior, but he brightened up when he learnt my name was De Ruiter. There was a big monument in the town of the famous Dutch Admiral, De Ruyter, and he thought I was related to him, and so was not such an insignificant person to escort him after all!

"On the first night after the landings it became known that fourteen German engineers and technicians who were working on a large ship in the dockyard were willing to surrender. The ship, which was under construction,

---

* De Naurois had escaped from France and had made his way to England via Spain, and was eventually attached to the French Commandos as their priest. But he also took a great interest in the British soldiers in the Commando and, despite his fractured English, got on very well with them – so much so that he learnt a number of words which were distinctly unclerical which he tended from time to time to use in conversation in the Officers' Mess. He was trained as a medical orderly and in Normandy he would insist on going out on night patrol with his flock. He was a fighting padre and always went armed. When he undertook one of these hazardous operations his bald head would be plastered with blacking, because, "If your cap falls off, Padre, it will shine like the beacon off Le Havre".[4] Sadly, de Naurois had a nervous breakdown after Walcheren and was hospitalized in England, but soon recovered. At the time of writing he is still alive, and is a world expert on the migration of sea-birds.

had been mined by the Germans and these technicians knew where the charges had been laid. So I went with two others and with a member of the Dutch Resistance who had tipped us off about the men. We started at 10pm and went over the Verbroon bridge. Before we went I told the Dutch Resistance man that he was to lead the way and that if we were fired on I knew it would be an ambush and that I would kill him. He still said he would go, but we got lost in the dockyard. Eventually, we found the technicians, disarmed them and removed the explosive charges – which in fact had already been rendered harmless by the shipyard personnel. As we led the way back I heard someone running towards us and expected trouble. But it was only a German sentry who had heard what was going on and wanted to be made a prisoner too!

"We recrossed the bridge at about 2.30 in the morning, which was much later than we had planned, and the Commando unit I had arranged to cover my return had been replaced by an army unit who knew nothing about us. We were challenged and though I was allowed across the bridge, my prisoners had to stay on the other side. While I was arguing with the officer in charge as to whose prisoners they were the Germans started mortaring the bridge and the prisoners scattered. The officer then said I could have them as he didn't know where they were anyway, but when I called across to them to follow me they all did!"[5]

The landing beach, codenamed Uncle, was right in Flushing, at Dokhaven. It was between two long piers and was very narrow, but was the only place the planners could find that fulfilled their requirements. The low cloud and persistent drizzle made heavy bombing impossible so for an hour before the first men went ashore the German defences in the area were pounded by heavy artillery and by low-flying Mosquito light bombers.

The plan was for No 1 and No 2 Troops, under the 2 i/c of the Commando, to land first and to move as quickly as possible to throw a secure perimeter round the landing area, before the main landing force, with Commando HQ, came ashore. Kieffer's task was to oversee the landing of the main part of the Commando before joining his two French Troops to co-ordinate their attack with No 3 Troop on their objectives. For ease of identification the town had been divided into various sectors, each named after an English or Scottish town.

One of the first ashore was Corporal Bill de Liefde of the Dutch section who at 5.45 landed as part of a reconnaissance party whose job it was to guide the rest of the landing force into the beach. This he managed to do with a lantern and at 0615 Kieffer landed, intending to set up his headquarters at the base of a windmill. "The enemy was firing from the windmill so I sent my HQ bren with Lieutenant Hattu to clear it; this was completed at 0710 and two prisoners were brought back. The bren and two men were left to hold the windmill. From 0730 until 0750 we were shelled violently. At about 0800 after a conference with the Commanding Officer, Lt-Colonel Dawson, I started moving my HQ to Bellamy Park to take up a HQ position for leading operations of Nos 3, 5 and 6 Troops."[6]

No 3 Troop touched down at 6.40 without difficulty and made straight for Bellamy Park, a town square 200 yards in length just inland of the Western harbour. The first French Troop to get ashore, No 5, under Lofi, landed under fire. The Troop had embarked in two LCAs, No 1 Section with Lofi and Lieutenant Chausse in one and No 2 Section with Lieutenant Amaury in the other. Both craft encountered machine-gun and light flak fire and the first LCA struck the pier out of control after the coxswain had been hit, and then sank. The second boat was also hit and several men, including two of the Dutch section, were wounded, and the rest had to wade through shoulder-high water to the shore.

Once ashore, No 5 Troop followed No 3 Troop to Bellamy Park and found it tough going. "Two prisoners were taken, one speaking French, who said that an important group had withdrawn to the barracks. The Troop moved forward, and on civilian information the church was attacked and one prisoner taken by Lieutenant Chausse. Route was now: Kerk Straat/Spuik Straat/Bree Straat/Bellamy Park, with No 2 Section (Amaury) in the lead. At the Groote Markt Crossroads No 2 Section was ordered to hold Bree Straat and No 1 Section was ordered to West Straat/Mossel Mans Gang to attack the barracks.

"The time was now approximately 0730. Lieutenant Amaury, with No 2 Section, was stopped by MMG and sniper fire. Lance-Corporal Montean and the prisoners were killed. House fighting forced the enemy to withdraw to the barracks leaving several wounded and dead behind."[7]

Chausse, with two of his sergeants, Messanot* and Paillet, now went forward to reconnoitre the barracks, but were ambushed en route with stick grenades and Chausse was slightly wounded. Lofi reported to Kieffer that he was held up and was informed that a company of the King's Own Scottish Borderers, which had landed behind the Commandos, would press home the attack on the barracks and the rest of Worthing Sector while Lofi moved on to attack Dover Sector.

The next French Troop, No 6, under Lieutenant Guy Vourc'h, was luckier when landing and lost only two men. With Captain van Nahuis, a former police inspector and now a local Resistance leader, as their guide, they made their way to their first objective, the main Post Office at the northern end of Wilhelmina Straat. At first they encountered only light sniper fire, but when they reached the Post Office they found it had been reinforced by, as it turned out, Germans

* It was during this heavy street fighting that Messanot behaved with such exemplary courage that he was later awarded the Military Medal. "In the course of street fighting," the citation read, "this NCO and his section were held up by strong, well-sited enemy pockets of resistance. Sergeant Messanot immediately dashed forward under heavy fire and destroyed the enemy with grenades. He then promptly broke into the position and took a number of prisoners."

who had been withdrawn from other parts of the town. The Troop's No 1 Section, under Lieutenant Senée attacked the position and took fifty prisoners, but a small group, under an officer, continued to hold out on the first floor and was only silenced when four or five Frenchmen climbed onto the roof and threw hand grenades in through the windows. Vourc'h and his Troop then made their way along Wal Straat to the big crossroads at the dockyard gates, Betje Wolf Plein in the Bexhill Sector, where they were to form a line between the Spui Kom lake and the docks to throw back any German counter-attack which might come from the new part of the town.

Vourc'h later wrote: "At about 0745 we were at Bexhill sector. The Dutch officer made a mistake at that time. He took a sub-section with him to a place near Dover sector and that sub-section got cut off by a party of Germans. Some of the men managed to escape and come back. Some had to hide for some time and joined the Troop only the day after.

"My plan was to occupy the block of houses which makes the corner between Badhuis Straat and Goosje Busken Straat. The first section of my Headquarters crossed the latter street, under fire from the pill box in Dover. The school in the street was occupied by the enemy, who had there large stores. We took seven prisoners. The second section was unable to cross the road, the fire being too strong. As we were just arriving a force of Germans about a company strong was coming towards us down Badhuis Straat. We opened fire on them from the street and stopped them. It was then about 0800.

"One of the sections was holding the corner of Badhuis Straat and Glacis Straat. They remained there alone with Lieutenant Senée in command for about two hours, stopping all attacks from the Germans and killing a great number of them. My losses were three killed. My headquarters was in the corner of Goosje Busken Straat and Badhuis Straat, the other section was in the building in front on the other side of Goosje Busken Straat, with Lieutenant G. de Montlaur. They made a recce of Aagje Keken Straat along the shipbuilding yard, but could not enter it. At about 0815 we were reinforced by the machine-gun section of No 4 Troop [the Heavy Weapons Troop]; one MG managed to come to my headquarters, the other staying with No 2 Section, having lost a man while trying to cross the road."[8]

At about 0900 another company of KOSB managed to contact the heavily beleaguered Frenchmen and an hour later got a platoon across the road to Vourc'h who despatched them to reinforce Senée. At about the same time the Germans again attacked in force, this time down Aagje Keken Straat, but they were again dispersed, the Heavy Weapons Troop MMG killing two of them before it jammed.

By noon Hove and Worthing sectors had fallen to the Commando, but Lofi was still unable to move forward through the narrow neck of land between the lake and the sea and at 1500 had come to a halt at the corner of Noord Straat and

Goosje Busken Straat. Kieffer now sent for Lofi and together they went to confer with Dawson. It was decided that Lofi should continue to advance as much as possible but later he was ordered to withdraw for the night so that a heavy barrage could be put down on the German positions.

At 0700 the next morning Lofi continued his advance along the Goosje Busken Straat. However, progress was slow for they found their way blocked by a 20mm quadruple-barrelled anti-aircraft gun in a concrete strongpoint at the far end of the street.

"It was always a pleasure to see the French in action," Dawson was to remark later. "They showed endless resource and contrivance, and were masters of individual action"; and what Lofi and his men did that morning is a shining example of what Dawson meant, for they took part in what was probably the classic street-fighting attack of the whole Flushing operation.

One section of the Troop managed to get into a cinema in the street and the PIAT team climbed on to the roof. From there it was able to give effective covering fire while the other section crossed the street and entered a building. Both sections now moved forward house by house by blowing holes in the garden walls – a method of advance called "mouseholing" – and clearing each house of any Germans, often in hand-to-hand fighting. Slowly the two sections moved closer and closer to the concrete blockhouse and were about to prepare themselves for the final assault when they were ordered to withdraw so that six Typhoons could attack the remaining German positions with rockets.

In the afternoon the advance was continued, with the Troop clearing houses and reaching the corner immediately overlooking the strongpoint. During this push forward they came across evidence of the ruthless manner in which the Germans behaved towards the local Dutch population. As mentioned earlier, one sub-section of No 6 Troop had been cut off the previous day and one member had been compelled to take refuge in a house which the Germans retook next day. When they found English equipment there they took the entire family who lived there outside and shot them.

The enemy were now confined to the strongpoint and to the house on the corner of the Boulevard Bankert. From this building they attempted to escape at about 1630, but ran into the concentrated fire of the whole of No 5 Troop and received several casualties.[9]

By now Lofi's No 1 Section had reached the anti-tank wall which blocked the end of the street and was firing PIAT bombs at very short range into the embrasures of the strongpoint, but as there was no sign of surrender from it Lofi decided the only thing to do was to lay an explosive charge by the armoured door.

One of his men, Lafont, had just volunteered for this hazardous mission when the armoured door opened and a white flag on a long stick poked out.

Then, moments later, three officers and about sixty soldiers stumbled out, their hands on their heads, many of them hardly conscious. By then Lofi's Troop had been reduced to three officers and forty-seven men.

2

While Flushing was under attack, the main assault on the island took place on the wind-swept dunes on either side of the ruined and partially flooded village of Westkapelle.

The Operational Orders for the Belgian and Norwegian Troops of the Inter-Allied Commando taking part in Infatuate II listed their role as being in support of No 41 Commando, which was to land north of the gap in the dyke and then move towards Domburg. However, one section of the Belgian Troop, commanded by Lieutenant Meny, was to be detached as protection for the tanks of the 1st Lothians which were also to land with the Commandos. On landing, at H-Hour + 25 minutes, the task of the two Inter-Allied Troops was to pass through the village of Westkapelle which, it was planned, would have been cleared by a Troop from No 41 Commando, and to "protect the left flank of 4 SS Bde and deny the enemy all approaches to N and NE of Westkapelle".

The two Troops, plus headquarters, were embarked with their LVTs at Ostend in four LCTs as follows:

1. Cdo Hq, No 4 (Belgian) Troop less one section, and one officer and 14 ORs of No 5 (Norwegian) Troop.
2. No 5 Troop, less one officer and 14 ORs.
3. One sub-section of No 4 Troop, Lieutenant Meny i/c, to act as tank protections.
4. One sub-section of No 4 Troop, as tank protection.[10]

These four vessels, in company with those carrying Nos 41, 47 and 48 Commandos, were protected by "T" Force, a Support Squadron commanded by Captain A.F. Pugsley RN which included LCFs, LCGs, and LCRs* for tackling the German defences at close range, as well the battleship HMS *Warspite* and two monitors for bombarding the beaches prior to landing and pounding the heavy German batteries that dominated the Scheldt.

Thanks to the bravery of the Close Support Squadron in going right inshore to tackle the German defences the LCTs carrying the Inter-Allied and Royal Marine Commandos approached the landing beaches, some twenty minutes behind schedule, relatively unscathed. Even so the enemy's fire became intense about a mile from shore and the LCT with one of the Belgian sub-sections in it received three direct hits, knocking out all the tanks in it and wounding the sub-section's Liaison Officer and two Belgians. Five minutes later it turned for home and passed the LCT containing the Commando's HQ. The sight of it, as the War Diary noted, "was not an aid to morale".

* Landing Craft (Flak), Landing Craft (Gun), and Landing Craft (Rocket).

The HQ ship, having narrowly missed being hit several times, grounded near the landing beach, codenamed White Tare, just north of the gap in the dyke at 1035. However, when an attempt was made to lower the ramp it was found that the LCT was rammed hard against some iron stakes. The vessel was now a sitting target for the German gunners but those aboard were heartened when a few minutes later the LCT containing the bulk of the Norwegian Troop passed inshore on the port beam and, with a rousing cheer from its occupants, beached safely. Some of the Norwegians, however, had to wade ashore. Lieutenant Gudmundseth, finding his wet trousers extremely uncomfortable, exchanged them for those belonging to the first German prisoner he came across.

The LCT carrying Lieutenant Dauppe's section of the Belgian Troop also became stuck on some underwater defences. The skipper wanted to back off and try again but the stern had already received a direct hit and Dauppe asked that the ramp be dropped and he and his section had to wade ashore.[11] Casualties among the Belgians on landing were light, though Stichnot was seriously wounded and Burggraeve, as he engaged the German beach defences with his bren gun, had his foot smashed by a shell. For this act of bravery under fire he was later decorated with the Belgian Croix de Guerre.

It was soon considered too dangerous to remain aboard the HQ ship any longer and orders were given for those on board to get ashore as best they could. The water was deep and the current strong, but despite heavy shelling and mortaring from the Germans, casualties were light. Corporal Hamilton, however, was killed as he stepped ashore and Captain Emmet was wounded while in the water. He was supported by Watson – who was wounded, too – until they were both picked up and taken back to Ostend.[12]

By 1050 the Commando's HQ had managed to establish itself at the top end of the beach near some reinforced concrete and shortly afterwards LVTs and Weasels which had been trapped in the LCT came ashore. At 1115 the situation was that the Belgians were ashore and mopping up the western area of Westkapelle in support of the No 41 Commando Troop assigned to clearing the village, and had suffered eight casualties, all wounded. At the same time the Norwegians were clearing up German opposition in the northern part of Westkapelle, and were advancing towards the large German battery, W.15, situated just north of the village, and had had ten casualties, two of them dead.

"The Norge Commander, seeing 41 Commando attack the battery W.15 from the landward, across open ground, attacked across the dunes and obtained a strategic position from which they had the defenders under fire, and forced them below ground, thus enabling 41 Commando to complete their advance and make the kill. They then took over the battery positions and made a screen around them to the north, while the Belge completed the mopping up of snipers with the aid of an AVRE,* which pumped a few 'dustbins' into the lighthouse, and finally set it on fire."[13]

With both Troops off the landing beach, HQ, which had by now been reduced to the CO, the 2 i/c, the Signals Officer and fifteen other ranks, moved into Westkapelle and set up in, of all places, a coffin-maker's shop, before moving later into the captured W.15 battery which had fallen at about 1215. One member of the Norwegian Troop had landed with a Norwegian flag wrapped around his stomach, and this was produced and flown on the battery.

With the No 41 Commando Troop assigned to clearing Westkapelle were two members of No 3 Troop, Sergeant Gray and Corporal Latimer. When Germans in the tall tower on the landward side of the village continued to fire, Gray gave his weapons to Latimer so that the Germans could see he was unarmed and walked out into the street. "I went along the main street shouting in German for the Germans to surrender, telling them they didn't have a chance. A German sergeant came out and said he'd lay down his conditions for surrendering. While I was arguing with him Latimer went into the tower. Latimer was a Czech socialist who thought that the common man was much better than those in charge, so he went behind my back, and the German sergeant's, and got the Germans in the tower to surrender without any conditions at all! He led them out the back way so their sergeant wouldn't see them and when they were out of the way told him he might as well surrender anyway as he had no troops left."[14]

While the two Troops of the Inter-Allied Commando took up defensive positions to ward off a possible counter-attack, No 41 Commando had advanced up the coast towards the next large battery, W.17, situated on the outskirts of the small town of Domburg, taking it before dark, and then moving on into Domburg itself.

While the attack north of the gap in the dyke could be said to be proceeding satisfactorily, Brigadier Leicester was being pressed to silence the batteries south of it as quickly as possible so that the minesweepers could enter the Scheldt and start their work. He therefore ordered all but two Troops of No 41 Commando to move back from Domburg to support Nos 47 and 48 Commandos, which had landed south of the gap, and at 1300 Laycock was ordered to move up the coast to take over No 41's positions. By 1630 the Belgians and Norwegians had moved to their new positions and the two remaining Troops from No 41 Commando came under Laycock's command.

At that time only half the town had been captured and there was a good deal of sniping and machine-gun fire. At 1730 a fighting patrol from the Belgian Troop, commanded by Lieutenant Roman, was sent out by Laycock to get, as

---

* Assault Vehicle Royal Engineers: this was a Churchill Mk IV tank which had fitted, instead of its gun, a 12-inch spigot mortar which fired a 25lb explosive charge up to 80 yards to break down concrete obstacles and defences.

the War Diary put it, the "lie of the land", and the Commando's position was much improved when half an hour later the remnants of the 1st Lothians that had managed to get ashore, two Sherman tanks and two AVREs, arrived on the outskirts of the town. Their presence soon put an end to snipers and any small arms fire, but mortar and shell fire continued to rain down throughout the night.

The tanks laagered at the southern end of Domburg for the night and were protected by a sub-section from the Norwegian Troop, and next morning they were put to good use by shelling a large water tower on the north-eastern outskirts of the town by the dunes that was being used by German snipers. Behind this tower were high dunes which were the centre of the German defensive positions.

After the Norwegians had reconnoitred the area in the morning they launched an attack on the German positions in the afternoon, supported by a rolling barrage from the Canadian guns at Breskens and by two of the Sherman tanks. The Germans had reinforced their positions by high barbed wire, among which they had laid mines, and in trying to surmount this, with the aid of a ladder, the Norwegian Troop Commander, Captain Rolf Hauge, was wounded in the arm by mortar fire. Eventually, a way was found through the wire and, though one man was killed and the Sergeant-Major wounded by the Germans' sporadic fire, the position was overrun.[15] Lieutenant Gausland started the Germans' surrender by lobbing a hand grenade with great accuracy through the entrance of one of the concrete emplacements and its occupants appeared with their hands held high.

Hauge now regrouped his Troop and, finding his way clear, pushed forward another half-mile into the dunes, taking two additional enemy positions. He then ordered Gausland to take his section further forward and Gausland advanced until he could see below him a group of buildings that lay in a dip inland from the next large battery which had to be taken, W.18. But by now the enemy's resistance had stiffened considerably and Gausland halted, reported his position, and was told to withdraw. During this action a total of 175 prisoners were taken. Though quite seriously wounded, Hauge continued in command until he had consolidated his Troop into defensive positions for the night. When he was eventually examined by the Medical Officer he was evacuated to the mainland and was later awarded the Military Cross for his leading part in this successful skirmish.[16]

"The attack was planned in three phases; each should have been reported by wireless, but the first message we received was that the Norwegians had just completed phase three. They had met with serious opposition, had attacked with the utmost disregard for danger, clearing out the lot, but casualties were fairly heavy."[17]

While the Norwegians advanced along the dunes, the Belgians continued to clear the wooded area on the southern flank of any remaining snipers. By nightfall, despite persistent mortaring and shelling, the two Troops had consolidated well to the north-east of Domburg, and had taken a total of 211 POWs. "The Kriegsmarine did not like close fighting," the War Diary commented succinctly.

To the south of the gap in the dyke No 47 Commando, along with Linzel and his men, had at last overrun the stubborn defenders of W.11. It had proved to be one of the fiercest battles of the whole operation and for No 47 Commando the position at one time had been critical. By the time they landed south of the gap the Support Squadron had been virtually wiped out and the German gunners had turned their attention to the LCTs bringing in No 47. As a result there were casualties and much confusion and delay, and at 0700 the next morning when the CO held an O Group he ordered Linzel and his men to join B Troop which had been depleted during the landing. The Commando's first attack on W.11, their main objective, was driven off that afternoon and had to be pressed home again the following morning. After a heavy artillery bombardment on the position, the Commandos charged and overran the German battery and bunkers, and their defenders began to surrender in droves. Then the Germans outside the position began to mortar the battery and seven of Linzel's men were wounded by shrapnel as they crouched by a casemate. Linzel himself had a narrow escape when a mortar bomb dropped right by him but did not explode.

With gathering momentum, the Commando swept on towards the final battery, W.4. But by now the Germans were in no mood to resist and the CO was soon accepting the surrender of the remants of the German garrison. "Captain Koll, handing me his Luger pistol, said. 'You will shoot me if you think I have not done my duty.' I was so relieved and delighted that I could have embraced him." Soon, No 47 Commando had linked up with No 4 Commando coming up from Flushing, and in the Scheldt the minesweepers could be seen at work clearing the estuary.[18] But the price had been high and Linzel remembers returning wearily through the dunes and seeing whole rows of dead bodies wrapped in army blankets, "looking like sardines waiting to be shipped back to Ostend. Since then I hate seeing an open tin of sardines and I never eat them anymore."[19]

But if the fighting to the south had ceased it had only just begun in the northern tip of the island. At 1215 on 4 November, No 41 Commando arrived back at Domburg and at 1300 the advance was resumed with the Belgians taking the southern half of the area through the wooded country and B Troop of No 41 Commando taking on the northern dune area, while the Norwegians, now under the command of Lieutenant Gausland, were rested. The attack was supported by both tanks and both AVREs. The going proved tough for the British Troop, but the Belgians were able to clear the wooded area quickly – though sniping and mines caused casualties, including the Troop's Adjutant, Lieutenant d'Oultremont – and by the end of the day the Germans had been pushed back between 800 and a thousand yards nearer to their next big battery, W.18.

The next morning, D+4, the Belgians were relieved by the Norwegians and it was agreed that No 41 Commando would be responsible for the northern, seaward, half of the front while the Inter-Allied Commando would be responsible for the wooded southern, inland, half. Offensive patrols were sent out into the wooded area and several prisoners were brought in. Sniping and mortar fire was constant.

In the afternoon effective air support was to be laid on for the attack on W.18 to the north of Domburg and the two Troops of the Inter-Allied Commando were put under command of No 41 Commando for it. The Norwegians were given the task of clearing the flank and advanced through this inland wooded area, while No 41 attacked the battery, which fell just before dark. That night a chance sniper's round hit Lieutenant Rommetvedt of the Norwegian Troop, wounding him in the chest, and his section was taken over by 2/Lieutenant Gudmundseth.

Early the next morning some Germans in an anti-tank position ahead of the Norwegians called out that they wanted to surrender. The Norwegians, fearing a trick, refused to go and collect them and told the Germans to come forward with their hands up, but the Germans did not come. Gausland reported this to the Belgians when they took over at dawn and a little later a sub-section of the Belgian Troop ran into an ambush and suffered casualties. However, the Belgians pressed on with tremendous *élan*, but were pinned down by fire from four different machine-gun positions. How they dealt with them must be put down as one of the most outstanding feats of arms performed by the Inter-Allied Commando in any of the operational zones in which its members fought during the war.

"The Belgians were ordered to clear the woods on the flank as far as the first bound of the next day's attack. This they carried in brilliant style, mopping up all opposition and occupying a feature which had been set as one of the first objectives for the next day, taking thirty POWs in the process."[20]

Even the unit's War Diary noted the Belgians' feat with unusually warm appreciation. "It can be noted here," it commented, "that this small battle was an absolute classic of determination to get through at all costs and obtain one's objective, and, after the objective had been taken, to appreciate the situation and realize that something further must be done in order to make the position tenable. This in fact was carried out, and there is no doubt at all that that extra piece of ground gained that night through 4 Troop Commander's own initiative made a vast difference to the speeding up of the final outcome of the battle for the north coast."[21]

It was not taken, however, without cost and the decorations awarded to the Belgian Troop for that one action shows how bravely they reacted to the Germans who so bitterly opposed them.* The woods through which they attacked that day were thick with undergrowth, ideal cover for the defenders. A Section, under Lieutenant Meny, who had already led a fighting patrol earlier on in the day to clear some machine-gun nests and snipers, was on the right of the advance, with B Section, under Lieutenant Roman, on the left. The Troop HQ, with Captain Danloy, was in the centre.

Just after A Section was forced to move further inland because of a minefield, intense enemy fire pinned them down and Lieutenant Meny was hit in the chest and killed. Moments later another Belgian, Dive, was also killed by a burst of machine-gun fire and the section sergeant, Artemieff, took command. He led his men forward and, though wounded twice in the shoulder, destroyed an enemy machine-gun position with his tommy gun, for which he was later decorated with a palm to the Croix de Guerre he had won in Italy.

With its two most senior leaders out of the battle and pinned down by heavy enemy fire, the position of the section was now desperate. Sergeant de Leener and Lance-Corporal Legrand now took over command of the two sub-sections and attempted to continue the advance, but, as Sergeant de Leener later recorded in his diary, "The enemy's fire at that time became so intense that we were forced to take cover. The least movement of one of us meant a hail of machine-gun fire. We were stuck and it became impossible to go forward or back."[22]

Danloy now acted by swinging his B Section to the right so that Roman and his men attacked the Germans on their flank. As they went in Legrand was ordered by Danloy to cover the attack and Legrand personally gave the fire orders to his sub-section. At 1530 he was wounded by a machine-gun bullet in his shoulder, but refused to relinquish command until the German machine guns were finally wiped out, which was done by Roman and his men "at the point of the bayonet", supported by covering fire from No 41's Heavy Weapons Troop.

Earlier in the day, Legrand, who was the NCO in charge of the mortar section of A Section, had been wounded in the back by shrapnel, but had said nothing about this until the task allotted his section had been completed. He was then treated by the Medical Officer but insisted that he return to duty with the Troop. For this, and for his leadership in covering Roman's attack while wounded in the shoulder, Legrand was later decorated with the Military Medal. "Lance-Corporal Legrand set a very fine example of leadership and courage to the men under his command," part of the citation read. "Although severely wounded, his devotion to his duty was such that he refused to leave his post, and continued to lead his men in the final assault."

* Besides the decorations mentioned in the text the Belgian Troop won no less than eight Croix de Guerre of various grades on that day.

Although the German machine guns had now been taken out, Danloy knew it was tactically essential to take the dunes that lay north of the wood. He therefore ordered Roman to advance and take this high ground, and Roman and his men successfully cleared it of Germans. Two hours later he led a patrol to find out what enemy activity there was in the adjoining wood east of the Belgians' positions. He carried this out successfully, too, and returned at 2000. For his leadership during that afternoon, and for successfully leading a reconnaissance patrol in the morning to report the position of a German mortar which was subsequently silenced, Roman was awarded the Military Cross. "Throughout this action," part of the citation read, "Lieutenant Roman showed a complete disregard for his personal safety, and by his fine qualities of leadership and courage, he set a splendid example to the men under his command."

The next morning, 7 November, No 41 Commando, which had been reinforced by the Heavy Weapons Troops of the other two Royal Marine Commandos, launched an attack on a commanding feature known as the Black Hut area which lay between W.18 and the last big battery, W.19, which was still holding out. The Norwegians took over from the Belgians and were given the task of clearing the wood that ran the length of the line of advance, and this was satisfactorily carried out, with "many prisoners taken, also many killed".[23]

The Black Hut area was taken in the afternoon but then No 41 Commando were caught in heavy machine-gun enfilade fire, and were also heavily mortared. It was then learned from a POW that the majority of the garrison in W.19 had moved out into the wood in the south, and that this was where the enfilade fire had been coming from. Air support was called for and the woods containing the Germans were plastered by rocket-firing Typhoons. Under cover of this fire the British Commandos who had been pinned down were withdrawn and Brigadier Leicester, with all his Commando units now at his disposal, began to plan a Brigade attack for the following morning.

Before dawn the next day Gray and Latimer were involved in what by now had become a typical No 3 Troop activity of infiltrating the enemy's lines and taking a prisoner. "We set out at about 3am, crossed the minefields and established ourselves behind the German lines. We picked up a few prisoners who were carrying coffee and interrogated them, and asked where their Commanding Officer was. They were very reluctant to tell us. I told them I'd shoot them and they cried. While I was interrogating them Latimer drifted off somewhere. Then I suddenly saw a figure come out of a bunker and stand there in the half light asking where his coffee was. I knew this was the man we wanted and was about to tackle him when out of the sky – or so it seemed – flew Latimer and landed right on this officer. Latimer was small and wiry but he was one of the world's best rugby tacklers. He knocked the man to the ground and that was the end of him. Then Palmer [the CO of No 41 Commando] arrived and I translated what he wanted to say to the German. He persuaded him to surrender and the German agreed to go round his own strongpoint to tell his men to give up, but he wouldn't go to any other strongpoint. We pushed on north but he refused to help any more, however much we threatened him. So we sent him back and pushed on towards W.19. Later we took another officer prisoner who assured us that the order had been given to surrender."[24]

This turned out to be no less than the truth for when, under cover of darkness the following morning, No 4 Commando passed through the position held by No 41 Commando and the Norwegians, W.19 fell with only a few shots fired, with many prisoners being brought in from the surrounding woods. The Commandos then moved to within a mile of Vrouwenpolder.

Soon after daybreak four Germans turned up in full battle kit at Dawson's HQ where all the surrendering enemy were being collected. When asked why they had not thrown down their weapons along with the other prisoners they produced a note written by Lieutenant Vourc'h whose Troop was right up near Vrouwenpolder. "These four enemy soldiers have the task of discussing the terms of surrender. They are not prisoners and I have therefore allowed them to keep their arms."[25] A ceasefire was arranged and the emissaries took an officer from No 4 Cdo to meet the senior German officer, and soon afterwards Dawson accepted the Germans' official surrender.

Epilogue

The success of Walcheren did not mean the end of Nazi Germany, but it was now not a matter of if the régime would be totally defeated but when. The Inter-Allied Commando played its part during these final months, and there was still a lot of hard, bitter fighting to be done.

After Walcheren the Belgian and Norwegian Troops returned to Belgium with No 4 SS Brigade for rest and refitting* before the Brigade was given its next task which was to bolster the line being held against the Germans in northern Holland. The two fighting Troops of the Inter-Allied Commando were stationed at Middleburg, the capital of Walcheren, under a Tac HQ led by Major Franks while the rest of the HQ returned to Eastbourne.

When the German counter-offensive began in the Ardennes on 16 December No 47 (RM) Commando, and later three Troops of No 48 (RM) Commando, were sent up to the front line on the River Maas, and just before Christmas No 47 Commando was reinforced by the Norwegian Troop. The Norwegians were stationed at Oosterhout and together with the Royal Marine Commando they carried out a number of raids on the German side of the river. On the night of 13/14 January they landed on Kapelsche Veer, a German-held island five miles long and one and a half miles wide in the middle of the river, about 20 miles north-east of Breda. On the north was a broad dyke 25 feet high which broadened out, at the defended point, to form quite a reasonable plateau. Here the enemy was well dug in. There was only one small cottage in the area, and all supplies etc. had to brought across the river. The defending troops came mostly from parachute divisions and were young and fanatical. They possessed

* On 6 December, 1944, all Special Service Brigades were renamed Commando Brigades.

a few LMGs but nothing larger, but there were a few batteries on the north side to support them. Most of the low ground was flooded, and, following snow, it had been freezing hard for some days. Forces of 1st Polish Armoured Division had twice attempted to move the enemy, first by a platoon recce, and then with a whole company, but in vain.

"The only possible means of approach to the enemy position was along the base of the dyke from the east or west. So it was decided to form two parties with Q and Norge Troops under the 2 i/c on the right and A, B, X, and Y Troops on the left."[1]

The Norwegian Troop had recently been reinforced with eighteen men from the Norwegian army under the command of a Norwegian officer, Lieutenant Gabriel Smith. After some hesitation Hauge, who had rejoined the Troop before its move to the Maas, decided to allow Smith and a handful of the new recruits to take part in the raid.[2]

An intense artillery barrage was laid down on the island and then the Norwegians, consisting of about seventy men, and the British Troop crossed over to the island by a temporary bridge which had been constructed by Polish Engineers. It was a bitterly cold, dark night with a heavy frost.

The attack almost immediately went wrong for the main force was detected at once and driven back so that the Germans could turn their full attention and fire power to the smaller diversionary force approaching the plateau. It was heavily attacked both by the Germans on the island and by those holding the far bank, and almost immediately one of the Norwegian bren gunners was killed by machine guns on fixed lines that covered the force's only way forward. Soon another fell dead and a third was wounded. Then, as the Norwegians closed on the plateau, hand grenades began to rain down on them from the other side of the dyke and when Smith stood up to throw a hand grenade back he was shot dead.

"Gudmundseth advanced fairly quickly with his section to within 100 yards of the enemy position, but they were then pinned down in the river – the temperature of which was minus 8 degrees Celsius – by severe fire and bombardment. Both sections kept down until the bombardment lifted and then Gudmundseth and his men attacked covered by Gausland's section. This attack got within 15–20 yards of the enemy positions, but then came under a hailstorm of fire and was forced back. Gausland now took over the attack, but he and his men were also driven back. Our positions were now so close to the enemy that we were throwing hand grenades at each other and any movement resulted in a storm of fire."[3]

The Troop from No 47 Commando had also run into heavy fire, but, though they received casualties, the Marines pressed home their attack on the German positions, with the Norwegians, now lying very close to the Germans, giving them covering fire. Three times they tried and three times they were thrown back. During the last attempt they actually got into the cottage but were driven back by a German counter-attack and lost their Troop Commander.

"By now we had four killed and around thirty wounded or disabled, seven seriously, out of a total of approximately seventy. We felt, to put it mildly, uneasy. Nevertheless, a decision from HQ to rally the rest of the Commandos capable of fighting, in order to try a last desperate storming of the enemy positions, was received. The remaining twenty-four available Commandos, under Lieutenant Gudmundseth, were rallied."[4]

But by now the position of both the British and the Norwegians seemed hopeless for both Troops had been severely mauled and those who were still on their feet were almost out of ammunition. What saved the Norwegians from being wiped out was the technique they had learnt at Walcheren which was to lie so close to the enemy that the mortars on the German-held bank did not dare open fire on them. Hauge, however, was a little behind his two sections and could not escape the German fire. A mortar bomb dropped near his small HQ, killing one man and injuring another.

Gudmundseth was about to launch his attack when orders came through on the radio for both Troops to withdraw. Gudmundseth said afterwards that he felt like a man condemned to death who had been unexpectedly reprieved and both Troops were able to withdraw under covering fire without further casualties.

Kapelsche Veer was not taken for another two weeks and it took two Canadian battalions from 10 Canadian Infantry Brigade, supported by tanks, to capture it, and it cost them around 350 casualties. They found there the graves of 140 Germans who had been killed in the fighting with the British and Norwegian Commandos. The Norwegians had suffered, too, for their casualties were, for them, the worst of the war, and two days later, along with No 47 Commando, they were withdrawn from the front to defend Walcheren which was in danger of being attacked by a German parachute division. For a short while the Norwegians were based at Flushing before returning to England on 8 February. They saw no further action in the war, but at the end of April reverted to the command of the Norwegian army. They were sent to Sweden to join other Norwegian units that were poised to cross the border into Norway in case the occupying Germans refused to surrender. Despite orders not to wear their Commando uniforms, Hauge, when the orders arrived for the Troop to return to its homeland, wore his, and each man continued to wear his green beret.[5]

While the Norwegians patrolled on the Maas the Belgian Troop was returned to the UK to join the two new Belgian Troops, and they, plus the reinforced Dutch Troop, now began a period of intensive training in preparation for joining in the final drive into Germany. On 26 April the Commando, consisting of the British Tac HQ, the Belgian HQ Troop, three officers and twenty-six men from No 3 Troop, and Nos 2, 4, 9 and 10 Troops, landed at Ostend, and then, with the exception of No 2 (Dutch), proceeded to join No 1 Commando Brigade in north-west Germany. The Dutch were attached to the three Troops of No 48 Commando patrolling the Maas opposite an area of swamp called the Biesboch. They were mostly used in liaison duties and in training an irregular battalion of Dutchmen which had been raised to try and strengthen the Allies' thinly-held positions. When the war ended they moved with the rest of No 4 Commando Brigade into Germany for garrison duties and were responsible for guarding the Recklinghausen camp which was full of SS wanted for war crimes.

The two French Troops were also employed in holding the line against the Germans in northern Holland and, with No 4 Commando, took part in raids on the German-held islands of Schouwen and Overflakee. It was while they were there that they were reinforced by reserves who had been made into a third Troop (No 7) under the command of Captain Willers, and it was to them that the honour fell of taking part in the first raid on the islands.

On the night of 17/18 January 1945, sixty-two officers and men embarked on three LCAs and two armed motor boats and at 0330 landed undetected on Schouwen. The raiding party split into two and went in opposite directions. The group led by Sergeant Demonet was spotted and fire opened on them and on the landing craft, and, when it was found that the main objective, a large blockhouse, was too well protected by a succession of barbed wire fences, Willers decided to retire. On returning to the beach he found Demonet's party with six civilians. The party had encountered a German patrol and one Commando had been wounded, but all embarked safely under covering fire from one of the armed motor boats.

The next major raid took place on the night of 14/15 February when two sections of No 5 Troop, commanded by Lieutenant Lofi, embarked in three LCAs and landed on Schouwen, though again without any positive results. This time ten civilians were brought back to provide information on the German positions but they proved to be, as the No 4 Commando Brigade War Diary noted, "astonishingly ill-informed and unobservant".[6]

The last attempt to raid Schouwen took place on the night of 13 March when Troop No 6, led by Captain Guy Vourc'h, landed and tried again to attack an enemy position. The Germans had now flooded the island, making movement difficult. It was also a very clear night so that the dykes and roads had to be avoided, and the French were forced to advance through the rushes. Very dense barbed-wire entanglements stopped their advance in front of their objective, and when the Germans spotted movement effective fire was opened and four of the Commandos were wounded. Vourc'h ordered his men to retreat and after only two hours ashore the Troop re-embarked. The next day No 4 Commando was withdrawn from North Beveland and spent a short period at

Middleburg on Walcheren where for three days the French Commandos served as Queen Wilhelmina's guard of honour.[7]

The three Belgian Troops and the detachment of No 3 Troop who joined 1st Commando Brigade were just too late to join in the fighting. On 8 May, VE-Day, they moved into Niendorf in support of No 45 (RM) Commando and then took over the Military Government of the southern half of the district of Eutin. The British Tac HQ and the Belgium HQ Troop were stationed at Niendorf, No 4 Troop at Timmerdorferstrand, No 9 Troop at Bad Schwartau and No 10 Troop at Ahrensbök.

"Problems were many and varied, and owing to lack of directives had to be dealt with on the spot and at the local Commanders' discretion. First essential was to show the local inhabitants that we were the conquering army and the second to establish some sort of check and control on the swarms of miscellaneous wanderers. This was done by the imposition of a 24-hour curfew, the organization of road pickets and stragglers' camps, the collection of arms, the appointment of a Bürgermeister and the presentation to him of a list of tasks which he was to set about without delay. The following day a Military Government Office was established, water and electricity supplies were regulated, instructions on the treatment and disposal of POWs were received from higher authority and a quick round-up of the local Nazis was made, aided by a flood of denunciations."[8]

Garrison duties continued until mid-July when most of the Belgians returned home for leave, taking with them groups of their fellow-countrymen who had served in the Waffen-SS and were being returned to their homeland for trial. The Dutch returned to the UK on 7 August and the Tac HQ followed a month later. Then on 9 September all the Belgians ceased to come under British command and returned to Belgium where they formed a Belgian Army Commando,* which was later to fight in Korea and the Belgian Congo.

Before leaving the Belgian Troop mention must be made of one of their most colourful nationals, Major the Vicomte Arthur de Jonghe. De Jonghe, described by his Brigade Commander, Mills-Roberts, as a tall, lean, sinister, wolf-like fellow, had been a prisoner of the Germans at the age of 15, an exeperience he did not forget. During the early part of the war he worked as an agent in Belgium, but when his description became known to the Gestapo he escaped to England and joined the Inter-Allied Commando as a Liaison Officer. From there he progressed to being Brigade Security Officer under Mills-Roberts who thought highly of him. "His vast knowledge of the Continent of Europe and his knowledge of those who lived there was of great use to us. He spoke English with an accent, protesting the while that he was in

---

* The Dutch and the French, too, became the nucleus for their countries' first Commando forces, but those members of the Norwegian Troop who did not opt for civilian life were integrated into the Norwegian army, and a Commando force was never formed from them.

fact more English than the English – and in many ways this was true. He had the charm and manners of a light cavalryman – which indeed he was."[9]

De Jonghe, helped by the three Belgian Troops, was an enthusiastic tracker-down of SS and Gestapo personnel wanted by the Allies, though he sometimes overstepped the mark, as Mills-Roberts on one occasion witnessed. On 4 April, 1945, his Brigade entered Osnabruck and were given orders to capture an Area Chief of the Gestapo alive. "We were given photographs and details of the man and told to get him at all costs," wrote Mills-Roberts in his memoirs. "It had been stressed that if he remained at large he was likely to make trouble for the Allies.

"I sent for Arthur de Jonghe and gave him his orders, adding: 'Now Arthur, at all costs don't let him slip through your fingers.'

"Arthur saluted and departed and I could see that this was a job which delighted him – but my crack about losing the man was almost more than he could stand.

"About 11am I noticed a macabre little procession filing down the street towards our headquarters in Osnabruck. The most noticeable thing about it was a stretcher with a body on it. Arthur was leading the procession.

" 'Here comes the Gestapo King,' said Donald Hopson. 'From what I see I doubt if he'll sabotage the Allied cause much now. It'll save us all a hell of a lot of trouble.

"Arthur came in and saluted. 'I have the man,' he announced a trifle smugly.

" 'Bring him in,' I said, and in came the stretcher. I raised the blanket and saw that it was the wanted man all right. 'Explain the circumstances of the arrest,' I said. 'Your orders were to capture him.'

" 'At all cost,' Arthur added.

" 'Yes,' I said.

" 'Of course, sir,' Arthur replied, 'when he does try to go from me I must prevent him.'

" 'You've certainly done that,' I said, with another look at the dead German."[10]

It was around this time that de Jonghe and another member of the Inter-Allied Commando were ambushed by the Germans. They were in a convoy of two jeeps and a motor cycle approaching Osnabruck when the windscreen of the leading vehicle was shattered by a burst of machine-gun fire. Its occupants, the driver and the Brigade Major, dived for the ditch and made it there without being wounded, but a corporal in the second jeep, which also contained de Jonghe, was hit in the face as they dived for cover. Though they returned the fire, they were pinned down and unable to move, and if Corporal K. E. Clarke,* a German-speaking member of the Inter-Allied Commando,

* It has not been possible to ascertain if Clarke was a member of No 3 Troop or not but he was certainly part of the Inter-Allied Commando at the time of the incident.

had not had the initiative to grab the bicycle of a passing German civilian and pedal away to get help the wounded corporal could well have bled to death. As it was he managed to find a British unit whose officer arranged for a barrage to be put down on the Germans' position so that the trapped party could extricate themselves. "Shortly before the enemy fire ceased, I noticed Corporal Clarke, now disguised in civilian clothes, riding the bicycle down the road towards us. He gave a brief wave, shouted the information we required to know, and cycled on towards the town. He told me later that he was then able to contact German civilians and ascertain what the exact positions of the enemy were. This was a very courageous act which required not only courage but initiative of the highest order. As a result of Corporal Clarke's actions no more of my party were killed or wounded, and he himself escaped unscathed. He was subsequently recommended for a Mention in Despatches."[11]

Clarke's bravery was typical of the German-speaking members of the Inter-Allied Commando who were attached to the two Commando Brigades during the closing months of the war and it seems only appropriate that this book should end on their activities during the final push into the country whose régime they had every reason to detest and despise, and what they did subsequently.

The casualties among the Troop were again high. Villiers and Seymour were both killed during the Rhine crossing; Howarth was killed in Germany, probably by a long-range shell, as he was returning from OCTU in England during the closing days of the war; and the Troop's Commander, Griffith,* now a Captain, was shot dead by a sniper only days before the end of the war. "He was a sound soldier," his Brigade Commander wrote of him later, "with an intimate knowledge of the German army. Such a man was invaluable in assessing the true value of any information about the enemy. Those Germans who had volunteered for the Commandos were of a high calibre and meant business. Their record was an impressive one."[12]

A number of the Troop were also wounded. One of them, Corporal Harris, who was with the Headquarters Troop of No 45 Commando for the crossing of the River Weser on 6 April, 1945, had one of his eyes shot out during an action which subsequently won him the Military Medal. "Immediately it left the existing bridgehead," his citation stated, "the Commando came up against extremely heavy and accurate small-arms fire from dug-in enemy positions to the front and left flank. Owing to the flat nature of the ground the only line of advance was along the river bank but every inch of ground was bitterly

---

* Griffith's place was taken by Monahan, who after D-Day had been detached from the Inter-Allied Commando to work with SOE. When he left, Lieutenant Bartlett took command of the Troop. Finally, Lieutenant Langley, the Troop's Administrative Officer, took over during the last days before the Troop was officially disbanded in September 1945. The last two officers had been, like Griffith, commissioned from the ranks of the Troop.

contested. Throughout Corporal Harris was always to the fore, seeking for every opportunity to engage the enemy at close range with his Thompson Machine Carbine. On one occasion the Headquarters found itself only five yards from three occupied enemy slit trenches up the river bank and on the other side of a hedge, and it was obvious that spontaneous action was necessary to save an awkward situation. Immediately, Corporal Harris climbed the bank and in full view of the enemy to his left flank fired his weapon at the enemy, killing two and taking one prisoner. Before he could return to the cover of the bank again he was wounded from a burst of Spandau fire from his left. The courage of this NCO has seldom been surpassed and he undoubtedly saved the lives of several of his comrades by his spontaneous action. His unceasing determination to get at the enemy will always be an inspiration to all."

By these final months quite a number of the Troop had been commissioned. Some, like Wilmers, who joined the SAS, left the Commandos; while others, like Kingsley, who was given a Mention in Despatches for his part in an operation in the Biesboch, became officers in army regiments but were then drafted into the Marine Commandos which were at that time desperately short of Troop officers.

Whether commissioned or not, the German-speakers on the Inter-Allied Commando continued their invaluable work right up to the collapse of Germany. For example, a number of the Troop were used as bait during Operation Cuckoo which took place on 11/12 April, 1945, at Zieriksee on the Dutch coast. "We simulated a German E-Boat in trouble off the coast with flares and some Austrians of 10(IA) Commando shouting for help."[13] The Germans sent out a patrol of six which was ambushed by the Commandos, killing two of them. The patrol leader was taken prisoner and the others were wounded. After Germany capitulated the unit's War Diary was found which showed the Germans had been totally deceived.

Sergeant Nelson was another member of the Troop who proved invaluable during those last months of fighting. He had been wounded in Italy with No 40 (RM) Commando but returned to duty in Europe with No 46 (RM) Commando, and had found important documents when he searched the Corps headquarters of Major-General Brunning in the village of Buchorst. One was a complete Order of Battle of the German forces east of the Elbe. This was immediately passed to VIII Corps and in due course Nelson received the Commander-in-Chief's Certificate of Commendation.

With the surrender of Nazi Germany on 8 May, 1945, most members of No 3 Troop became part of Intelligence units tracking down SS and Gestapo wanted for war crimes or as interpreters and interrogators, vetting personnel of the German armed forces and questioning those suspected of being Nazi sympathizers. One man vividly remembers his time with a Commando Intelligence team based in Essen and his story is a good illustration of the invaluable work carried out by the Troop in the first fragile months of peace. "Part of our job was to arrest and interrogate German businessmen – steel magnates and so on – who had helped the German war effort. It was also part of our job to hunt down and arrest small Resistance groups, and to find wanted SS men. To this end I once had to spend some days in a lunatic asylum pretending to be an inmate as we had been tipped off that some wanted SS men were hiding there. I had to try and interrogate one man who sat naked in a totally bare cell with just a Tyrolean hat on his head, but he refused to speak to me because we had not been introduced. However, I was soon able to come to the conclusion that he was genuine, but the men we wanted were there and we found them eventually.

"To find out about one Nazi Resistance group I joined it, pretending to be an interpreter with the Military Government who was sympathetic to their cause. They wanted to dig up some weapons which they had buried, so I offered to find a car and take them to the place. I then arranged for a road block to be set up on our way back. But as we came to it one of them put a pistol to my head and told me to drive straight through it, which I did. However, I was then able to slow the car down on the pretence that it had been damaged, and those on the road block were soon able to overtake us, and all the group was arrested.

"On another occasion we arrested an ex-paratrooper, who, under interrogation, admitted he was meeting a Resistance group in Bremen who were going to try and blow up some Allied shipping in the harbour with some explosives which they had. My job was to take him to Bremen and to shadow him, and when he made contact with the group we were then to go in and arrest them all. But things went wrong. He walked up to the group all right, but a tram came in between him and me and he got away. But I became friendly with his girl friend and eventually I got him. They caught the Resistance group, too, in the end."

This man was obviously so good at his job that after he was demobilized he joined British Intelligence in Germany and worked in that capacity until his retirement in 1984, but only a few, very few, of the others went back to live there. One of them who did so was Ken Lincoln who took back his old name and returned to teach. "I was with Intelligence until August, 1947, and during that time I met quite a few Germans who had performed what I would call heroic deeds against Nazism and I felt obliged to return to Germany to help people like that. So I became a teacher as there was an extreme shortage of them at that time. I went to a school in Schleswig-Holstein and eventually became a headmaster. I still live in the area, near Hamburg."[14]

For others the memories were too grim to return. One of the newer recruits to the Troop, Fred Jackson, had to interrogate a former commandant of Auschwitz, Rudolf Hoess, who had been found hiding in the kitchen of a farmhouse. "I was drunk for a week," Jackson later wrote. "I just could not live with myself. He was the man who had killed my mother."[15]

Nearly all the Troop applied for, and were granted, UK citizenship after demobilization. Many settled down in Britain and returned to University or went into business or the Law. Others emigrated to the United States and Canada. A few went to Australia and New Zealand. What strikes one meeting them now after all this time is that many of them have been as successful after the war as they were during it. Among their numbers are, or were, a judge, a QC, a Fellow of Balliol College, Oxford, a vice-president of American Express, an international chairman of Ogilvy-Mather, a president of the Institution of Chemical Engineers, a Fulbright scholar . . . The list is a long and distinguished one, and gives one hope that the true worth of the Inter-Allied Commando, as estimated by Hilton Jones after the war, may yet be realized. "Although the sentiment is not very original," he wrote, "it is certainly true to say that chief amongst the means whereby the world may be saved from future unhappiness and chaos is sincere, everyday co-operation between ordinary people of different countries. It is for this reason that interest and importance must attach to No 10 (Inter-Allied) Commando as a unit, quite apart from its activities and achievements in the field; for it was an example in a warring world of real international goodwill and fellowship."[16]

Notes

CHAPTER 1

1. *The Unknown Warrior* by James Leasor, p2.
2. From synopsis written by the late James Monahan CBE for a book he intended to write on No 3 (Misc) Troop whose Intelligence Officer he was. Lent to the author by Mrs Gail Monahan.
3. Letter from the Archivist, Broadlands, to the author dated 11 October, 1985.
4. Philip Ziegler in conversation with author, September, 1985.
5. From memo written to the Chiefs of Staff on 3 June, 1940, in PRO CAB 120/414.
6. *News Chronicle*, 7 January, 1943.
7. From "No. 10 (Inter-Allied) Commando" by C. R. Featherstone in PRO DEFE 2/977.
8. The details of how the French Troop was founded come from the first chapter of *Beret Vert* by Commandant Philippe Kieffer. Kieffer says he was interviewed by Haydon when the latter was Chief of Staff to Mountbatten, but his meeting with him preceded Haydon's promotion and appointment by some months.
9. *Castle Commando* by Donald Gilchrist, pp60–1.
10. Many of the details about the Inter-Allied Commando in this chapter come from the unit's War Diary in PRO WO 218/40.
11. Leasor, op.cit., p3. Leasor was told this by Mountbatten.
12. Quoted from the *Daily Express*, 24 October, 1946.
13. From "No. 3 Troop, 10 Commando: A Brief History" by Bryan Hilton Jones in PRO DEFE 2/977.
14. Obituary printed in the ICI magazine.
15. Hilton Jones, op.cit.
16. Featherstone, op.cit.

17. *Clash by Night* by Brigadier Derek Mills-Roberts, pp180–1.
18. Featherstone, op.cit.
19. Letter from Peter Masters written to the author, 19 May, 1983.
20. *March Past* by Lord Lovat, pp223–4.
21. Hilton Jones, op.cit.
22. Dr J. G. Coates DSO in conversation with author, November, 1982.
23. Tazelaar's colourful wartime career is taken from *Soldier of Orange* by Erik Hazelhoff Roelfzema, *The Square Moon* by Gerald Dogger, and from a conversation the author had with Tazelaar in April, 1985.
24. *SOE in France* by M. R. D. Foot, pp122–3.
25. From letter to author from Paul Streeten, May, 1986. "Peter was my room mate in Aberdovey, and one of my best friends. He painted, drew and wrote poetry, and had a delightful sense of humour. He was shy and almost retiring, and very good looking. His story is probably the most heroic one of any member of X-Troop."
26. From 10(IA) War Diary in PRO 218/40, appendix B dated 22/9/42.
27. From 10(IA) War Diary in PRO 218/40, appendix C dated 23/10/42.
28. *Raiders from the Sea* by Rear-Admiral Lepotier, p127.
29. Report by Leading Seaman Maurice César, dated 5 May, 1943, in TTF 1 bis, Service Historique de la Marine, Château de Vincennes, Paris, from which his story, up to the time he left St Quentin, has been taken. However, he ends his report, "At this point in my story I must stop as I am not allowed to tell the rest or I shall be liable to imprisonment if I say anything at all." Details of how he was subsequently rescued by SOE were given to the author during a conversation with Félix Grispin, Laurent Casalonga and Dr Guy Vourc'h, March, 1986.
30. Kieffer, op.cit., p54, though he does not mention Balloche carrying a wounded commando to the landing craft. This is recorded in *Raiders from the Sea*, p134. Lepotier writes that he interviewed Balloche after the war.

CHAPTER 2

1. Extracted from letter to author from Colonel Rommetvedt, dated 17 December, 1985.
2. Information from letter to author from Arne Sørbye, dated 8 January, 1986.
3. *Klar Til Storm* by Arnfinn Haga, p22.
4. Gausland, in conversation with the author, November, 1985.
5. *Na Sciezkach Polskich Komandosow* by Miroslaw Derecki, p26.
6. Unless otherwise stated the information about Dutch and Belgian escapees comes from interviews with the people concerned.
7. Contained in letter to author from de Waard, dated 8 March, 1983.
8. From narrative supplied to author by Brigadier-General Jan Linzel, March, 1986, and from the *News Chronicle* dated 19 September, 1941.
9. From narrative supplied to author by Colonel Noel Dedeken, February 1986.
10. *Donnez-Nous Un Champ de Bataille* by Carlo Segers, pp16–52.
11. *Don't Cry for Me* by Donald Gilchrist, p42.

12. Chauvet's escape is told in his picture book, *Lancelot, Soldat de la France-Libre*, pp5–12.
13. From an article by Maurice Chauvet in the Journal of the French Navy, *Cols Bleu*, No. 230, 16 February, 1951.
14. *Nous Etions 177* by Gwenn-äel Bolloré, pp47–76.
15. From *Castle Commando* by Donald Gilchrist, pp55–7, which has been read and corrected by Dr Guy Vourc'h, March, 1986.

CHAPTER 3

1. From privately printed booklet by Bill Watson, Darlington, 1979, pp9–12.
2. George Saunders, in conversation with author, October, 1985. Unless otherwise stated, quotations in this chapter are from interviews.
3. *Deemed Suspect* by Eric Koch, p7.
4. ibid, pp9–10.
5. *Collar the Lot* by Peter and Leni Gillman, *Deemed Suspect* by Eric Koch, and *The Dunera Scandal* by Cyril Pearl.
6. *I Understand the Risks* by Norman Bentwich, pp13–15.
7. From letter received by author from Peter Masters, 30 July, 1983.
8. From letter in the *Spectator* (8 June, 1945) from Sir Alexander Paterson.
9. ibid.
10. Extracted from narrative supplied by Professor Paul Streeten, August, 1984.
11. Quoted in letter from Peter Terry to the author, dated 26/11/82.
12. Letter from SOE archivist to author dated 22 January, 1986.
13. Extract from the diary of His Honour Judge Brian Grant.
14. From "No. 3 Troop, 10 Commando: A Brief History" by Bryan Hilton Jones in PRO DEFE 2/977.
15. From conversation with Colin Anson and Miss Pat Cleland, January, 1986.
16. Extracted from manuscript supplied to author by Peter Terry, 26/11/82, and from interviews with other members of X-Troop.

CHAPTER 4

1. *The Commandos: 1940–1946* by Charles Messenger, p175.
2. In PRO DEFE 2/122.
3. *Klar Til Storm* by Arnfinn Haga, p52.
4. Report by Military Force Commander, Operation Cartoon, in PRO DEFE 2/221.
5. Haga, op.cit., p62.
6. *The Green Beret* by Hilary St George Saunders, p212.
7. From "Summary of the Activities of No 5 Troop 10(IA) Commando" in DEFE 2/977.
8. Report by Lt Rommetvedt in PRO WO 218/56.
9. Olav Gausland, in conversation with author, November, 1985.
10. Memo in PRO DEFE 2/1231.
11. In PRO DEFE 2/211.
12. Messenger, op.cit., p246.

13. Harry Nomburg, in conversation with author, June, 1984.
14. Details of these raids are in PRO DEFE 2/208–13.
15. The details of this raid all come from the Raid Commander's report in PRO DEFE 2/209 and from Casalonga's translated report in the same file.
16. Report loaned to author by Mrs J. Wilmers. It was evidently written at a later date when Wilmers was a captain in the SAS as he is given that rank at the top of the report. A few extracts from it were used by Hilary St George Saunders in *The Green Beret*, p214, who in the first edition of his book wrongly named Wilmer(s) as the Military Force Commander. Later editions were corrected.

CHAPTER 5

1. Memo in PRO DEFE 2/1093.
2. Memo to GOC SS Group from COHQ dated 29 January, 1944, in PRO DEFE 2/1093.
3. The story of Hardtack 11 is taken from Major Leahy's report which is in PRO DEFE 2/345.
4. The story of the five French Commandos stranded in France after Hardtack 11 has been pieced together from the reports each of them wrote. Madec's report is in PRO DEFE 2/1074; those written by Navrault and Pourcelot were given to the author by Dr Guy Vourc'h; and those of Caron and Meunier are in file TTF 1 bis, Service Historique de la Marine, Château de Vincennes, Paris.
5. McGonigal's report is in PRO ADM 202/74.
6. Hulot's report is in PRO DEFE 2/345.
7. I. D. C. Smith's report is in the Layforce II War Diary, which is in PRO 208/167.
8. No Force Commander's report exists on this raid, but mention of what happened is in DEFE 2/209.
9. Francis Vourch's report is in PRO DEFE 2/345.
10. *Clash by Night* by Brigadier Mills-Roberts, p123.
11. "Il y a sept ans disparaissait en raid Charles Trepel, Capitaine Commando" by Maurice Chauvet, K17249 in the Imperial War Museum archives.
12. "Intelligence Requirements – Operation Premium: Questionnaire for Raid Commander" in PRO DEFE 2/520.
13. Memorandum, dated 13 September, 1943, in PRO DEFE 2/352.
14. The story of Operation Premium is contained in two reports: one by Commandant Kieffer to Chief of Staff of French Naval Forces in Britain, dated 8 March, 1944, in the possession of Colonel Robert Dawson, based on the account of the dory coxswain; the other by Major Peter Laycock, in PRO DEFE 2/520, based on the accounts given by the two members of X-Troop on the operation, Farr and Sayers. Additional facts were also supplied to the author during interviews with the CO of MTB 682, William Beynon, his No. 1, John Miller-Stirling, and with the Flotilla Commander, Donald Bradford, in February and March, 1986.
15. Letter from Hulot to Monsieur l'Officier des Equipages Delveaux, dated May, 1945, which is in the archives of the Musée des Fusiliers-Marins at L'Orient, France.

16. *The Green Beret* by Hilary St George Saunders, p221.
17. *Het Drama Bij Wassenaarse Slag*, a detailed analysis of Operation Premium and the mysterious deaths of its participants, was written in 1985 by P. H. Kamphuis, a Dutch historian who is the assistant to the Head of the Historical Branch of the Royal Netherlands Army. This has been translated into French under the title *Le Drame de Wassenaar*, and it is from this edition that the author has gleaned some facts about the aftermath to the operation. Dr Kamphuis also kindly supplied the author with the German reports and with a copy of Lieutenant Hulot's letter.
18. Letter from Félix Grispin to Colonel Robert Dawson dated 30 December, 1985.
19. Saunders, op.cit., p264.
20. ibid, p264, but Saunders has a different list of possible types of mines than appears in the report of the raids to the Prime Minister which is in PRO PREM 3/330/8. The author's list is taken from this latter reference.
21. The records of these raids are in PRO PREM 3/330/8, DEFE 2/612, and WO 106/43.
22. From report of Naval Force Commander for Tarbrush 10 in PRO WO 106/4343.
23. From report on interrogation of Sergeant E. Bluff RE in PRO WO 106/4343. This report also remarks that "the most notable thing about this operation was the apparent hesitancy on the part of the German patrols to engage the landing party".
24. This narrative is based on the sources quoted for 22 and 23.
25. From information in letter written by Lieutenant Wooldridge in PRO DEFE 2/612.
26. From written narrative supplied by George Lane to author.
27. Saunders, op.cit., p217.
28. The reconstruction of this conversation comes partly from the author's interview with George Lane and partly from *Secret Agents, Spies and Saboteurs: Famous Undercover Raids of World War Two* by Janusz Piekalkiewicz, pp392–7. Rommel's interview with Lane was apparently recorded and notes on it were found after the war in the relevant German High Command files.
29. Letter from PRO DEFE 2/612.

CHAPTER 6

1. From narrative "July 1943: On the Night of the 9th" written by Professor Paul Streeten and supplied by him to the author, August, 1984.
2. From narrative by Paul Streeten, sent to the author August, 1984.
3. Letter from Lister to Laycock in PRO DEFE 2/1016.
4. From p1 of annexure 2 to *History of the Commandos in the Mediterranean*, headed "Report on the Activities of the Polish and Belgian Troops of 10(IA) Commando in Italy" in PRO DEFE 2/700.
5. Interim report on the activities of the Polish and Belgian Troops of 10(IA) Commando for period 13 December, 1943, to 21 December, 1943, by Brigadier T. B. L. Churchill in PRO DEFE 2/1231.

6. From *Na Sciezkach Polskich Komandosow* by Miroslaw Derecki, pp82–5.
7. From *Donnez-Nous un Champ de Bataille* by Carlo Segers, pp96–103.
8. From p4 of annexure 2 to *History of the Commandos in the Mediterranean*, headed "Report on the Activities of the Polish and Belgian Troops of 10(IA) Commando in Italy" in PRO DEFE 2/700.
9. ibid.
10. Extract from letter from George H. Kendal to the author dated 10/9/84.
11. Stephan Ross in conversation with author, June, 1984.
12. Derecki, op.cit., pp113–17.
13. From Polish Troop War Diary in Sikorsky Institute, London, quoted in *Poles in the Italian Campaign* by Olgierd Terlecki, p14.
14. From *Zielony Talisman* quoted in Derecki, p124, op.cit. *Zielony Talisman* is an anthology of pieces written by members of the Polish Troop about their wartime experiences between 1942 and 1944. It was published in 1946 in Bologna, a town which the Troop fought to free and where they ended the war.
15. From Lieutenant Czyński's section log book quoted in Derecki, p127, op.cit.
16. Memos in PRO DEFE 2/1231.
17. Segers, op.cit., p143.
18. ibid, pp144–8.
19. Memo in PRO DEFE 2/1231.
20. Segers, op.cit., p150–1.
21. Laycock's and the Raid Commander's reports in PRO WO 218/88.
22. From *The Historical Encyclopedia of World War II*, p605–6.
23. Segers, op.cit., p134. Sturges' memo is in PRO DEFE 2/1231. The relevant Yugoslavian authorities, the Muzej Revolucije in Beograd, have no information on the eventual fate of the members of the Yugoslavian Troop nor any details of its activities in the Mediterranean.
24. The narrative of the Polish Troop's activities between May and August, 1944, is gleaned from *Na Sciezkach Polskich Komandosow* by Miroslaw Derecki and from *Spopielone Komandosy* by Tadeusz Monsior, parts of which Monsior kindly translated for the author in 1983.

CHAPTER 7

1. Lt-Colonel Robert Dawson in conversation with author, January, 1986.
2. *The Longest Day* by Cornelius Ryan, p60.
3. Lt-Colonel Robert Dawson in conversation with author, January, 1986.
4. *Beret Vert* by Commandant Philippe Kieffer, p84.
5. *The Green Beret* by Hilary St George Saunders, p267.
6. Ryan, op.cit., p83.
7. *D-Day 1er B.F.M. Commando* by Maurice Chauvet, pp14–16.
8. *The D-Day Landings* by Philip Warner, pp230–3.
9. From "Chronicles of D-Day" an unpublished manuscript by Rupert Curtis, who was the Senior Naval Officer of Convoy S9, which landed 1 SS Brigade on Queen Red and Queen White beaches at La Brèche.

10. From an account of the part played by the Bataillon de Fusiliers-Marins Commandos in the Normandy campaign by Guy de Montlaur. It was obviously written after the war when de Montlaur was an officer attached to the Service Historique de la Marine, Château de Vincennes, Paris, and is in file TTF 1 there.
11. From a report by Philippe Kieffer on the actions of the Bataillon de Fusiliers-Marins Commandos, 6–10 June, 1944, which is in file TTF 1 bis, Service Historique de la Marine, Château de Vincennes, Paris. It is dated 14 June, 1944, and was dictated to Commandant Bernard Laporte at Warwick emergency hospital.
12. *Don't Cry for Me* by Donald Gilchrist, p53.
13. See 10 above.
14. From narrative supplied to Colonel Robert Dawson by Alex Lofi, December, 1985.
15. *Le Commando du 6 Juin* by Raymond la Sierra, p154.
16. See 11 above.
17. See 11 above.
18. See 10 above.
19. *Nous Etions 177* by Gwenn-Aël Bolloré, p141–6.
20. From article *"Les Premiers Jours en France du 1er Bataillon Fusilier-Marin Commando"* by Commandant Hubert Faure, a Warrant Officer with the No 1 French Troop during the Normandy campaign.
21. See 10 above.
22. See 11 above.
23. See 20 above.
24. See 20 above.
25. From narrative supplied to Colonel Robert Dawson by Alex Lofi, January, 1986.

CHAPTER 8

1. From letter written by His Honour Judge Brian Grant.
2. *Story of 45 Commando*, p12, in Royal Marines Museum, Eastney.
3. ibid, p20. According to another member of No 3 Troop, Peter Masters, the Commando had accidently fired at a German ambulance which in the half-light they had taken to be a military vehicle and the Germans had retaliated by firing at Arlen.
4. Peter Masters, in conversation with the author, June, 1984.
5. J. E. Day, in letter to author, November, 1985.
6. George Saunders, in conversation with the author, November, 1985.
7. *Story of 45 Commando*, p25.
8. Peter Masters, in conversation with author, June, 1984.
9. *March Past* by Lord Lovat, p314.
10. Harry Nomburg in conversation with author, June, 1984.
11. Peter Masters, in conversation with author, June, 1984.
12. Manfred Gans, in conversation with author, June, 1984.
13. Peter Terry, in undated letter to author.
14. Manfred Gans, in conversation with author, June, 1984.

15. Narrative by Peter Terry supplied by author.
16. From an early draft of the narrative of 47 (RM) Commando's History written by the Adjutant, Captain Spencer. Curiously, this passage, plus considerably more detail about Terry's exploits, was excluded from the final version which is in the Royal Marines Museum, Eastney.
17. Narrative by Peter Terry supplied to author.
18. Peter Terry, in undated letter to author.
19. Narrative by Peter Terry supplied to author.
20. "Operation Overlord: An Account of the Part Taken by 1 SS Brigade", p8, lent to author by Gerald Nichols.
21. Peter Masters, in conversation with author, June, 1984.
22. Lovat, op.cit., pp350/1.
23. Manfred Gans, in conversation with author, June, 1984.
24. Contained in letter from Ken Bartlett to the author, March, 1986. Bartlett was one of those who returned to live in Germany after the war. His first post was as Music Officer to the Broadcasting Control Unit of the then Nordwestdeutsche Rundfunk in Cologne, and he subsequently had a distinguished musical career.
25. In conversation with Manfred Gans and Peter Masters. The capture of Lawrence is also mentioned in *I Understand the Risks* by Norman Bentwich, p107, who says that Lawrence "was recognized by his captors and shot". It is not clear how Bentwich could have known this.
26. From the patrol report in possession of Ken Phillot and quoted in *The Commandos: 1940–46* by Charles Messenger, pp280–2, and from a slightly different version quoted in *The Green Beret* by Hilary St George Saunders, pp276–7.
27. Saunders, op.cit., p276.
28. Narrative by Peter Terry supplied to author.
29. Ian Harris in conversation with author, February, 1985.

CHAPTER 9

1. From the English MS of *Rudy, Een Strijdbare Jood* by Rudy Blatt, lent by Rudy Blatt to the author.
2. Mountbatten signal in PRO DEFE 2/1231.
3. Memos in PRO DEFE 2/1231.
4. "De Nederlandse Commandotroep Nr:2 (Dutch) Troop van Nr:10 (Interallied) Commando", p11, a pamphlet by Major-General b.d. V. E. Neirstrasz, published at The Hague in 1959 by the Military History Department of the Department of Defence.
5. Martin Knottenbelt, in conversation with author, August, 1983.
6. *Escape from Arnhem* by Leo Heaps, pp67–8.
7. Martin Knottenbelt, in conversation with author, August, 1983.
8. Heaps, op.cit., pp73/4 and 87.
9. Letter from A. Beekmeijer to the Commission for Military Awards at The Hague, dated 6 January, 1950.
10. Extract from a letter from W. de Waard to author dated 9 January, 1984.

11. From article on No: 2 Dutch Troop at Arnhem by W. Boersma printed in "Maandorgaan van de Documentatiegroep '40–45' no: 119 (September, 1974)", a pamphlet given to author by Martin Knottenbelt.
12. Hendrik Beekhuisen, quoted in "August F. M. Bakhuys Roozeboom, the forgotten Commando of Arnhem, 1944", an article published in 1980 by Major A. L. J. van Vliet, Military History Section, Royal Dutch Army Service Corps.
13. From letter of recommendation printed in "Maandorgaan van de Documentatiegroep '40–45' no: 119 (September, 1974)".
14. From English MS of *Rudy, Een Strijdbare Jood*, lent by Rudy Blatt to author.
15. ibid.
16. de Koning, in conversation with author, August, 1983.
17. William van der Veer, in conversation with the author, July, 1984, and from narrative supplied by him. Van der Veer has written several best-selling books in Holland about his wartime experiences.

CHAPTER 10

1. *I Understand the Risks* by Norman Bentwich, pp105–6.
2. *Donnez-Nous un Champ de Bataille* by Carlo Segers, p166.
3. ibid, p167.
4. *Don't Cry for Me* by Donald Gilchrist, p44.
5. De Ruiter, in conversation with the author, 1983. De Ruiter was awarded the Dutch Bronze Cross for this episode.
6. Kieffer narrative in PRO DEFE 2/40, which is part of a much longer account of how Flushing was taken. The exploits of the French during Infatuate I is almost wholly taken from this definitive history though I have also drawn on accounts given by Kieffer in *Beret Vert*, pp167–87 and by Major-General J. L. Moulton given in *Battle for Walcheren*, pp143–9.
7. ibid, Lofi narrative in PRO DEFE 2/40.
8. ibid, Vourc'h narrative in PRO DEFE 2/40.
9. ibid, in PRO DEFE 2/40 from which the rest off the description of No 5 Troop's attack on the Dover strongpoint is also taken.
10. War Diary in PRO 218/40. Except where otherwise noted, the narrative in this chapter is taken from the War Diary, from *The Battle for Antwerp* by Major-General J. L. Moulton, and from the narrative "No 10(IA) Commando's Role in the Walcheren Operation" by C. R. Featherstone in PRO DEFE 2/977.
11. Van der Bossche in conversation with the author, 1983.
12. Privately printed booklet by Bill Watson, p35.
13. Narrative of "No 10(IA) Commando's Role in the Walcheren Operation" by C. R. Featherstone in PRO DEFE 2/977.
14. Manfred Gans in conversation with author June, 1984.
15. *Klar Til Storm* by Arnfinn Haga, p117.
16. Details from Hauge's citation for the MC and from a conversation with Olav Gausland, November, 1985.

17. Narrative of "No 10(IA) Commando's Role in the Walcheren Operation" by C. R. Featherstone in PRO DEFE 2/977.
18. Official narrative of action by No 47 Commando at Walcheren by Lt-Colonel C. F. Phillips. He prefaced his description of the attack on W.11 with the words, "a complete and accurate account can never be written, so great was the confusion".
19. From narrative supplied to author by Brig-General Jan Linzel, March, 1986. Linzel had a distinguished career in the Dutch army. He fought in Korea and was reported killed there during one battle.
20. Narrative of Infatuate II in PRO ADM 202/407. This also contains detailed accounts of the individual actions of the Support Squadron.
21. The War Diary of 10(IA) Cdo erroneously states that W.18 was taken on 6 November when in fact it was taken on 5 November.
22. Segers, op.cit., pp173–4. The narrative for this action is taken from the War Diary and from the citations for the decorations awarded Lieutenant Roman and Lance-Corporal Legrand which are given in full in the above book, pp205–7.
23. War Diary in PRO 218/40.
24. Manfred Gans in conversation with author, June, 1984.
25. Kieffer, op.cit., p201.

EPILOGUE

1. Typescript of "History of No. 47 (RM) Commando", p29, in author's possession.
2. *Klar Til Storm* by Arnfinn Haga, p161.
3. Narrative supplied to author by Colonel Kaspar Gudmundseth, January, 1986.
4. ibid.
5. Haga, op.cit., p171.
6. In PRO DEFE 2/843.
7. Details of these raids are in "Les operations de Schouwen par le 1er bataillon de F.M. commandos" which is in the file TTF 1 bis, Service Historique de la Marine, Château de Vincennes, Paris.
8. Report on activities of 10(IA) Commando between 29 April 1945 and 13 September 1945 in PRO DEFE 2/977.
9. *Clash by Night* by Derek Mills-Roberts, p119.
10. ibid, pp170–1.
11. Details of this incident come from letters written to the author by Sir Maxwell Harper Gow, who was the Brigade Major, and by Mr Keith Thompson, who was his driver.
12. Mills-Roberts, op.cit., p107.
13. Letter from Major-General A. P. Willasey-Wilsey RM, dated 18 September, 1970, in the Archives of Royal Marines Museum, Eastney. Willasey-Wilsey was the patrol leader during Operation Cuckoo.
14. *The Unknown Warrior* by James Leasor, p257.
15. Peter Levy during interview with author, June, 1984.
16. "No 10 Commando – An International Experiment" by Bryan Hilton Jones in PRO DEFE 2/977.

Index